How To Read Character:

A

New Illustrated Hand-Book

OF

Phrenology and Physiognomy,

FOR

STUDENTS AND EXAMINERS;

WITH

A DESCRIPTIVE CHART.

I LOOK UPON PHRENOLOGY AS THE GUIDE TO PHILOSOPHY AND THE HANDMAID OF CHRISTIANITY. WHOEVER DISSEMINATES TRUE PHRENOLOGY IS A PUBLIC BENEFACTOR.
Horace Mann.

THE PROPER STUDY OF MANKIND IS MAN.
Pope.

NEW YORK:

FOWLER & WELLS, PUBLISHERS,

753 BROADWAY.

1883.

PREFACE.

THE first Phrenological CHART ever produced was printed on a single sheet, the size of our common note paper, and was sold for a cent. It simply gave the names of the organs then discovered by Dr. GALL. The next was larger, and gave both the names and definitions of the organs; still later, the charts of Drs. GALL and SPURZHEIM embraced all the above, together with some account of the Temperaments. But as it was with the inventors of the steam-engine, the locomotive, and the steamboat, so it has been with phrenologists. Each succeeding author is supposed to have availed himself of all that has been proved to be true and useful, adding thereto his own observations and experiences. Thus the improved charts of to-day are as unlike those first printed as are the modern steamers, locomotives, and engines to those first invented.

During our thirty years' experience in the practical application of scientific rules to character reading, we have used many different charts, revising old ones year after year, and adding one improvement after another. The present work embodies our latest and best ideas on the subject, so far as they can be set forth in this condensed and popular form.

It contains not only all of the PHRENOLOGY of previous charts or hand-books for self-instruction, but it embraces much more of PHYSIOLOGY and PHYSIOGNOMY than any former book of the kind.

In this Illustrated Hand-book we have endeavored to incorporate just that kind of matter best suited to both the EXAMINER and the EXAMINED, and to put it in the smallest possible compass compatible with completeness of statement and ample illustration. We have endeavored to be systematic in our arrangement, succinct and clear in our expositions, and popular rather than technical or professional in our style. We do not claim that this work is free from error. Our knowledge of Anatomy, Physiology, Chemistry, Astronomy, etc., will, we doubt not, increase with our years and with more careful study; so we intend it shall be with our knowledge of Phrenology and Physiognomy. We hope to revise this and all our other works when time may permit. We ask examiners and readers to kindly point out errors and to suggest improvements, that we may correct the former and incorporate the latter in future editions.

That this little work may be the means of encouraging the reader to correct any errors of judgment or improper habits he may possess—to cultivate and develop all the higher qualities of mind and heart—and to make the most of his opportunities and of himself, is the desire of

                                        THE AUTHOR.

NEW YORK, *January*, 1869.

INTRODUCTION.

THE BRAIN AND THE SKULL.

THE HUMAN SKULL.

SOME knowledge of the structure of the human brain, and of its appearance when exposed, as well as of the general forms of the skull, will be useful to the learner. We can here merely give very brief descriptions, referring those who desire further information to our larger and more elaborate works.

The human brain is an oval mass filling and fitting the interior of the skull, and consisting of two substances, a gray, ash-colored, or cineritious portion, and a white, fibrous, or medullary portion. It is divided, both in form and function, into two principal masses—the cerebrum and the cerebellum.

The cerebrum is divided longitudinally into two equal hemispheres, and each of these, in its under surface, into three lobes. But the most remarkable feature in the structure of the cerebral globe is its numerous and complicated convolutions, the furrows between which dip deeply down into the brain. By means of these foldings the surface of the brain is greatly increased, and

BRAIN IN THE SKULL.*

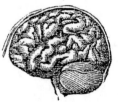

BRAIN EXPOSED.

---

* The side and top of the cerebrum are seen in this engraving. A A. The scalp turned down. B B. Edge of the base of the skull. the top having been sawed off and removed. C. Dura Mater, a part of the lining membrane of the skull raised up from the brain. D. Left hemisphere of the brain. E. Right hemisphere. F. The longitudinal cleft or fissure which divides the hemispheres.

In the next engraving the brain is fully exposed.

power gained with the utmost economy of space; for it is a demonstrated fact, that in proportion to the number and depth of these convolutions is the mental force. "The mind's revolvings," as Wilkinson

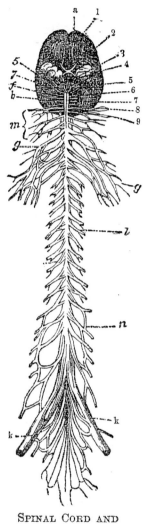

beautifully expresses it, "are here represented in moving spirals, and the subtile insinuation of thought, whose path is through all things, issues with power from the form of cerebral screws. They print their shape and make themselves room on the inside of the skull, and are the most irresistible things in the human world."

The cerebellum lies underneath the posterior half of the cerebrum, and is about one-eighth the size of the latter organ. It is divided into lobes and lobules, and consists of a gray and a white substance, like the cerebrum, but is not convoluted on the surface like the cerebrum; the gray matter somewhat darker than that of the cerebrum occupies the surface of the cerebellum, the white being interiorly disposed.

Extending from the base of the brain to the atlas or bony pivot on which the head rests, is the medulla oblongata. It is conical in shape, and may be considered as merely the head or beginning of the spinal cord, which continues it, and, in fact, extends the brain down the vertical canal, and by means of the nerves which it gives off, and which pass through notches between the vertebræ, connects it with every-part of the body. There are generally reckoned eleven pairs of nerves arising from the brain, and thirty-one from the spinal marrow. It is thus seen that the whole nervous apparatus is included in the mental system, and that the brain, as the organ of the overruling mind should be, as it unquestionably is, is omnipresent in the human body.

SPINAL CORD AND NERVES.*

Now, as is the soul which is incarnate in it, so is the brain in texture, size, and configuration; and as is the brain, so is its bony casement, the cranium, on which may be read, in general forms and special elevations and depressions, and with unerring certainty, a correct outline of the intellectual and moral character of the man.

---

* a. The brain. b. Cerebellum. f. Medulla oblongata. g, g. Nerves distributed to the arms. k, k. Great sciatic nerve, distributed to the lower limbs. l. Dorsal nerve. n. Lumbar nerve. m. Plexus of cervical nerves. 1. Olfactory nerve. 2. Optic nerve. 3, 4, 5, 6. The third, fourth, fifth, and sixth nerves. 7. Portio dura of the seventh nerve. 8. Auditory nerve and par vagum. 9. Hypoglossal nerve.

The heads of the sexes differ in shape as much as do their bodily forms. The engravings here presented are from two skulls in our possession, and were copied by daguerreotype, and show their relative size and shape. The first is from the skull of a man, and is a fair specimen of the male head. It rises high from the opening of the ear, *a*, to Firmness, *b*. It is large in the social region, particularly at Amativeness, *c*. The phrenological organs of force, pride, energy, and self-reliance are predominant. The second

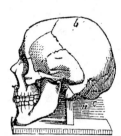

MALE SKULL.

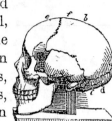

FEMALE SKULL.

is of a well-balanced female skull, and is fine, smooth, and even. The leading developments are at *d*, in the region of Philoprogenitiveness, Adhesiveness, and Inhabitiveness, while at *b* and *c* it is much less than in the male. At *e*, Benevolence, and at *f*, Veneration, the female is relatively more developed, but less so at Firmness and Self-Esteem, *b*.

The skulls of races and nations also differ widely in form, and these differences are found to correspond with known differences of character. In the Caucasian it will be seen that the forehead is prominent and high, the coronal region elevated, and the back-head moderately projected. The facial angle, measured according to Camper's method, is about 80°. It indicates great intellectual power, strong moral or spiritual sentiments, and a comparatively moderate development of the propensities. The special organs in which the Caucasian brain most excels, and which distinguish it

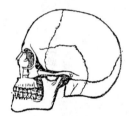

CAUCASIAN SKULL.

from those of all less advanced races, are Mirthfulness, Ideality, and Conscientiousness, the organs of these faculties being almost invariably small in savage and barbarous tribes.

See what a contrast between the Caucasian skull and those of the North American Indian and the negro here represented! One of the most distinctive traits of the aboriginal American skull is roundness. This quality is very manifest in every aspect, but still more so in the vertical and back views than in the one here presented. Great breadth immediately

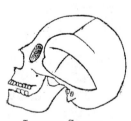

INDIAN SKULL.

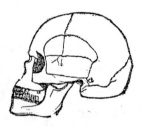

NEGRO SKULL.

above the ears and in the region of Cautiousness and Secretiveness, and a lofty coronal region, are also prominent characteristics. The forehead is broad and very prominent at the lower part, but retreating, and not high. The back-head in the region of the affections is, in general, only moderately developed, but there is almost always a large and sharply defined occipital protuberance.

The negro cranium is long and narrow. Compared with that of the Caucasian, the difference is seen to be striking. In the side view of the former the frontal region is less capacious than in the latter, the forehead more retreating, and the occiput comparatively more full. The facial angle is about 70°, the jaws being large and projecting, and forming what is called the prognathous type. Here the animal feelings predominate over both the intellect and the moral sentiments. The top view shows the facial bones compressed laterally, but projecting enormously in front.

We might carry these comparisons still farther, and show that each nation has its peculiar type of skull, the English differing strikingly from the French, and the American from both, and so on, but space will not here permit, and we must refer the reader to "New Physiognomy" for additional particulars on this and kindred topics.

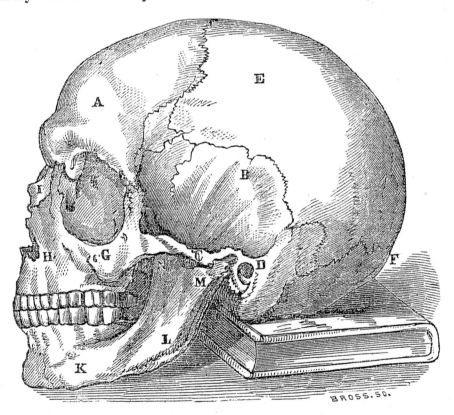

BONES OF THE HEAD AND FACE.*

* A. Frontal bone. B. Temporal bone. C. Zygoma. D. Mastoid process. E. Parietal bone. F. Occipital bone. G. Malar bone. H. Superior maxillary bone. I. Nasal bone. K. Inferior maxillary bone. L. Angle of the jaw. M. Condyles. N. Coronoid process.

HOW TO READ CHARACTER.

I.

FIRST PRINCIPLES.

I. PHRENOLOGY DEFINED.

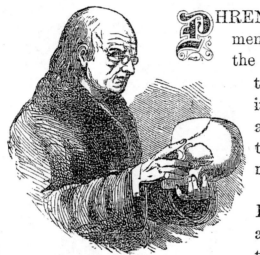

FIG. 1.—"THE DOME OF THOUGHT."

PHRENOLOGY is a system of mental philosophy founded on the physiology of the brain. It treats of mind, as we know it in this mortal life, associated with matter and acting through material instruments.

In its practical application, Phrenology becomes an art, and consists in judging from the head itself, and from the body in connection with the head, what are the natural tendencies and capabilities of the individual.

Phrenology does not now claim to be entirely complete as a science or perfect as an art, and it demands recognition and acceptance only so far as it has been firmly established on the broad and immovable basis of the constitution of man.

The chief principles of Phrenology—every one of which is supported by an array of unquestionable facts and susceptible of the clearest proof—are the following:

1. The Brain is the Organ of the Mind.
2. Each Faculty of the Mind has its separate or special Organ in the Brain.

1*

3. Organs related to each other in Function are grouped together in the Brain.
4. Size, other things being equal, is the Measure of Power.
5. The physiological conditions of the Body affect Mental Manifestation.
6. Any Faculty may be Improved by Cultivation and may deteriorate through Neglect. ·
7. Every Faculty is normally Good, but liable to Perversion.

II. BRAIN, THE ORGAN OF MIND.

While in this material world, where the all-wise Creator has seen fit to place it, mind can neither act nor be acted upon except through an organized apparatus. Impressions of external objects must be received through the organs of sense and their delicate nervous filaments, and thought can find expression only by means of the physical instruments under its control.

Now, if we go behind these instrumentalities, tracing back the nerves which ramify through all the bodily organs to their focus in the interior of the cranium, what do we find? Not mind, but brain—not the immaterial intelligence which receives, analyzes, and compares the impressions transmitted through these nerves, but a material apparatus—an organ. Without this organ, no mental manifestation would be possible while mind remains linked to matter.

That the brain is the organ of the mind is now universally admitted, and it is necessary merely to mention a few of the facts by means of which the truth of the proposition has been established.

1. Consciousness localizes the mind in the brain, giving a clear conviction that it is there, and nowhere else.
2. Deficiency of brain is always connected with a low degree of mental power.
3. The brain is found to be larger and more complicated in proportion to the strength and variety of the faculties manifested.
4. Mental disturbances always accompany affections of the

brain, a fever or a blow on the head often changing an intelligent and gifted individual into a raving maniac.

5. The rapid withdrawal of the blood from the brain causes a swoon, and temporarily suspends consciousness.

6. Where a part of the skull has been removed and the brain laid bare by an injury, it has been found that consciousness could be suspended by merely pressing on the brain with the fingers, and restored by withdrawing the pressure.

7. It has been observed also, in cases where the brain has been exposed to view, that in dreamless sleep it is motionless; that dreams agitate it in proportion to their vividness, and that when awake the motion is still greater.* Cases coming under this head are quoted at length by Mr. Combe in his "System of Phrenology," to which the curious reader is referred.

It being proved and conceded that the brain is the organ of the mind, it follows that every mental affection must be accompanied by a corresponding state of the organ, and that every state of the organ must be attended by a certain determinate condition of mind; and secondly, that the manifestations of mind will bear a strict relation in power and variety to the size and quality of its instrument.

III. THE BRAIN A CONGERIES OF ORGANS.

The brain, as a whole, is admitted to be the organ of the mind, as a whole. The mind is made up of many separate faculties, from which fact alone it might be inferred that the brain has a corresponding separate organ for each. That such is the case is conclusively proved by evidence which can not be set aside or successfully controverted. A small

---

* A writer in the *Medico-Chirurgical Review* mentions that many years ago he had "frequent opportunities of witnessing similar phenomena in a robust young man, who lost a considerable portion of his skull by an accident which had almost proved mortal. When excited by pain, fear, or anger, his brain protruded greatly, so as sometimes to disturb the dressings, which were necessarily applied loosely; and it throbbed tumultuously, in accordance with the arterial pulsations."

The cause of these appearances obviously was, that the brain, like the muscles and other organs of the body, is more copiously supplied with blood when in a state of activity than while at rest; and that when the cerebral blood-vessels were filled, the volume of the brain was augmented, and the protrusion above noticed took place.

portion of this evidence—all that our space will allow—may
here be cited:

1. In all other parts of the system—throughout all nature,
in fact—each function has an organ for itself. Sight has the
eye; hearing, the ear; digestion, the stomach; and it may be
further observed, that wherever the function is compound, the
organ is correspondingly so, as in the case of the tongue, in
which there is one nerve the office of which is to move the
member and thus subserve the purpose of speech, a second
which communicates the sense of feeling, and a third which
conveys the sense of taste.* In short, in the whole human
frame there is, so far as we know, not a single instance of one
nerve performing two functions. Reasoning analogically,
therefore, we infer that functions so essentially different as
observing and comparing—not to speak of others still wider
apart—must have separate cerebral organs.

2. Individuals frequently exhibit extraordinary capabilities
for some particular pursuit or branch of study, while in regard
to all other departments of mental effort they never rise above
mediocrity. If the brain were a unit in function, each faculty
should be manifested with equal efficiency through its agency.

3. The various mental powers in man do not appear simul-
taneously. The child loves and fears long before he has any
notion even of veneration or of moral responsibility. He
observes, too, the qualities of external things almost from the
commencement of his existence, but the power to reason concerning them comes later. This seems to show that loving,
for instance, requires the exercise of one part of the brain, and
venerating another—that observing has one organ, and
reasoning a different one.

4. In dreaming, one or more faculties may be in active
exercise, while all the others are apparently dormant. Emo-

---

* But the most interesting example of distinct functions being dependent on distinct
organs, is furnished by the spinal marrow. This is composed of two double columns,
the anterior being appropriated to motion, the posterior to sensation. This, Sir Charles
Bell clearly proved in the following manner: he cut an anterior nerve at its root in an
ass, and the parts through which it ramified lost the power of motion, though feeling
remained unimpaired. He cut a posterior nerve in another, and the parts through
which it ramified lost the power of feeling, but retained that of motion.

tions of love, fear, anger, and jealousy may arise and succeed each other, coming and going without order or restraint (the controlling organs being asleep), or a thousand vivid but disjointed conceptions may fill the mind—sometimes rational, but oftener absurd, and always differing from the ordinary and orderly operations of the fully awakened brain. If the brain were a single organ, these partial manifestations could not occur, but all the faculties would be asleep or awake together.

5. Partial idiocy and partial insanity are plainly contradictory to the doctrine of the organic unity of the brain. Some idiots, utterly deficient in intellect, have strong moral feelings. Others manifest only the propensities. In many, perfectly idiotic in everything else, some particular faculty is strongly developed—as Time, Tune, or Calculation. Pinel mentions an idiot girl who manifested wonderful propensity and talent for mimicry—could imitate anything she saw or heard, but who displayed no intellectual faculty in a perceptible degree, and evidently attached no ideas to the sounds she uttered.* Were deficiency of brain, as a whole, the cause of idiocy, these phenomena could not occur, for whatever brain might exist would be as competent to manifest one faculty as another. Partial insanity furnishes equally conclusive evidence on the same point.

6. Partial injuries of the brain result in a suspension of one or more faculties, while the others retain their normal activity, which could not be the case if the brain were a single organ.

7. Referring to our own individual consciousness, we may satisfy ourselves at any time that the faculties must act through a plurality of organs, for we find ourselves feeling and manifesting not only different but opposite emotions at the same time. This would be clearly impossible with but a single organ for all the faculties.

---

* Mr. Combe mentions an idiot in Liverpool, named Jones, who manifested great facility in learning languages; "Show him," he says, "a passage in the Bible, and he will point out and read the parallel passage in seven or eight other languages. But about the meaning he has no idea. Now if the brain were a single organ, this would be the same as if a man had the power of walking east, without having the power of walking west."

III. GROUPS OF ORGANS.

The location of any particular organ being known, it would naturally be inferred that other organs having related functions might be found in the same region of the brain. This inference is in accordance with the fact as established by observation, and furnishes another evidence of the truth of Phrenology, for this arrangement is the natural one, and the one which best serves the purpose of facilitating the action of the faculties through their organs, each being thus enabled to support and co-operate with the other members of the same class. It will also be seen, further on, that the arrangement of the groups in the cranium is in accordance with the same beautiful natural order.

IV. SIZE THE MEASURE OF POWER.

That size, other things being equal, is the measure of power, is a universal and undisputed law, and requires no detailed exposition here. It is the basis of all our calculations and reasonings in mechanics and natural philosophy as well as in Physiology and Phrenology.*

V. PHYSIOLOGICAL CONDITIONS.

In stating the general law, that size is the measure of power, we are always careful to add the qualifying clause—"other things being equal." The "other things" which modify this law in the case of the brain are certain physiological conditions, such as Temperament; Quality; Health; Respiration; Circulation; Digestion; Activity; Excitability; and Balance or Harmony, all of which affect mental manifes-

---

* When the brain is below a certain size, idiotism is the invariable result. In the lowest class of idiots, the horizontal circumference of the head, taken a little higher than the orbit, varies from 11 to 13 inches; in a full-sized head, the circumference is 22 inches; in Spurzheim's skull it is 22¼. In such idiots the distance from the root of the nose, backward over the top of the head to the occipital spine, is only 8 or 9 inches; in a full-sized head it is 14; in the skull of Spurzheim it is 15 6-10. Let those who deny the influence of size reconcile these facts with their belief. "But," say some, "we know idiots who have large heads." Our reply is—so do we; but, then, in these cases, the brain is not healthy. A large leg is usually indicative of strength; but this is not the case when the leg is large from disease. But though disease be absent, if the size of the brain be very deficient, idiocy is invariable, and men remarkable for great force of character, as Bruce, Cromwell, Bonaparte, Franklin, Webster, and Burns, invariably have heads of unusual magnitude.

tation in a greater or less degree, and must always be taken into account in estimating character.

VI. IMPROVABILITY.

Every faculty of the human mind is susceptible of being improved by judicious culture. This is a principle of great practical importance, and affords opportunity and encouragement to every one (for all have more or less need of improvement), and especially to those who have marked and embarrassing deficiencies of character. It is only applying to the mind through its organ, the brain, or to a faculty of the mind through its special organ, the same means we make use of to strengthen the arm or increase the flexibility of the fingers—properly adapted exercises. The improvement of man does not imply the extinction of any faculty or the creation of new faculties, but the development and training of all existing mental powers. The means through which each faculty may be strengthened, if too weak or restrained, if too active or influential, will be pointed out in another place.

VII. ALL THE FACULTIES GOOD.

Each faculty is in itself good, and was given by the Creator for the benefit of its possessor and the world, but may be perverted and distorted, and thus made an instrument of evil, or stunted and dwarfed, so as to become impotent for good. When rightly developed, acting in harmony, and with the lower faculties duly subjected to the higher, each contributes its share to the welfare and happiness of man.

There is no organ of murder, but there is a faculty intended to impart energy, executiveness, force and effectiveness in character and action, which, when large, active, and not restrained by the more conservative powers of the mind, may lead to violence and bloodshed. So the property-getting, accumulating propensity, given us for the laudable purpose of making a wise provision for the future, may, by perversion and lack of moral control, become the instigator of fraud and theft. In all cases the evil is the result of a disorderly manifestation, and not the legitimate action of the faculty.

II.

PHYSIOLOGICAL CONDITIONS.

I. BODY AND BRAIN.

IT has been stated in the previous chapter that mental manifestation, depending primarily upon the size of the brain for its power and efficiency, is modified by certain bodily conditions which affect the action of the organs. These conditions are so important in their practical bearings, that the student of Phrenology, especially if he have in view any application of the science either in public or merely among his friends and acquaintances, should not fail to make himself familiar with them.

The intimate connection between body and brain is illustrated in many ways, and in the experience of every one. They act and react upon each other. The nerves which ramify through every part of the body, all have their focus in the brain. If the body be ill, weak, or exhausted, the brain gives but feeble manifestations. If the body be stimulated or exhilarated, the brain shares its strengthened or quickened action. The influence of mind upon body is not less potent. Hope and joy quicken the circulation, brace the nerves, and give firmness and tension to the muscles. Grief and despondency have a relaxing tendency, weakening the limbs and deranging all the functions of the body, and especially those of digestion and secretion. In the same way other conditions of body and mind, whether constitutional and permanent or pathological and temporary, act and react upon each other, making it necessary for him who would study mind and read human character to make himself familiar with the conditions of the body, and equally so for him who would minister to the needs of the body, either in sickness or in health, to make himself acquainted with the existing state of the mind as well as its permanent characteristics.

II. TEMPERAMENT.

First in order, in noting the physiological conditions which affect mental manifestation, is temperament, which may be defined as " a particular state of the constitution depending upon the relative proportion of its different masses and the relative energy of its different functions."

Temperament has generally been looked at from the standpoint of physiology and pathology rather than from that of anatomy, and the classification of the various constitutional conditions now generally accepted by physiologists is founded on the distinct influences of the stomach, the lungs, the liver, and the brain, either of which predominating gives its peculiar conformation and complexion to the body and its specific tone to the mind.   We have, then, under this arrangement, four temperaments.   They are called: the Lymphatic Temperament; the Sanguine Temperament; the Bilious Temperament; and the Nervous Temperament.

1. The lymphatic temperament, depending on the predominance of the stomach, is characterized by roundness of form; repletion of cellular tissue; softness of the flesh; a weak pulse, and a languid condition of the system generally. The complexion is pale, the hair generally light, and the eyes light and dull.

2. The sanguine temperament, depending upon the predominating influence of the arterial system, is indicated by a moderate plumpness of parts; tolerably firm muscles; light or chestnut hair; blue eyes; a strong, full pulse; and an animated countenance.   Persons with this temperament are ardent, lively, and impressible, and possess more activity and energy than those having the lymphatic temperament.

3. The bilious temperament, having the liver for its basis, has for its external signs black hair; a dark yellowish skin; black eyes; firm muscles; and harshly expressed forms.   It indicates great activity, energy, and power.

4. The predominance and abnormal activity of the nervous system gives rise to the nervous temperament, a constitutional condition marked by light, thin hair; slenderness of form; delicate health; general emaciation; rapidity of muscular

action; and vivacity in sensation. It imparts great sensibility and mental activity.

This classification has clearly a physiological foundation, but the nomenclature adopted (drawn from pathology rather than from anatomy or physiology) is objectionable, and two of the conditions or temperaments themselves—the lymphatic and the nervous—as usually described, are diseased and abnormal, and not healthy states of the constitution. While, therefore, we acknowledge its value in a pathological point of view, and take into account the morbid conditions it embraces, we prefer to base our examinations on what we deem a simpler, and at the same time a more comprehensive, system founded on anatomy.

There are in the human body three grand classes or systems of organs, each having its special function in the general economy, namely: the Motive or Mechanical System; the Vital or Nutritive System; and the Mental or Nervous System. On this natural basis rests our doctrine of the temperaments, of which there are primarily three, corresponding with the three classes of organs just mentioned, namely:

1. The Motive Temperament;
2. The Vital Temperament; and
3. The Mental Temperament.

Each of these temperaments is determined by the predominance of the class of organs from which it takes its name. The first is marked by a superior development of the osseous and muscular systems, forming the locomotive apparatus; in the second, the vital organs, the principal seat of which is in the trunk, give the tone to the organization; while in the third, the brain and nervous system exert the controlling power.

THE MOTIVE TEMPERAMENT.

In the motive temperament the bones are comparatively large, and generally long rather than broad, and the form manifests a tendency to angularity. The muscles are only moderately full, but dense, firm, and possessing great strength. The figure is generally tall; the face long; the cheek-bones high; the front teeth large; the neck rather long; the shoulders broad, and the chest moderately full. The complexion and eyes are generally, but not always dark, and the hair dark, strong, and rather abundant. The features are strongly marked, and the expression striking and sometimes harsh or stern. The whole system is characterized by strength and toughness, and is capable of great endurance. Persons in whom this temperament predominates possess great energy, physical power, and capacity for work. They have strongly marked characters, and are the acknowledged leaders in the sphere of active life. They are men for the field rather than the council chamber, and are often found at the head of public works and of armies. They are observers rather than thinkers; are firm, self-reliant, constant in friendship and in

FIG. 2.—WM. REEVES, D.D.*

love; executive, ambitious, and persevering. They love power and conquest, and often pursue their ends with a reckless disregard for their own or others' physical welfare. As speakers, they use strong expressions, emphasize many words, and talk to the point, hitting the nail on the head with a heavy blow.

There is an abnormal development of this temperament, in which both the vital and mental systems are sacrificed to mere animal strength. It is marked by a small head, deficient in the coronal region and broad at the base; a short, thick, neck; broad shoulders; expanded chest, and large, dense muscles, the tendons of which are apparent through the skin. The possessor of this excessive development is remarkable for brute strength, and for nothing else, unless it be stupidity. Muscle is a good thing, but it is not well to absorb all of one's brain in producing an excess of it.

Full or large Firmness, Combativeness, and Destructive-

---

* William Reeves, a popular Methodist clergyman, is noted as an active, energetic, and efficient worker in his chosen profession. His character is as strongly marked as his features. He has black hair, dark brown eyes, and a dark complexion.

ness, and a strongly developed perceptive region are characteristic of the motive temperament.

The motive temperament is generally predominant and strongly marked among the North American Indians, and is very common in Scotland, Ireland, Wales, and France. In America, the States of Vermont, Maine, Kentucky, Tennessee, Missouri, and Arkansas are noted for its development. It prevails in mountainous regions.

THE VITAL TEMPERAMENT.

This temperament, depending upon the predominance of the vital organs which occupy the great cavities of the trunk, is necessarily marked by breadth and thickness of body, rather than by length. Its prevailing characteristic is rotundity. The chest is full; the abdomen well developed; the limbs plump and tapering, and the hands and feet relatively small. The neck is short and thick; the shoulders broad, but not angular; and the head and face corresponding with the other parts of the system, incline to roundness, as seen in fig. 3. The complexion is generally florid, the eyes and hair light, and the expression of the countenance pleasing and often mirthful.

FIG. 3.—REV. CHARLES H. SPURGEON.*

Persons in whom this temperament predominates are both physically and mentally active, and love fresh air and exercise as well as lively conversation and exciting debate, but are, in

---

* Rev. Charles Haddon Spurgeon is a very popular English minister of the Baptist denomination. He is ardent, impulsive, persuasive, and very effective as a preacher.

general, less inclined to close study or hard work than those in whom the motive temperament takes the lead. They are ardent, impulsive, versatile, and sometimes fickle; and possess more diligence than persistence, and more brilliancy than depth. They are frequently passionate and violent, but are as easily calmed as excited, and are cheerful, amiable, and genial in their general disposition. Being fond of jovial company and good living, they are more liable than others to become addicted to the excessive use of stimulants, as well as to over-eating, and should be on their guard against this danger, and curb their appetites with a strong will.

Phrenologically, the vital temperament is noted for large animal propensities generally, and especially Amativeness, Alimentiveness, and Acquisitiveness. Benevolence, Hope, and Mirthfulness are also generally well developed.

An undue and abnormal preponderance of the absorbent system, and a sluggish action of the circulatory organs, produce the unhealthy condition called in the old classification the lymphatic temperament, characterized, bodily and mentally, by insurmountable languor, sloth, and apathy.

The vital temperament is the prevailing one in Germany, Holland, and England, and in low countries and valleys generally; also among the negroes.

THE MENTAL TEMPERAMENT.

The mental temperament, depending upon the predominance of the brain and nervous system, is characterized by a frame relatively slight and a head relatively large; an oval or pyriform face; a high, pale forehead, broadest at the top; delicately cut features; an expressive countenance; fine, soft hair; a delicate skin, and a high-keyed flexible voice. The figure is often elegant and graceful, but seldom striking or commanding.

Sensitiveness, refinement, taste, love of the beautiful in nature and art, vividness of conception, and intensity of emotion mark this temperament in its mental manifestations. The thoughts are quick, the senses acute, the imagination lively, and the moral sentiments generally active and influential.

In the mental temperament, the superior portions of the forehead together with the coronal region are most fully developed. Causality, Comparison, Ideality, Spirituality, and Veneration are generally prominent, while the organs which lie in the basilar and posterior regions of the cranium are not so fully developed.

FIG. 4.—ALGERNON CHARLES SWINBURNE.*

It is the excessive or morbid development of this temperament — unfortunately very common in this age and country — which corresponds with the nervous temperament of the pathologists. It is characterized by emaciation of muscles, weakness of body, intensity of sensation, and a morbid impressibility. The foundation for this diseased condition is laid in the premature and disproportionate development of the brain, and it is built up by sedentary habits; the immoderate use of tea, coffee, tobacco; and other hurtful indulgencies.

The mental temperament is the prevailing one among scholars everywhere, and especially in Ireland, France, and America.

BALANCE OF TEMPERAMENTS.

Where either of the temperaments exists in great excess, the result is necessarily a departure from symmetry and harmony, both of body and mind, the one, as we have seen, always affecting the character and action of the other. Perfection of constitution consists in a proper balance of temperaments, and whatever tends to destroy this balance or to increase existing excesses should be carefully avoided.

---

* A young English poet of undoubted genius, whose head is something like that of Edgar A. Poe. Is he not sadly wanting in vitality?

Fig. 5 is a tolerably good illustration of a well-balanced temperament and a harmonious organization.

FIG. 5.—CHARLES A. MACY.*

A thorough practical knowledge of the temperaments alone will enable one to form a correct general estimate of character. The practical difficulty (by no means unsurmountable, however) lies in measuring accurately the relative proportion of the different elements in each individual temperament, so as to give each its due influence on the character. Study, careful observation, and the necessary practice will enable the student to do this in time, however, with great exactness.

III. QUALITY.

The next physiological condition to be considered, as affecting mental manifestation and modifying the law of size, is quality. A piece of wrought iron is much more tough than a piece of cast iron of the same size. Density gives weight and strength. Porous, spongy substances are light and weak. The lion is strong because his muscles, ligaments, and bones are dense and tough. It is the same in man as in beast, in brain as in muscle. Real greatness can exist only where a bulky, compact brain is combined with strong nerves and a dense, tough, firmly-knit body. Men with small heads may be brilliant, acute, and, in particular directions, strong, but they can not be comprehensive, profound, or commanding; and, on the other hand, men with large heads may be dull, if not stupid, on account of disease or low organic quality. Both high quality and large size are essential to the highest order of power, whether of body or of mind.

---

* Formerly a merchant, now a banker in New York. He is a "Friend," or Quaker.

It is difficult to illustrate by means of wood-cuts the conditions denominated high and low quality respectively, but

HIGH QUALITY.   LOW QUALITY.

FIG. 6.—REV. F. W. ROBERTSON.*   FIG. 7.—ANTOINE PROBST.†

figs. 6 and 7 will convey an imperfect idea of their external manifestations. Observe the features of the two characters, and note the difference.

IV. HEALTH.

Having taken note of the size of the brain and the original organic quality of the body (with which the brain must correspond), the existing condition of the whole, as regards health, must be taken into account.

All states of the body affect the mind, as we have shown in a previous section. The strong thoughts which have moved the world have not been sent forth among men through the agency of weak, sickly bodies. The motive power of muscle and of brain is the same. We can no more write, study, or think energetically and effectively when sick, than we can wield the ax, the sledge hammer, or the scythe.

---

* An English clergyman who resided in Brighton, of singularly refined tastes, fervent piety, and impressive eloquence. He died in 1863.

† Antoine Probst, a brutal murderer, confessed that he killed seven persons—the Deering Family. He was executed in Philadelphia in 1866.

Animal power is not mind, but it is something which mind requires, in this life, for its manifestation. Memory, reason, eloquence, poetry, philosophy, and even morality, are affected by disease. A disordered body involves disordered or weakened mental manifestations. In some diseases, as in consumption, for instance, there is often great clearness and vividness of conception and a high tone of moral feeling, but there is, at the same time, lack of power and continuity, and a fitful and vacillating state of mind. "A sound mind in a sound body" is the law; and in the sickly body, a weak and inefficient state of mental action.

V. RESPIRATION.

Respiration is one of the most important functions of the physical system. Breath and life are one. When the former fails, death supervenes. Even plants breathe, in their way, and die at once if air be excluded from them.

The power of respiration depends upon the size of the chest and the condition of the lungs. The size of the chest is readily ascertained by measurement.* This, other things being equal, will be the measure of the breathing power. The general health as well as the condition of the lungs must be taken into account as modifying the energy of respiration. The signs of good breathing power, in addition to a broad or deep chest, are considerable color in the face, warm extremities, elastic movements, and vigorous functions generally. Where it is deficient, there is general pallor, with occasional flushing of the face, cold hands and feet, blue veins, and great liability to colds and coughs.

Our vitality is in proportion to our respiration. The assertion of a distinguished physician, that "many people die for want of breath—when it is their own carelessness alone that prevents them from breathing," is no less true than startling. If we only half breathe—and many scarcely do that—we only half live. To expand the chest, therefore, and to increase our breathing power where it is deficient, is of the utmost import-

---

* Military regulations require the circumference of the recruit's chest to be equal to one half his height.

ance. Whether, as Alphonse Le Roy and others have contended, the development of the chest be actually an absolute standard of the length of life or not, it is clear enough that by expanding it, life may be prolonged and health and beauty promoted.*

VI. CIRCULATION.

Respiration and Circulation are closely related. Lungs and heart co-operate harmoniously in the work of manufacturing vitality. Between the heaving of the chest and the beating of the pulse, there is a definite relation both in strength and rapidity.

Good blood is the result of pure food properly assimilated and fully oxygenated by the copious breathing of pure air, and it is the office of the heart to propel this blood through the system. From the blood is made muscle, nerve, and brain. If the blood be good, these are strong, healthy, and efficient. If the blood be poor, or charged with impurities, the structures built up by it will be weak and disordered; for "the blood is the life thereof."

The signs of a good circulation are—a healthy color in the face, warm extremities, and a slow, strong, steady pulse.

VII. DIGESTION.

Digestive power depends primarily upon the condition of the organ of digestion—the stomach; but is affected by both circulation and respiration. If the former be deficient, the proper quantity of blood may not be sent to the stomach during the process of digestion; and if the latter be imperfect, the blood sent to the stomach will lack its full quickening and strengthening power. Copious breathing promotes the process of digestion and strengthens the digestive organs as well as the lungs.

A good development of firm, solid flesh and a healthy color are signs of sound digestive organs and an effective

---

* To cultivate breathing power and expand the chest, practice the following exercise: Stand erect, throw the shoulders back, and then breathe slowly, freely, and deeply, *filling the lungs to their utmost capacity at every inspiration*. Do this several times a day in the open air if practicable, and if not, in a well-ventilated room.

performance of the digestive process. Emaciation, paleness, a sallow or pimpled skin, and a peevish and desponding state of mind are indications of deranged or imperfect digestion.

VIII. ACTIVITY.

Activity is a matter of temperament mainly, and is greatest where the motive and the mental temperaments are both strongly developed. Its indications are length of body and limb, with very moderate fullness of muscle. The deer, the greyhound, and the race-horse illustrate the fact that activity and ease of action are associated with length and slenderness, and delicacy of structure.

IX. EXCITABILITY.

This is another condition depending upon temperamental combinations, and has its greatest normal manifestations in those in whom the vital and the mental temperaments are both well developed. It is morbidly active in persons whose nerves are disordered and whose systems have been subjected to the stimulation of alcoholic liquors, tobacco, and strong tea and coffee. In the lymphatic temperament there is the opposite condition,—a general coldness and apathy, which nothing seems to arouse into a genuine feeling of interest in present things and passing events.

X. BALANCE OF CONDITIONS.

It is essential to a harmonious character, and the most efficient action of the faculties, that all the developments of the body and brain and all the physiological conditions of both be well balanced—that there be no marked excesses or deficiencies; and in estimating the influence of the body upon the mind in any given case, we must not only consider its individual developments and conditions, but the proportions and relative activity and power of each. Where all act together harmoniously, the effective strength of each is increased; while, on the other hand, lack of balance or harmony impedes the action of all.

III.

GROUPING OF THE ORGANS.

I. PLAN OF THE GROUPS.

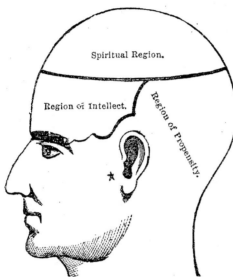

FIG. 8.—THREE REGIONS.

THE arrangement of the various organs of the brain in groups furnishes a beautiful illustration of that perfect adaptation of means to ends which characterizes all the works of God, and which man can only approximate in his most skillfully contrived inventions. The place of every organ of body and brain is just that which best fits it for its special function, and grouped around it for its support, and for co-operation with it in action, are those organs most closely related to it in function. Observe, for instance, the relations so admirably indicated in the arrangement in contiguity of Amativeness, Parental Love, Friendship, and Inhabitiveness; or of Acquisitiveness, Secretiveness, Destructiveness, and Combativeness. So Individuality, Form, Size, Weight, Color, Order, and the rest of the Perceptives, indicate by their locations not only their matter-of-fact tendencies, but their relationship to each other and to the external senses—seeing, hearing, etc.

In accordance with the same principle, we find the groups so placed that the location of each indicates its rank in the graded scale of functions. The propensities or animal organs (fig. 8) are placed next to the spinal column, in the base of the brain, and in close connection with the body. Rising above these, we come into the region of intellect; while above

that, in the coronal region, are the moral or spiritual sentiments, through which we are brought into relation with God.

II. THE GROUPS AND THEIR FUNCTIONS.

The first division of the faculties of the mind and the
organs of the brain is into three grand classes:

1. The Propensities;
2. The Intellectual Faculties; and
3. The Moral or Spiritual Sentiments.

How these great classes of faculties are arranged, each in
its special region of the brain, may be seen in fig. 8. The
Propensities, having to do with natural things, and being
closely related to the physical system, are placed nearest to
the body, with which their connection is intimate through the
spinal marrow and its ramifying nerves. In front, the Intellectual Faculties are arranged in appropriate order. They are
not in quite so close connection with the body as the Propensities, nor yet too far removed, and have their out-look, as it
were, upon the external world. Above these, and crowning
all, are the MORAL SENTIMENTS, occupying the highest place,
as they are highest in function and relation. Through them,
as through windows opening toward heaven, the soul gets
glimpses of things lying above and beyond its present narrow
environments—of a better life, and of the joys to which it
can here only aspire.

The Propensities give force and efficiency in all actions;
adapt us to our fellows; and lead us to take care of ourselves.
The Intellectual Faculties enable us to obtain knowledge of
men and things; to compare and arrange facts; and to invent
and construct what we need for the practical application of
our knowledge. The Moral or Spiritual Sentiments are
meant to control all the rest by subjecting them to the
tribunals of kindness, justice, and the Divine Law.

The grand classes or orders of faculties and organs we
have thus described and illustrated are each divisible into
smaller groups, the members of which bear a still closer
relation to each other than to the members of other sub-
groups.

LARGE.   MODERATE.

FIG. 9.—YANKEE SULLIVAN.   THE PROPENSITIES.   FIG. 10.—REV. DR. BOND.

LARGE.   SMALL.

FIG. 11.—REV. H. M. GALLAHER.   FIG. 12.—A PARTIAL IDIOT.

LARGE.   THE INTELLECTUAL FACULTIES.   SMALL.

   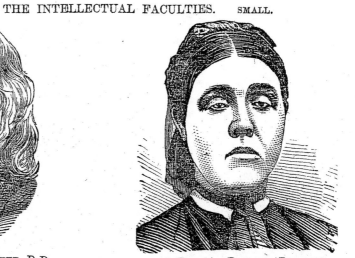

FIG. 13.—T. WORCESTER, D.D.   FIG. 14.—BRIDGET DURGAN.

THE MORAL SENTIMENTS.

The classification we adopt gives us the following arrangement of classes and groups:

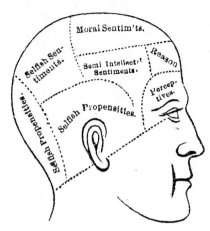

FIG. 15.—GROUP OF ORGANS.

I.—THE PROPENSITIES.
1. The Social Group.
2. The Selfish Group.

II.—INTELLECTUAL FACULTIES.
1. Group of the External Senses.
2. The Perceptive Group.
3. The Reflective Group.
4. The Literary Group.

III.—THE MORAL SENTIMENTS.
1. The Selfish Group.
2. The Semi-Intellectual Group.
3. The Religious Group.

1. The Social Group has for its collective function the manifestation of those affections which connect us with country and home, and attach us to relations, conjugal companions, family, and friends.

2. The office of the Selfish Group is to make proper pro-

SMALL.   LARGE.

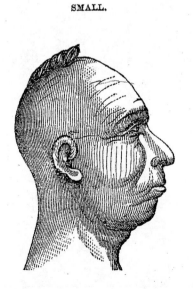

FIG. 16.—BLACK HAWK.   FIG. 17.—JOSEPH SMITH.

THE SOCIAL GROUP.

vision for the animal wants, and to secure the preservation of life, the defense of the person, and the accumulation and protection of property.

3. The External Senses have for their appropriate work the conveying to the brain of intelligence concerning the world of material things outside of the brain itself, acting, therefore, in direct co-operation with the perceptive faculties.

4. The Perceptive Group, through the senses, brings man into direct communication with the physical universe, gives a correct judgment of the properties of things, and leads to the practical application of the knowledge obtained.

5. The Function of the Reflective Group is to analyze, compare, and classify the facts collected by the perceptives, and to philosophize, contrive, invent, and originate ideas.

LARGE.   NOT LARGE.

FIG. 18.—LOUIS AGASSIZ.   FIG. 19.—MISS CARMICHAEL.
THE PERCEPTIVE GROUP.

6. The Literary Group imparts memory, and the ability to communicate ideas and feelings by means of written or spoken words.   (Included among the perceptives in diagram, fig. 15.)

7. The Group of Selfish Sentiments gives regard for character, love of distinction, self-reliance, independence, stability, and perseverance.   They have an aspiring and governing tendency.

8. The Semi-Intellectual Group has for its function self-improvement, and the love and production of whatever is beauti-

ful. It is elevating and chastening in its influences, and acts in co-operation with the strictly religious group, to which it is closely allied.

9. The Religious Group has the highest office of all, and tends to elevate man into fellowship with angels, and beget aspirations after holiness and heaven, while making him at the same time meek and humble—even as a little child—

LARGE.   SMALL.

FIG. 20.—EMANUEL KANT.   FIG. 21.—A NEGRO.
REFLECTIVE GROUP.

toward God. When large and active, and holding the leading place which belongs to it, all the other groups are sanctified through its action.

Our illustrations, so far as they go, tell their own story too well to need much comment. We select extreme cases when we can, in order to make the contrast as great as possible, and thus impress the fact illustrated upon the mind. Some of the sub-groups are not susceptible of pictorial illustration.

CLASSIFIED LIST OF ORGANS.

I.—THE PROPENSITIES.

I. THE SOCIAL GROUP.

1. Amativeness.   3. Adhesiveness.
2. Philoprogenitiveness.   4. Inhabitiveness.
5. Continuity (not grouped).

2*

II. THE SELFISH GROUP.

E. Vitativeness.
6. Combativeness.
7. Destructiveness.

8. Alimentiveness.
9. Acquisitiveness.
10. Secretiveness.

II.—THE MORAL SENTIMENTS.

I. THE SELFISH GROUP.

11. Cautiousness.
12. Approbativeness.

13. Self-Esteem.
14. Firmness.

II. THE RELIGIOUS GROUP.

15. Conscientiousness.
16. Hope.

17. Marvelousness.
18. Veneration.

19. Benevolence.

III. SEMI-INTELLECTUAL GROUP.

20. Constructiveness
21. Ideality.
C. Human Nature.

22. Imitation.
23. Mirthfulness.
D. Agreeableness.

III.—INTELLECTUAL FACULTIES.

I. GROUP OF THE EXTERNAL SENSES.

Feeling.
Sight.

Hearing.
Taste.

Smell.

II. PERCEPTIVE GROUP.

24. Individuality.
25. Form.
26. Size.
27. Weight.

28. Color.
29. Order.
30. Calculation.
31. Locality.

III. THE LITERARY GROUP.

32. Eventuality.
33. Time.

34. Tune.
35. Language.

IV. THE REFLECTIVE GROUP.

36. Causality.

37. Comparison.

DEFINITION OF THE ORGANS.

1. AMATIVENESS, Love between the sexes—desire to marry.
A. CONJUGALITY, Matrimony—love of one—union for life.
2. PARENTAL LOVE, Regard for offspring, pets, etc.
3. FRIENDSHIP, Adhesiveness—sociability—love of society.
4. INHABITIVENESS, Love of home and country.
5. CONTINUITY, One thing at a time—consecutiveness.
E. VITATIVENESS, Love and tenacity of life—dread of annihilation.
6. COMBATIVENESS, Resistance—defense—courage—opposition.
7. DESTRUCTIVENESS, Executiveness—force—energy.
8. ALIMENTIVENESS, Appetite—hunger—love of eating.
9. ACQUISITIVENESS, Accumulation—frugality—economy.
10. SECRETIVENESS, Discretion—reserve—policy—management.
11. CAUTIOUSNESS, Prudence—provision—watchfulness.
12. APPROBATIVENESS, Ambition—display—love of praise.
13. SELF-ESTEEM, Self-respect—independence—dignity.
14. FIRMNESS, Decision—perseverance—stability—tenacity of will.
15. CONSCIENTIOUSNESS, Integrity—love of right—justice—equity.
16. HOPE, Expectation—enterprise—anticipation.
17. SPIRITUALITY, Intuition—faith—"light within"—credulity.
18. VENERATION, Reverence for sacred things—devotion—respect.
19. BENEVOLENCE, Kindness—goodness—sympathy—philanthropy.
20. CONSTRUCTIVENESS, Mechanical ingenuity—sleight of hand.
21. IDEALITY, Refinement—love of beauty—taste—purity.
B. SUBLIMITY, Love of grandeur—infinitude—the endless.
22. IMITATION, Copying—patterning—mimicry—following examples.
23. MIRTHFULNESS, Perception of the absurd—jocoseness—wit—fun.
24. INDIVIDUALITY, Observation—desire to see and examine.
25. FORM, Recollection of shape—memory of persons and faces.
26. SIZE, Cognizance of magnitude—measuring by the eye.
27. WEIGHT, Balancing—climbing—perception of the law of gravity.
28. COLOR, Perception and judgment of colors, and love of them.
29. ORDER, Perception and love of method—system—arrangement.
30. CALCULATION, Cognizance of numbers—mental arithmetic.
31. LOCALITY, Recollection of places and scenery.
32. EVENTUALITY, Memory of facts and circumstances.
33. TIME, Cognizance of duration and succession of time—punctuality.
34. TUNE, Sense of harmony and melody—love of music.
35. LANGUAGE, Expression of ideas—memory of words.
36. CAUSALITY, Applying causes to effect—originality.
37. COMPARISON, Inductive reasoning—analysis—illustration.
C. HUMAN NATURE, Perception of character and motives.
D. AGREEABLENESS, Pleasantness—suavity—persuasiveness.

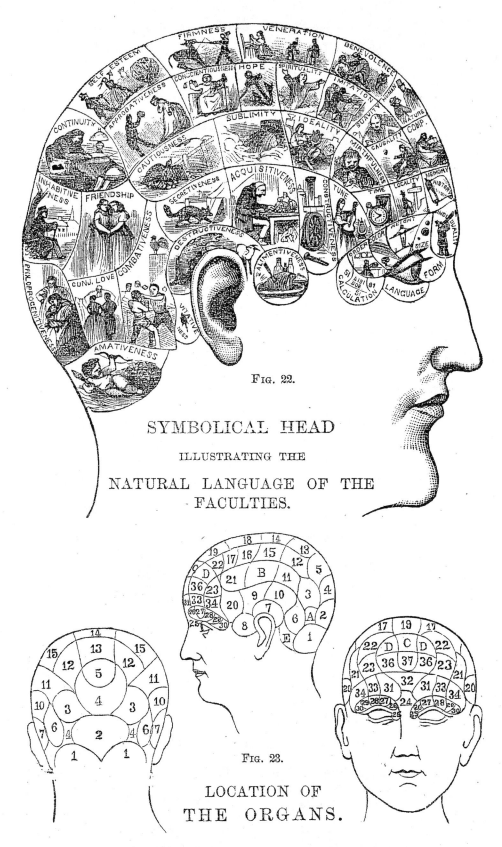

FIG. 22.

SYMBOLICAL HEAD

ILLUSTRATING THE

NATURAL LANGUAGE OF THE
FACULTIES.

FIG. 23.

LOCATION OF
THE ORGANS.

NAMES AND NUMBERS OF THE ORGANS.

IV.
THE ORGANS AND THEIR FUNCTIONS.

I. AMATIVENESS. (1.)

Be fruitful, and multiply, and replenish the earth, and subdue it.

1. **L**OCATION.—The organ of Amativeness occupies the cerebellum, situated in the base of the back-head, as shown at 1, figure 23. To find it, feel on the middle line toward the base of the skull, at the back part of the head, and you will discover a small bony projection called the occipital process. Below this point, and between

LARGE.   SMALL.

FIG. 24.—AARON BURR.*   FIG. 25.—GEORGE BANCROFT.†

two similar protuberances (the mastoid processes) behind the bottom of the ears, lies the organ in question. Its size is indicated by the extension of the occipital swellings backward and inward of the mastoid processes, and downward from the occipital process. Observe the striking contrast

---

* Aaron Burr, third Vice-President of the United States, was noted for his debauchery in private life, as well as for his unscrupulous conduct as a statesman.

† George Bancroft, American historian, is best known for his "History of the United States," the most complete and elaborate work of the kind yet produced. He was never married. Observe how short and narrow the head back and below the ears, in the organ of Amativeness. See also Rev. Dr. Pusey, fig. 97.

between figs. 24 and 25 in respect to this region; how full the head behind the ears in the one case, and how small in the other! The characters of the two men correspond with their developments. When it is large, the neck at those parts between the ears is thick, and it gives a round expansion to the nape of the neck, as shown in fig. 26. Fig. 27 shows it small.

2. PHYSIOGNOMICAL SIGNS.—A large cerebellum and a full neck are usually accompanied by a prominent if not massive chin, indicative of the strength of circulation, vital stamina, and ardor of passion we expect to find in persons thus characterized. Another and an unfailing

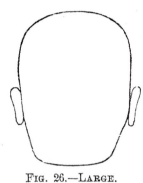

FIG. 26.—LARGE.

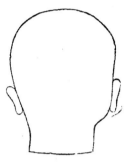

FIG. 27.—SMALL.

sign of Amativeness is the breadth and fullness of the lips. Their redness indicates present activity of the organ. The absence of color indicates inactivity.

3. NATURAL LANGUAGE.—The action of Love on the chin, constituting what may be called its natural language, consists in throwing it forward or sidewise, the former movement being the more natural to woman and the latter to man. These movements of the chin are accompanied by a slight parting and considerable humidity of the lip

4. FUNCTION.—The function or use of Amativeness is to manifest sexual feeling, and give the desire to love and be loved, and to marry.

There is no phrenological organ of more importance, or which has a greater influence upon human character and human destiny, or the bearings and relations of which are more extensive. It increases greatly in size and becomes active at the age of puberty. In males, it nearly doubles in size between the ages of ten and twenty, and the feelings and emotions dependent upon it undergo a corresponding change. The gentler sex, which before were viewed with comparative indifference, now seem invested with every charm. Their forms seem the perfection of grace, their faces all but divine, their voices enchanting, and their smiles bewitching beyond expression. The fair ones, at the same period, are conscious of similar feelings, and both sexes discover their greatest bliss in each other's society.

Dr. Spurzheim, speaking of this propensity, says: "Its influence in society is immense. It may excite various feelings, such as Combativeness, Adhesiveness, and Destructiveness, inspire timid persons with great moral courage, and at other times and under different circumstances mitigates our nature, and increases the mutual regards of the sexes toward each other."

5. PERVERSION.—The abuse and disorderly gratification of this propensity is fraught with innumerable evils, physical, intellectual, and moral, destroying the health of the body and debasing the tone of the mind; and so great is the influence of the amative propensity, that only the full development and proper activity of the higher intellectual faculties and moral sentiments are sufficient to hold it in subjection and make it duly subservient to the great end for which it was created.

6. CULTIVATION.—Where this organ is small, its size and activity may be increased, like those of any other organ or part of the body, by judicious exercise; and this exercise consists in a manifestation of the feeling of love for the opposite sex, which should be encouraged and promoted by social intercourse and the contemplation of the advantages and pleasures of the conjugal union. Any one desiring to cultivate Amativeness, then, should go into society as much as convenient, make it a point to be as agreeable as possible to those persons of the other sex with whom he or she may be brought into contact, trying to appreciate their excellences and to admire their personal charms. A well-developed man or woman—one in whom all the elements of masculine or feminine organization and character are present in due proportion—will exert a strong influence upon the love feeling of the other sex and help largely to awaken and develop the organ of Amativeness. Such persons should be sought, and a warm intimacy established with them. Marriage, when

founded on constitutional fitness and true affection, awakens and develops this organ greatly in those in whom it is deficient or inactive.

7. RESTRAINT.—The excesses and abuses to which this propensity often leads are by no means always referable to the excessive development of the organ in the brain. The true cause is often—perhaps in a majority of cases—a pathological one—gastric irritation and an inflamed state of the blood. A too stimulating diet; liquors, wines, tea, coffee, and tobacco; and the excitements of the feverish sensational life of our fast age are the principal causes of this unhealthy condition. The first step, then, is to remove these causes. Abandon the stimulants, withdraw from the sphere of social excitements, and cultivate the society of people who are living a quieter and more sober, earnest, and natural, but not less happy, life. Bathing and exercise in the open air, with a rather spare and cooling diet, will greatly aid in restoring the system to a healthy tone. Beyond these hygienic measures, the only means to be relied upon are the restraining influences of the aspiring and governing intellectual faculties and the moral sentiments. These must be cultivated, and their controlling influence brought to bear upon the unruly propensity. Make good use of the means God has placed within your reach for the government of your passions, asking Him to aid you, and you will not struggle in vain.

II. CONJUGALITY. (A.)

Therefore shall a man leave his father and his mother, and shall cleave unto his wife; and they shall be one.

1. LOCATION.—The organ of Conjugality or Union for Life is situated in the lower part of the back-head (A, fig. 23), just above Amativeness. It does not admit of pictorial illustration, except merely to indicate its place, as in fig. 28.

2. FUNCTION.—The instinct of permanent union between the sexes which it is the function of Conjugality to manifest, though closely related to Amativeness, is a distinct faculty, and each may be exercised independently of the other. In fact, Conjugality very often comes into activity before Ama-

tiveness, and the young heart pants to find its mate, and really does select, meets with a response, and never regrets the choice, or changes in the least. Some of the most perfect and happy of unions ever known have been of this sort, formed in childhood, perhaps five years before the promptings of Amativeness were experienced.

3. ILLUSTRATIVE EXAMPLES.—Some birds and animals choose a sexual mate, and remain faithful to that mate for life, as the lion and the eagle. The sheep and horse associate promiscuously, and do not choose mates at all. The lion and eagle manifest one faculty that the horse and sheep do not evince, consequently the disposition to choose a sexual mate for life is a distinct and special faculty. Among the lower animals, those that pair for life are just as constant in affection the whole year round as they are during the procreating season, showing that for ten months in the year Amativeness is by no means their bond of union.

FIG. 28.—FEMALE HEAD.

4. CULTIVATION.—One desiring to develop this organ should strive to center all his or her hopes, interests, and plans for life in the one already beloved, and not let new faces awaken new loves. Be as much as possible in the company of the chosen companion, and when absent cherish every memorial, association, and reminiscence connected with him or her, not allowing the affections to wander, but keeping ever in view the good qualities and charms of person and mind which first attracted you.

5. RESTRAINT.—Should the chosen one die, or love be blighted in any way, it may be necessary to restrain an excessive manifestation of this faculty leading to despondency and broken-heartedness. Try, then, to appreciate the excellences of others; seek society, and try to find a suitable

object upon which to bestow your affections, remembering that "there are as good fish in the sea as ever were caught."

III. PARENTAL LOVE.   (2.)

Can a woman forget her sucking child?

1. LOCATION.—The organ of Parental Love or Philoprogenitiveness is situated above the middle part of the cerebellum (2, fig. 23), and about an inch above the occipital protuberance. When large, it gives fullness to the back-head above

LARGE.   SMALL.

FIG. 29.—QUEEN VICTORIA.*   FIG. 30.—A. JOHNSON.†

Amativeness, as seen in fig. 29, which may be contrasted with fig. 30, in which the organ is small.

2. FUNCTION.—Parental Love, as its name implies, is the peculiar feeling which watches over and provides for the wants of offspring. Its primary function is to impart love for the young, and particularly for one's own children; but it also leads to a fondness for pets generally, as an incidental manifestation. It gives a softness of manner in treating the feeble and the delicate, even in advanced life; and persons in whom this organ is large in combination with Benevolence, are better fitted for the duties of a sick-chamber than those in whom Philoprogenitiveness is small. The natural language of the faculty is soft, tender, and endearing. It is essential

---

* Queen Victoria is known to have been a loving wife, and to be the excellent but perhaps over-fond mother of many children.

† Johnson was a bachelor, no lover of children—and children, we are sure, would avoid him—and is said to have been a woman-hater. Observe his lips and mouth.

to a successful teacher of children. Individuals in whom the organ is deficient, have little sympathy with the feelings of the youthful mind, and their tones and manner of communicating instruction repel, instead of attracting, the affections of the pupil. It is particularly well developed in the negro, who makes an excellent nurse. In selecting a person to take care of children, always, if possible, take one in whom this organ is full or large.

3. PERVERSION.—A perverted manifestation of Parental Love spoils children by excessive indulgence or pampering, or by allowing them to rule, instead of yielding that obedience which is due from offspring to parent.

4. ILLUSTRATIVE EXAMPLES.—Those who possess the feeling of parental love in a high degree, show it in every word and look when children are concerned; and these, again, by a reciprocal tact, or, as it is expressed by the author of Waverly,

 by a kind of 'free-masonry,' discover at once persons with whom they may be familiar, and use all manner of freedom. It is common, when such an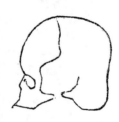

FIG. 31.—FEMALE SKULL. individual appears among FIG. 32.—MALE.

them, to see him welcomed with a shout of delight. Other individuals, again, feel the most marked indifference toward children, and are unable to conceal it when betrayed into their company.

The organ of Parental Love is more prominently developed in the female than in the male head. It is this, in part, that gives its proportionally greater length from the forehead to the occiput in the former. Figs. 31 and 32 indicate this and other differences between the heads of the two sexes. Of course there are exceptions to this general rule. Sometimes the back-head is small in women, and also occasionally very large in man. In these cases it will generally be found that the woman resembles her father and the man his mother.

5. CULTIVATION.—To cultivate the organ of Parental Love one should court the society of children, play much with

them, and try to enter into the spirit of their sports and games, and to sympathize with them in their little joys and griefs, being always tender and indulgent toward them. Those who have no children of their own should, if they have the means to support them, adopt one or more, or provide some suitable pets. The organ is large in Ralph Wells, a teacher.

6. Restraint.—If there be a tendency to idolatrous fondness or to undue and hurtful indulgence, the restraining influence of reason and moral sentiment must be brought to bear. It should be impressed upon the mind that the good of the child requires the exercise of the parents' authority, and that they are responsible for all the evils which come from their neglect to exercise it.

IV. FRIENDSHIP. (3.)

The soul of Jonathan was knit with the soul of David, and Jonathan loved him as his own soul.

LARGE.

1. Location.—The organ of Friendship or Adhesiveness is situ-

NOT SO LARGE.

FIG. 33.—MLLE. N.*

FIG. 34.—ISAAC T. HECKER.†

ated at the posterior edge of the parietal bone (3, fig. 23), just above the lambdoidal suture. It projects at the pos-

---

* Mlle. N., a young Parisienne, was so tenderly attached to a lady of her own age, that neither marriage nor the solicitations of her mother could induce her to leave her. Her friend died at a time when such an event was least expected, but Mlle. N. did not immediately exhibit any marked signs of grief, so that her friends deemed her resigned

terior and lateral part of the head, on each side of Inhabitiveness, and a little higher than Philoprogenitiveness, and when very large produces two annular protuberances there.

2. PHYSIOGNOMICAL SIGN.—Friendship (*Adhesiveness*) holds fast, clings, adheres, and is represented by the round muscle which surrounds the mouth and *draws together* or closes the lips. When this muscle is large and strong it produces slightly converging wrinkles in the red part of the lips, sometimes extending slightly into the white part. Small perpendicular wrinkles in the red part of the lips indicate a smaller degree of Friendship, but not a deficiency.

3. NATURAL LANGUAGE.—The great activity of this organ disposes persons to embrace and cling to each other; two children in whom it is active will put their arms round each other's necks, and lay their heads together, causing them to approach in the direction of the organ of Adhesiveness, or assuming this attitude as nearly as possible. A dog, when anxious to show his attachment, will rub his head at the seat of this organ on his master's leg.

4. FUNCTION.—This organ gives the instinctive tendency to attachment and delight in the return of affection. It causes one to seek company, love society, and indulge friendly feelings. Those in whom it is strong feel an involuntary impulse to embrace and cling to any object which is capable of experiencing fondness. It gives ardor and a firm grasp to the shake with the hand. In boys, it frequently displays itself in attachment to dogs, rabbits, birds, horses, or other animals. In girls, it adds fondness to the embraces bestowed upon the doll. The feelings which it inspires abound in the

---

to the loss of her companion. A day or two elapsed after the burial when she was found in her chamber quite dead, having committed suicide. A letter, addressed to her parents, disclosed the state of her mind previous to the fatal act, the substance of which was that she could not survive the loss of her friend. In scanning the conformation of the back-head of Mlle. N., it must be at once seen how very large the region of the social sentiments appears. Mark the great distance from the ear backward. It is an extraordinary instance, and the above account furnishes the surprising fact in connection with so great a development.

† Father Hecker is a Roman Catholic priest of New York, of German and English stock, noted for learning, talent, energy, and strength of character.

poetry of Moore.   He beautifully describes its effects in the following lines:

> The heart, like a tendril accustomed to cling,
>   Let it grow where it will, can not flourish alone;
> But will lean to the nearest and loveliest thing
>   It can twine with itself and make closely its own.

5. PERVERSION.—Perverted Friendship leads to bad company and the formation of attachments for the unworthy.

6. CULTIVATION.—Friendship may be cultivated by associating freely with those around us, going much into society, and keeping the heart open to all social influences.   One should strive to be as companionable as possible, and not too exclusive and fastidious in regard to associates.

7. RESTRAINT.—Friendship hardly needs restraining, but should be kept under the guidance of the intellect and moral sentiments, so as not to be bestowed upon unworthy objects.

V. INHABITIVENESS.   (4.)

The Lord forbid it me, that I should give the inheritance of my fathers unto thee.

LARGE.   NOT LARGE.

FIG. 35.—REV. T. O. PAINE.*   FIG. 36.—REV. G. H. HEPWORTH.†

1. LOCATION.—Inhabitiveness is located between Parental Love and Continuity, on the back part of the head.   Where

---

* Mr. Paine is a Swedenborgian preacher, and author of a work well known and esteemed in his church, " Of Restoring the Holy Tabernacle," etc.

† Mr. Hepworth is a popular and eloquent Unitarian minister of Massachusetts.

it is large or very large and Continuity moderate, an angle is formed near the union of the lambdoidal sutures, between which and the occipital bone there will be considerable distance.

2. FUNCTION.—The function of this organ is to give love of home and country, a desire to have a permanent abode, and attachment to any place where one was born or has lived. The feeling is particularly strong in the Swiss, and in the inhabitants of mountainous countries generally.

3. CULTIVATION.—To increase the activity of this organ, one should make home as attractive as possible, and cultivate a love of it by planting trees, vines and shrubs, and by dwelling on the associations and memories connected with it. Reading the history of one's country, and cherishing a just pride in its greatness and glory, has a tendency to arouse and increase feeling.

4. RESTRAINT.—Where this feeling is very strong and active, absence from home or country often causes a terrible feeling of home-sickness. This excessive local attachment may be weakened by going frequently abroad, reading books of travel, and becoming interested in foreign countries.

VI. CONTINUITY. (5.)

Let every man abide in the same calling wherein he was called.

1. LOCATION.—Continuity or Concentrativeness is situated next above Inhabitiveness and below Self-Esteem. When large, it gives a general fullness to that region; and when moderate or small, a marked depression will be perceptible.

2. FUNCTION.—The function of Continuity is to give connectedness to thought and feeling, and thoroughness in the elaboration of ideas or the working out of the details of any plan. It enables us to keep the other faculties concentrated upon a single object, and to follow a train of thought uninterruptedly through all its phases till we reach the legitimate conclusion. It gives unity and completeness to mental operations.

3. EXCESS.—A too strong development of this feeling leads to excessive amplification and tedious prolixity.

4. ILLUSTRATIVE EXAMPLES.—Continuity is very largely developed in the German head, and only a little less so in the English, and the people of these nationalities generally stick to one thing—one trade or profession through life, and in literature and art produce elaborate and finished works, noted for unity and completeness. The American has in general but a moderate endowment of the faculty, is correspondingly versatile, and often changes his occupation. He is,

LARGE.   SMALL.

FIG. 37.—THOMAS HUGHES.*   FIG. 38.—ELIHU BURRITT.†

perhaps, first a lawyer, then a doctor, and finally a merchant or a farmer—possibly all these at once; and this is one of the greatest defects in the American character, and accounts, in fact, for the superficial nature of much of our literature, and the want of thoroughness in our studies and in our scientific investigations. The defect is increased in those schools where a great many studies are pursued at one time.

5. CULTIVATION.—Such an arrangement of work or business as will compel continuous attention to one thing, or a steady adherence to one line of conduct, will tend to increase the activity of the faculty under consideration, and promote the growth of its organ in the brain. Let it be " one thing at a time."

---

* Thomas Hughes, member of the British Parliament, and author of " Tom Brown's School Days," etc., manifests in his works the influence of this organ.

† Well known as " the Learned Blacksmith." Observe also his large Individuality.

6. RESTRAINT.—To restrain the excessive or too influential manifestation of Continuity, one should reverse the directions given in the preceding paragraph, and compel, by some arrangement of occupation, a frequent transfer of the attention from one thing to another. In writing or speaking, where there is a tendency to prolixity, it is well to prescribe to one's self, before commencing, rather narrow limits, and make it a point not to overstep them.

VII. VITATIVENESS. (E.)

All that a man hath will he give for his life.

1. LOCATION.—The organ of this faculty is located just behind the ear, below Combativeness, and forward from Amativeness (fig. 23, E). See also fig. 39.

2. FUNCTION.—It gives a love of existence for its own sake, tenacity of life, dread of death, and resistance to disease.

3. ILLUSTRATIVE EXAMPLES. — There is a remarkable difference among men in regard not only to the love of life and the dread of death, but to the actual hold upon life. One passes through cholera or yellow fever; gets shipwrecked, and goes for days without food and lives, while others "give up" and let go of life when they might have held

FIG. 39.—THOMAS H. BENTON.*

on. Some yield readily to disease, and resign themselves to die with little reluctance, while others struggle with the utmost determination against death, and by the power of the will often recover from a sickness that would quickly prove fatal to another with the same degree of constitution and vital power, but lacking this faculty of resistance to death. This difference is believed, on the evidence of thousands of observations, to be due to the different degrees of development of

* An American politician and statesman, noted for his independence, persistence, and tenacity as well as for physical and mental vigor.

a fundamental faculty which we call Vitativeness. It is not recognized by the European writers on Phrenology.

4. CULTIVATION.—The constant contemplation of the pleasures and advantages of life, and the formation of plans to secure these pleasures and advantages in the largest possible measure, or to do good by living, will tend to increase the size and influence of this organ.

5. RESTRAINT.—A morbid love of this life should be held in check by cultivating faith in God and in a better life to come. Let us cheerfully accept the inevitable.

VIII. COMBATIVENESS. (6.)

Whatsoever thy hand findeth to do, do it with thy might.

1. LOCATION.—Combativeness lies behind and above the ears, as shown in the diagram (fig. 23) at 6. To find it on the

LARGE.

MODERATE.

FIG. 40.—J. H. HOPKINS, D.D.*   FIG. 41.—HORATIO POTTER, D.D.†

living head, draw a line from the outer angle of the eye to the top of the ear, and thence straight backward from an inch and a half to an inch and three quarters, and you will be on

---

* Dr. Hopkins was for some years Presiding Bishop of the Protestant Episcopal Church of the United States, and was distinguished for energy, industry, and *controversial* ability.

† Horatio Potter, D.D., is Protestant Episcopal Bishop of New York, and is much beloved and admired by his people for intelligence, devotion, mildness. and magnanimity.

the place of the organ.   On the cranium it corresponds with the inferior posterior angle of the parietal bone, above and a little behind the mastoid process, and when large, gives great breadth to the head at that point, as shown in fig. 42.   Fig.

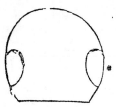

43 shows the form of the head when this organ is small.

2. PHYSIOGNOMICAL SIGNS.—In connection with the breadth of the back part of the side-head at the point we have indicated, there

FIG. 42.

FIG. 43.

may generally be observed a marked enlargement of the neck below, as in Marshall, the English boxer (fig. 44).   This sign, when present, we consider infallible, and as it is not often covered by the hair, is readily seen.

Prominence of the ridge of the nose is believed to be another sign of Combativeness.   It is certainly a well-defined characteristic of most great warriors, pugilists, and other fighters.

3. NATURAL LANGUAGE. —The action of Combativeness tends to throw the head backward and a little to the side in the direction of the organ, and to give the person the attitude of a boxer.   It also, when excited, gives a hard thumping sound to the voice, as if each word were a blow.

4. FUNCTION.—Combativeness is not primarily a fighting faculty, and might

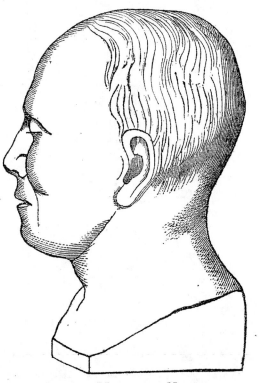

FIG. 44.—MARSHALL—MURDERER.

have received a better name.   Its office is to give the will and ability to overcome obstacles, to resist aggression, contend for rights, and to protect person and property.   If it be necessary to fight for these objects, it gives the pluck to do it.   A considerable endowment of it is indispensable to all great and magnanimous characters. Even in schemes of charity, or in plans for the promotion of religion or learning, opposition will arise, and Combativeness inspires its possessor with that

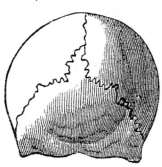

FIG. 45.

instinctive boldness which enables the mind to look undaunted on a contest in virtue's cause, and to meet it without the least shrinking. Were the organ very

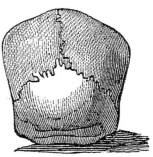

FIG. 46.

deficient in the promoters of such schemes, they would be liable to be overwhelmed by contending foes, and baffled in all their exertions.

5. PERVERSION.—When too energetic and ill-directed, Combativeness produces the worst results. It then inspires with the love of contention for its own sake. In private society it produces the controversial opponent, who will wrangle and contest every point, and, "e'en though vanquished, argue still." When thus energetic and active, and not directed by the Moral Sentiments, it becomes a great disturber of the peace in the domestic circle; contradiction is

FIG. 47.

then a gratification, and the hours which ought to be dedicated to pure and peaceful enjoyment are imbittered by strife. On the great field of the world its abuses lead to quar-

FIG. 48.

rels, and, when combined with Destructiveness, to bloodshed and devastation.

6. ILLUSTRATIVE EXAMPLES.—This organ is generally more developed in men than in women, and in male than in female animals. It is constantly found large in military commanders

and others who have shown remarkable valor and disregard of danger. Napoleon's generals Ney and Murat are examples in point. Look, too, at the skull of General Wurmser (fig. 45), who defended Mantua so obstinately against Napoleon! See how broad it is from side to side in the region of the organ we are illustrating! and compare it with that of the Cingalese boy (fig. 46) which we have placed near it. Our own great commanders, Grant, Sherman, Sheridan, Hancock, and Thomas (fig. 49), are remarkable for this development and for th qualities it indicates.

FIG. 49.—GENERAL THOMAS.*

The ancient artists seem to have known that there exists some connection between this configuration and animal courage, for they have given it to the heads of their gladiators and wrestlers.

The heads of courageous animals between and behind the ears are wide, as in fig. 48, while those of timid and shy ones are narrow at the same place, as in fig. 47.

7. CULTIVATION.—To cultivate this organ where deficient, one should rather court than avoid encounters with whatever has a tendency to call out a spirit of defiance, resistance, or opposition; and should make it a point to engage in debates and mental contests on every suitable occasion.

8. RESTRAINT.—To restrain Combativeness, requires the controlling power of the intellect and the Moral Sentiments, which should be placed as guards over it, to quell at once, before it burst into flame, the rising spirit of anger and contention. As precautionary measures, we should avoid exciting discussions and conflicts of opinion, as well as scenes and places where temptations to quarrel and fight would be likely to assail us

* Major-General George H. Thomas is an officer in the United States Army. who greatly distinguished himself during the late civil war.

IX. DESTRUCTIVENESS.   (7.)

Be ye angry, and sin not; let not the sun go down on your wrath.

1. LOCATION.—Destructiveness (7, fig. 23) is situated immediately above the ear, and its development gives prominence

LARGE.   NOT LARGE.

FIG. 50.—LEONARD BACON.*   FIG. 51.—ALBERT BARNES.†

to the skull at that point, and breadth to the center of the
basilar region of the head, as shown in fig. 52. Fig. 53 shows
the form given to the skull by its deficiency. When well

developed it is easily
distinguished.

2. PHYSIOGNOMICAL
SIGN. — In carnivo-
rous animals — the
lion, the tiger, and
the wolf, for instance
— the upper jaw
projects forward of
the lower; while in

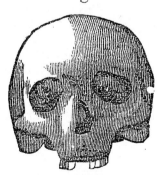

FIG. 52.—DESTRUCTIVENESS
LARGE.

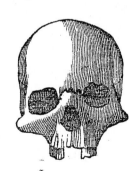

FIG. 53.—DESTRUCTIVE-
NESS SMALL.

vegetable eaters the reverse is true, as seen in the sheep, the
goat, the cow, etc.   In carnivorous birds, the upper mandible

---

* A prominent minister of the Congregationalist denomination in New Haven,
Conn., regarded as the champion of his sect in New England.

† Dr. Barnes, formerly of Western New York, now of Philadelphia, is well and widely
known as an author, and as a pulpit orator of the Presbyterian denomination.

is much longer than the lower, bending over, as in the eagle, the hawk, etc. It is believed that in man analogous physical peculiarities indicate dispositions allied to those of the class of animals to which the resemblance may be traced. Thus an individual, like that represented in fig. 54, in whom the upper jaw projects slightly beyond the lower, will be found to have large Destructiveness and to be particularly fond of animal food; while fig. 55 represents one who prefers vegetable food, and is adverse to the shedding of blood, Destruc-

FIG. 54.—DESTRUCTIVENESS LARGE.   FIG. 55.—DESTRUCTIVENESS SMALL.

tiveness being small. This sign, however, requires the confirmation of more extensive observations.

3. NATURAL LANGUAGE.—When very active, this propensity produces a quick step, a drawing up of the body to the head, and a stamping or striking downward, also a wriggling of the head, like the motion of a dog in the act of worrying. It gives a dark expression to the countenance, and harsh and discordant tones to the voice. If in a friendly converse with a person in whom the organ is large and Secretiveness small, one happens to touch on some irritating topic, in an instant the softness of Benevolence and the courtesy of Love of Approbation are gone, and the hoarse growl of Destructiveness indicates an approaching storm.

4. FUNCTION.—This is one of the organs given to man for self-preservation. It imparts the energy and executiveness necessary to enable us to overcome obstacles and remove or

crush whatever is inimical to our welfare; to tunnel mountains, fell trees, blast out rocks, and face the storm. It impels us to destroy in order not to be ourselves destroyed; to endure and to inflict pain, when necessary, as in a surgical operation; to kill the animals necessary for our subsistence; and even to take human life in defense of our own lives, our liberties, or our country's safety.

5. PERVERSION.—A delight in destruction, in giving pain for its own sake, in killing through revenge, malice, or a mere thirst for blood, are perversions of a beneficent faculty. Professor Bruggmans, of Leyden, told Dr. Spurzheim of a Dutch priest whose desire to kill and

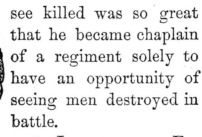
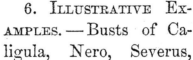

see killed was so great that he became chaplain of a regiment solely to have an opportunity of seeing men destroyed in battle.

6. ILLUSTRATIVE EXAMPLES. — Busts of Caligula, Nero, Severus,

FIG. 56.—BULLDOG.

FIG. 57.—DEER.

Charles XII., and Catherine de Medicis present remarkable prominences in the place of this organ. It was large in the ancient Roman head generally, but comparatively small in the Greek. It is large in the heads of most savage nations, and especially so in those of the Caribs. The Hindoos generally have it small.

All deliberate murderers, in common with carnivorous animals, such as the lion, the tiger, and the wolf, have a large development of Destructiveness. Observe fig. 56 in contrast with fig. 57. It is also larger in men than in women, as indicated by the broader heads of the former, and the manifestations correspond.

7. CULTIVATION.—The killing of noxious animals, the extirpation of weeds, the clearing of forests, the breaking up of the land, hunting, fishing, and so forth, help to exercise and develop Destructiveness. We may also cultivate a whole-

some indignation when wronged, fight against public evils, and exercise our energy in striving to remove or destroy whatever impedes our progress.

8. RESTRAINT.—To restrain Destructiveness, cultivate Benevolence and a mild and forgiving spirit, avoid killing anything if possible, and take but little animal food and no alcoholic liquors.

X. ALIMENTIVENESS. (8.)

For one believeth that he may eat all things; another, who is weak, eateth herbs.

1. LOCATION.—It is situated, as may be seen by reference to our diagram (fig. 23), immediately in front of the upper part

LARGE.   SMALL.

FIG. 58.—ALEXANDER DUMAS.*   FIG. 59.—MR. ——.

of the ear (8). In the brain, it occupies the anterior convolutions of the middle lobe, and externally corresponds with the anterior part of the temporal bone. To find it on the living head, take the upward and forward junction of the ear with the head as the starting-point, and draw a line half an inch forward, inclining a little downward, and you will be upon it. It lies nearly parallel with the zygomatic arch, which is often rendered prominent by it, when large, but the distance of the arch from the proper walls of the skull is variable, and it therefore furnishes no certain guide. The temporal muscle also opposes an obstacle to a correct judgment of its degree

---

* Well known as a very prolific French novelist of the modern sensational school.

of development, but may itself be taken as a sign of character in relation to this propensity, as it is almost always large in connection with large Alimentiveness, and its lower part is pushed outward, making it appear as if lying on a pyramidal instead of a vertical-sided cranium.

2. PHYSIOGNOMICAL SIGN.—In addition to the size and strength of the temporal muscle, and the broadness of the head on and above the zygomatic arch already alluded to, we find accompanying large Alimentiveness a greater or less enlargement of the lower part of the cheeks, as shown in fig. 58, sometimes, when excessive, resulting in an overlapping of flabby integument, which gives a gross animal look to the face. Fig. 59 shows these signs small.

3. FUNCTION.—The function of this propensity is to prompt us to select food and to take nourishment. Its action creates the sensations of hunger and thirst, and when unperverted, and the stomach in a healthy condition, furnishes a sure guide as to the quality and quantity of food necessary for the purposes of nutrition and health.

4. PERVERSION.—Perverted Alimentiveness leads to gluttony and drunkenness, to the use of condiments, coffee, tea, tobacco, and other unnatural stimulants, such as opium, arsenic, and morphine, and through these to disease, suffering, and premature death.

5. CULTIVATION.—To increase the activity of this faculty, when it is weak or dormant, one should make his table and its belongings as attractive as possible, provide the best and most finely flavored dishes his means will permit, and then sit down with the determination to enjoy the meal as much as possible. If the inactivity of Alimentiveness result from disease of any kind, its restoration will come with that of health. The latter requires the first attention.

6. RESTRAINT.—To restrain this propensity is difficult, and requires the exercise of the higher organs, whose action has a tendency to hold the appetites in check. In addition to this, the temptations of sumptuous tables and rich, highly seasoned food should be avoided. You should " eat to live, rather than live to eat."

XI. BIBATIVENESS. (F.)

Look not on the wine when it is red. At the last it biteth like a serpent, and stingeth like an adder.

1. LOCATION.—This organ is situated in front of Aliment-iveness. It is not marked on our diagrams. (See fig. 60.)

2. FUNCTION.—It gives a fondness for liquids; a love of water, and a desire to drink, bathe, swim, etc.

3. PERVERSION.—In its perverted action, it leads to excessive drinking, unquenchable thirst, and drunkenness.

4. CULTIVATION.—The practice of bathing, swimming, boating, and the moderate drinking of pure water will tend to increase the action of this faculty.

5. RESTRAINT.—To restrain a too strong

FIG. 60.—WILLIAM COBBETT.*

appetite for drink, abstain wholly from all beverages except water, and cultivate the higher faculties; a love for literature, art, and nature, or whatever else has a refining and elevating tendency; and especially seek the help from above which comes only through the awakened and sanctified moral sentiments.

XII. ACQUISITIVENESS. (9.)

If any provide not for his own, and especially for those of his own household, he hath denied the faith, and is worse than an infidel.

1. LOCATION.—The organ of Acquisitiveness is situated on the side of the head next above Alimentiveness (9, fig. 23). To find it on the living head, take the middle of the top of the ear as a starting-point, and move the finger directly upward one inch, and then horizontally forward the same

---

* An English writer and politician who spent a portion of his life in America, and was noted for his controversial tastes and abilities.

distance, and it will rest upon the place of the organ. On the skull, Acquisitiveness corresponds with the anterior inferior angle of the parietal bone. Figs. 63 and 64 show how its

LARGE.   SMALL.

FIG. 61.—GEORGE PEABODY.*   FIG. 62.—J. D. B. DE BOW.†

development affects the form of the head as seen in front, giving greater *width*, when large, to this portion of the brain.

2. PHYSIOGNOMICAL SIGN.—Persons noted for their love of gain and ability to acquire property are observed to have, as a general rule, massive noses, and it is believed that thickness of the nose above the wing (fig. 65, *a*) is the true facial sign of Acquisitiveness. The sign is promi-

FIG. 63.   FIG. 64.

nent in likenesses of the Rothschilds, Billy Gray, John Jacob Astor, and in the living faces of the men of our day who have made or are making fortunes. The noses of the Jews are

---

* Mr. Peabody, the American banker, is as well known for his princely munificence as for his immense wealth.

† The late Mr. De Bow, best known as the editor of *De Bow's Review*, was a good commercial and statistical writer, and had great talent for business, but never accumulated money.

generally thick as well as arched, and the arched or hawk nose has, not inaptly, been called the Commercial Nose; though it is not in the form of the profile, as some have asserted, but in the thickness of the trunk, which almost invariably accompanies it, that the sign of the trading or money-getting propensity resides.

3. FUNCTION.—Acquisitiveness prompts to acquire, to accumulate, to store our surplus, to make provision for the future. It incites the farmer, the mechanic, the manufacturer, the merchant, and the professional man to diligence in their respective callings, and is one of the sources of the comforts and elegances of life. Its regular activity distinguishes civilized man from the savage. The latter is, in general, content with the satisfying of his present wants, while the former looks thoughtfully forward to the possible necessities of the future. Consuming but a portion of what he earns, the industrious and prudent citizen contributes to the national wealth, and leaves something behind him for the benefit of posterity. The objects of Acquisitiveness may be various—in one, money or lands; in another, books or works of art; in a third, old coins and other objects of antiquity, the propensity taking its direction from other faculties with which it is combined.

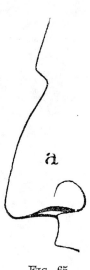

FIG. 65.

4. PERVERSION.—Excessively developed, Acquisitiveness engenders a miserly, grasping penuriousness, and an all-absorbing love of gain for its own sake; and when not controlled by the moral sentiments, results in theft and other dishonest means of acquiring the coveted lucre.

5. CULTIVATION.—When the organ is small, and there is too little economy, and a tendency to lavish and careless expenditure, some plan, devised by the intellect, must be put into operation to compel, as it were, a more prudent and saving course. Keeping a strict account of expenditures, and especially personal expenses, and looking over and balancing cash accounts frequently, will serve to remind one how the money goes and wherein much of it might readily be

saved.   Making up one's mind to get rich, if there be a strong
will to back the resolution, sometimes arouses Acquisitiveness,
and finally greatly increases its power.

6. RESTRAINT.—The only way to restrain this or other
powerful propensities, is by cultivating the higher faculties
and sentiments, and bringing their influence to bear upon
them, thus keeping them in due subjection.   Benevolence,
Conscientiousness, Ideality, and the reflective faculties tend
to counteract a miserly tendency or a too great love of money.

XIII. SECRETIVENESS.   (10.)

He that keepeth his mouth, keepeth his life; but he that openeth wide his lips shall
have destruction.

1. LOCATION.—The organ of this propensity is situated at
the inferior edge of the parietal bone (10, fig. 23), immediately above Destructiveness, or in the middle of the lateral

LARGE.   SMALL.

FIG. 66.—F. D. HUNTINGTON, D.D.*   FIG. 67.—J. C. SMITH, D.D.†

portion of the brain.   When this organ and Destructiveness
are both highly developed, there is a general fullness of the
lower and middle portion of the side-head, as in the outline,
fig. 68.   Fig. 69 shows it small.

2. PHYSIOGNOMICAL SIGN.—The breadth of the wings of

* Francis D. Huntington, D.D., formerly of Boston, well known both as an author
and as a preacher, is Bishop of the Protestant Episcopal Church of Maine.

† Dr. John Cotton Smith is an eminent leading Protestant Episcopal clergyman of
New York.

the nose next to the face indicates Secretiveness. This is in accordance with the physiological action of this faculty, which tends to shut the mouth and expand the nostrils. This sign is large in the Negro, the Chinese, the North American Indian, and in most savage and half-civilized tribes.

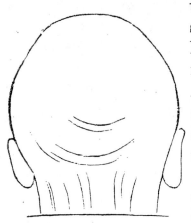

FIG. 68.—SECRETIVENESS LARGE.

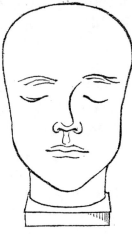

FIG. 69.—CLARA FISHER.

3. NATURAL LANGUAGE. — Persons who have Secretiveness large, manifest its natural language in various ways—buttoning up the coat to the chin, wearing a high, tight cravat; or, if a woman, a dress fitting high up on the neck. Those who possess little Secretiveness wear their clothes more loose and open. This propensity, when predominantly active, produces a close, sly look, admirably exemplified in our likeness of Constance Emily Kent, the murderess; the eye rolls from side to side; the voice is low; the shoulders are drawn up toward the ears, and the footstep is soft and gliding. The movements of the body are toward the side. Sir Walter Scott accurately describes the look

FIG. 70.—CONSTANCE EMILY KENT.*

* An English murderess, who showed a great deal of cunning.

produced by this faculty and Cautiousness in the following lines :

> "For *evil* seemed that old man's eye,
> *Dark and designing, fierce yet shy.*
> *Still he avoided forward look,*
> *But slow and circumspectly took*
> *A circling, never-ceasing glance,*
> *By doubt and cunning marked at once,*
> Which shot a mischief-boding ray
> From under eyebrows shagged and gray."

4. FUNCTION.—The Good Book says : "A fool uttereth all his mind, but a wise man keepeth it till afterward." The fool thus characterized has no Secretiveness.

This faculty gives the wise man his prudence—restrains expression till "afterward"—till a suitable occasion. It imparts, in fact, an instinctive tendency to conceal, and the legitimate object of it is to restrain the outward expression of our thoughts and emotions, giving the understanding time to pronounce judgment on its propriety. Some instinctive tendency to restrain within the mind itself—to conceal, as it were, from the public eye—the various emotions and ideas which involuntarily present themselves, was necessary to prevent their outward expression; and nature has provided this power in the faculty of Secretiveness. Those in whom it is deficient are characterized by a lack of tact, great bluntness of manner, and an instantaneous expression of every thought and feeling ; and they seldom suspect any hidden purpose in another. Othello is described by Iago as such a person. He says :

> "The Moor is of a free and open nature,
> That thinks men honest that but seem to be so ;
> And will as tenderly be led by the nose
> As asses are !"

5. CULTIVATION.—Where the instinct of concealment is not sufficiently developed, the intellect should, so far as possible, supply the necessary policy. There must also be a constant effort to suppress injudicious out-gushings of feeling. Impulse must be kept in check by Cautiousness and reason. Everybody is not to be trusted.

6. RESTRAINT.—To restrain the too influential action of this faculty, a more frank, open, and straightforward manner should

be cultivated, and constant effort be made to give hearty expression to thought and feeling.

XIV. CAUTIOUSNESS.   (11.)

A prudent man foreseeth the evil, and hideth himself.

1. LOCATION.—The place of the organ of Cautiousness is on the upper, lateral, and posterior part of the head, and near

LARGE.   MODERATE.

FIG. 71.—JOHN DOWLING, D.D.*   FIG. 72.—REV. J. G. BARTHOLOMEW.†

the middle of the parietal bone (11, fig. 23). When large, the head is very broad at that point, as in figs. 71 and 73, while a deficiency gives quite another shape to the skull, as in figs. 72 and 74. To find Cautiousness on the living head,

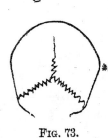

take the back part of the ear as the starting-point and draw a perpendicular line upward, and where the head begins to round off to form the top is the location of the organ.

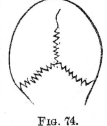

FIG. 73.

2. NATURAL LANGUAGE.—The

FIG. 74.

action of this faculty raises the head and body and gives the former a rotary motion, as in looking on all sides, whence the

---

* Dr. Dowling, an Englishman by birth, is pastor of a Baptist Church in New York, and author of a work on the Christian Martyrs.

† A Universalist preacher in Brooklyn, N. Y., of marked talent, and much respected and esteemed by all who know him.

French name given to the faculty by Spurzheim—*Circonspec-tion*, to look around one's self.

3. FUNCTION.—It is the function of Cautiousness to give prudence, watchfulness, carefulness, and provision against danger. It is one of the restraining powers of the mind, and prevents the propelling forces of our nature from plunging us into difficulty and danger. Persons having it well developed are habitually on their guard; they know that it is more difficult to sustain than to acquire reputation, and, consequently, every new undertaking is prosecuted as carefully as the first. They look forward to all possible dangers, and are anxious to anticipate every occurrence; they ask advice of every one, and often, after having received much counsel, remain undecided. They put great faith in the observation, that of a hundred misfortunes which befall us, ninety-nine arise from our own fault. Such persons never break any article; they may pass their lives in pruning trees, or in working with sharp tools, without cutting themselves.

4. EXCESS AND PERVERSION.—When the faculty is too largely developed, with moderate Hope, it produces doubts, irresolution, and wavering, and may lead to absolute incapacity for any decisive and vigorous action. A great and involuntary activity of it produces *panic*—a state in which the mind is hurried away by an irresistible emotion of fear, for which no adequate cause exists.

5. ILLUSTRATIVE EXAMPLES.—In armies and other large bodies of men, a panic becomes contagious, and results in the abandonment of everything else in obedience to the one absorbing instinct of self-preservation. A large development of this organ, combined with large Destructiveness, predisposes to suicide. Dr. Andrew Combe examined a number of suicides in the *Morgue* (dead-house) of Paris, and found in them Hope generally small, with Cautiousness and Destructiveness large. Cautiousness is larger in the Germans, English, and Scotch than in the Celtic French or Irish.

6. CULTIVATION.—By an intellectual effort, one may arouse Cautiousness into activity and promote its development. The disastrous results of indiscretion, carelessness, rashness, and

recklessness should be kept before the mind, and a more prudent and watchful policy resolved upon. Causality and Firmness should be called to the aid of weak Cautiousness.

7. RESTRAINT.—Causality and Firmness should be brought into action to restrain as well as to encourage this faculty. Reason should tell us that excessive or over-active Cautiousness inclines us to magnify dangers, and to be irresolute and over-anxious, and we should therefore try to adopt a more bold and decided course of action than mere feeling would suggest. Combativeness and Destructiveness may also be made to partially offset this faculty, and promote a more daring spirit.

XV. APPROBATIVENESS.   (12.)

Do good, and thou shalt have praise.

1. LOCATION.—Approbativeness is located on the upper and back part of the top side-head, at the point marked 12 in

LARGE.   MODERATE.

FIG. 75.—R. HANKS, D.D.*   FIG. 76.—JOHN P. DURBIN, D.D.†

the diagram (fig. 23). When large, it produces a remarkable fullness and breadth in the upper and back part of the head. On the skull, it commences about half an inch from the lambdoidal suture.

---

* Dr. Hanks is an impressive and eloquent preacher of the Protestant Methodist denomination.

† Dr. Durbin is one of the most powerful and controlling leaders of the Methodist Episcopal denomination in the United States.

2. PHYSIOGNOMICAL SIGN.—Approbativeness manifests itself in the face by the lifting of the upper lip, sometimes exposing the teeth, as shown in fig. 77. It is generally largely developed in the French, the Irish, and especially in the Negro. The latter is no less remarkable for his love of praise than for showing his teeth.

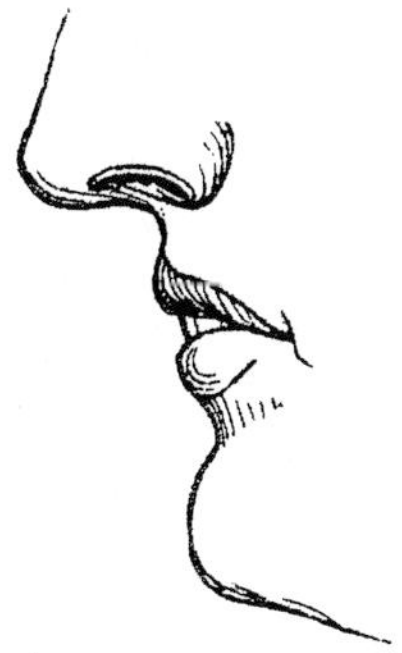

3. FUNCTION.—This faculty gives regard for character, desire to excel and be esteemed, love of praise, ambition, affability, and politeness. Mr. Combe calls it "the drill master of society;" and in this capacity it leads to acts of moral tendency, as our ill feelings and selfishness are restrained to please others; but it does not

FIG. 77.

decide what actions are praiseworthy and what are not, but merely judges these actions in reference to some conventional standard set up by custom or by the dictates of the other faculties, and praises or blames accordingly as they do or do not conform to this standard.

4. PERVERSION.—No faculty is more prone to run into excess than Approbativeness. It leads to self-praise, vanity, and egotism. The diversified forms in which its activity appears are well exposed in Young's "Love of Fame."

> " The love of praise, howe'er conceal'd by art,
> Reigns, more or less, and glows in every heart:
> The proud to gain it, toils on toils endure;
> The modest shun it, but to make it sure.
> O'er globes and scepters, now on thrones it swells,
> Now trims the midnight lamp in college cells;
> 'Tis Tory, Whig; it plots, prays, preaches, pleads,
> Harangues in senates, squeaks in masquerades;
> It aids the dancer's heel, the writer's head,
> And heaps the plain with mountains of the dead;
> Nor ends with life, but nods in sable plumes,
> Adorns our hearse, and flatters on our tombs."

5. ILLUSTRATVE EXAMPLES.—The French are remarkable for a large development of this organ, while the English are more noted for Self-Esteem. The influence of Approbativeness shows itself in the manners, institutions, and daily literature of France in an extraordinary degree. Compliments and praises are the current coin of conversation, and glory

the condiment of the feast of life.   Americans also generally have the faculty largely developed.

Approbativeness is generally more active in woman than in man, shown in her greater love for display, fashions, etc., and it has been observed that a greater number of women than of men become insane through excess of this feeling.

6. CULTIVATION.—One who finds himself too careless of reputation and of the opinions of his fellow-men, should strive intellectually to arrive at a true estimate of the real value of public opinion, and of the importance of one's character and standing among men.   The cultivation of manners and the strict observance of the etiquette of social intercourse will help to develop the organ of Approbativeness.

7. RESTRAINT.—To restrain Approbativeness, one must cultivate Self-Esteem and Conscientiousness, and, doing what is right, try to not care too much what people say about it. Have less fear of " Mrs. Grundy."   Too great sensitiveness to praise and blame must be overcome by allowing reason to show how little either is generally worth, and by recalling to mind how often the feelings have been hurt in the past, when, as has been afterward seen, there was no real cause.

XVI. SELF-ESTEEM.   (13.)

What ye know, the same do I know also ; I am not inferior unto you.

1. LOCATION.—The organ of Self-Esteem is situated at the back part of the top-head (13, fig. 23), where the coronal surface begins to decline toward the back-head, and a little above the posterior angle of the parietal bones.   When it is large, the head rises far upward and backward from the ear in the direction of it, as in fig. 78.   Fig. 79 shows the form of the head when Self-Esteem is small.

2. NATURAL LANGUAGE.—The action of this faculty throws the head back in the direction of its phrenological organ, as shown in fig. 81, and gives a dignified and upright carriage to the body.   Fig. 80 shows the attitude induced by a deficiency of the faculty.

3. FUNCTION.—The function of Self-Esteen is to inspire self-

respect, self-reliance, independence, dignity, magnanimity, pride of character, and an aspiring and ruling disposition.

LARGE.   MODERATE.

FIG. 78.—GEN. E. KIRBY SMITH.*   FIG. 79.—GEN. ROSECRANS.†

Its due endowment produces only excellent results, and we find that in society, that individual is uniformly treated with most lasting and sincere respect who esteems himself so

FIG. 80.—DEFERENCE.

FIG. 81.—DIGNITY.

highly as to scorn every mean action. By communicating a feeling of self-respect, it frequently and effectually aids the

---

* A noted "Confederate" officer in the American Civil War.
† Distinguished in the army of the Union in the American Civil War.

moral sentiments in resisting temptation to vice. Several individuals in whom the organ is large, have stated to us that they have been restrained from forming improper connections by an overwhelming sense of the degradation which would result from doing so; and that they believed their better principles might have yielded to temptation had it not been for the support afforded to them by the instinctive impulses of Self-Esteem."

4. PERVERSION.—Perverted Self-Esteem manifests itself in insupportable pride, hauteur, forwardness, superciliousness, imperiousness, and an insatiable love of power.

5. DEFICIENCY.—A predisposition to excessive humility and a painful lack of self-confidence are the results of deficient Self-Esteem. A person thus constituted has no reliance upon

FIG. 82.—PRIDE.

himself; if the public or his superiors frown, he is unable to pursue even a virtuous course, through diffidence of his own judgment. Inferior talents, combined with a strong endowment of Self-Esteem, are often crowned with far higher success than more splendid abilities joined with this sentiment in a feebler degree.

6. ILLUSTRATIVE EXAMPLE.—At Heidelberg Dr. Gall saw a girl of eighteen, of a remarkable character. Every word or gesture in the least familiar revolted her. She called on God on every occasion, as if he took a special interest in her affairs. When she spoke, assurance and presumption were painted in her features; she carried her head high, and a little backward, and all the movements of her head expressed pride. She was not capable of submission; when in a passion, she was violent, and disposed to proceed to all extremities. Although only the daughter of a quill merchant, she spoke her native language with extraordinary purity, and communicated with none but persons of a rank superior to her own.

7. CULTIVATION.—By assuming the attitude of Self-Esteem

and trying to imbibe its spirit at the same time, the faculty may be strengthened and its activity promoted. The too low self-valuation which arises from a deficient development of this faculty, should be corrected by bringing prominently into view the best traits of one's character and reflecting on the exalted nature of those endowments. "I am a man," Black Hawk said to Jackson. "I am a man," or "I am a woman," should be the proud assertion of the too modest reader, who must learn to hold up the head in all company. A correct phrenological delineation of character will do more than anything else to correct false, and especially too low estimates of character.

8. RESTRAINT.—To restrain forwardness, pride, excessive self-confidence, and an overbearing, domineering spirit, cultivate the moral sentiments, and especially Veneration, seeking in religion that grace which maketh humble like a little child. Correct too high estimates of yourself by the exercise of reason and the help of Phrenology.

XVII. FIRMNESS. (14.)

Be ye steadfast, unmovable; always abounding in the work of the Lord,

1. LOCATION.—The organ of this faculty is situated at the back part of the coronal region (14, fig. 23), on the median line, and between Veneration and Self-Esteem. Figs. 85 and 86 show how its degree of development affects the form of the skull.

2. PHYSIOGNOMICAL SIGNS.—The facial sign of Firmness, corresponding with the situation of its phrenological organ, is the perpendicular straightness or convexity and stiffness of the center of the upper lip (fig. 87). To tell a man to "keep a stiff upper lip" is equivalent to telling him to be firm—to hold his ground. This faculty has also one of its most striking indications in the size and strength of the cervical vertebræ, or bones of the neck, and in the perpendicularity of the neck itself.

3. NATURAL LANGUAGE.—The action of Firmness throws the head, face, and neck into the line of the phrenological

organ of the faculty. When it predominates, it gives a peculiar hardness to the manner and stiffness and uprightness

LARGE.   MODERATE.

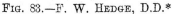

FIG. 83.—F. W. HEDGE, D.D.*   FIG. 84.—W. H. RYDER, D.D.†

to the gait (the foot being brought down heavily on the heel), and an emphatic tone to the voice.

4. FUNCTION.—Firmness imparts stability of character, tenacity of will, perseverance, and an aversion to change. It seems to have no relation to external things, its influence terminating on the mind itself, and it adds only a quality to the manifestations of the other powers: thus, acting along

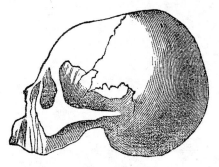
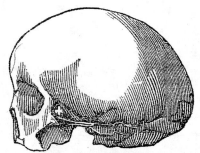

FIG. 85.—LARGE.   FIG. 86.—SMALL.

with Combativeness, it produces determined bravery; with Veneration, sustained devotion; and with Conscientiousness,

---

* A Unitarian preacher and an author of reputation. His scholarship is of the highest order. Noted for determination and strength of will.

† A Universalist minister of high culture, fervid eloquence, and great kindness of heart.

4

inflexible integrity. It gives perseverance, however, in acting only on the other faculties which are possessed in an available degree.

5. ILLUSTRATIVE EXAMPLES.—Firmness is much larger in some nations than in others. The English have it much more fully developed than the French. The latter, under the influence of large Combativeness and moderate Cautious-

ness, make lively and impetuous charges, shouting and cheering as they advance; but if repulsed or steadily resisted, their ardor abates, they become discouraged, and any serious reverse is apt to become a total defeat; while the English, on the other hand, are less impetuous and dashing, but hold steadily to their purpose, and if repulsed, return undiscouraged to the charge, or, if com-pelled to fall back, obstinately dispute the enemy's advance step by step. Americans of the Northern States resemble the English in this respect, though they unite with this persevering steadfastness some of the impetuosity of the French. The men of the South have less Firmness and show less persistency; acting more under the influence of Self-Esteem and Approbativeness, they fight for glory, and refuse to yield through pride rather than from genuine steadfastness.

FIG. 87.

6. CULTIVATION.—Firmness may be developed by a well-considered and wise assumption of positions which are clearly important to be held. The faculty is then stimulated by Conscientiousness, Self-Esteem, and Approbativeness. One must constantly remember his weakness in this matter, and strive to have a mind of his own, and to overcome difficulties instead of turning aside to avoid them.

7. RESTRAINT.—To restrain Firmness, we must subject it to the influence of reason and the moral sentiments. Listen, at least, to advice, and if good try to profit by it. The needless losses and humiliations to which obstinacy and an unreason-able persistence in a line of conduct proved to be wrong or impracticable has subjected us, should be constantly recalled to mind when we are tempted to be willful or stubborn.

XVIII. CONSCIENTIOUSNESS.   (15.)

Till I die I will not remove mine integrity from me. My righteousness I hold fast, and will not let it go.

1. LOCATION.—The organ of Conscientiousness is situated on the posterior and lateral parts of the coronal region (at the point marked 15 in fig. 23), upward from the fore part of

LARGE.   SMALL.

FIG. 88.—THE GOOD BOY.   FIG. 89.—THE BAD BOY.

Cautiousness and forward from Approbativeness. On the skull, its place is on the upper and forward part of the parietal bone, about three inches above the opening of the ear, and about one and a half inches from the middle line of the head. When large, with deficient Firmness, it gives the head the shape shown in fig. 90.   Fig. 91 represents it small.

2. FUNCTION.—Conscientiousness imparts a perception and love of right, an innate sense of accountability, and a dis-

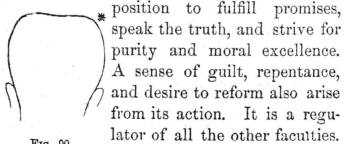

position to fulfill promises, speak the truth, and strive for purity and moral excellence. A sense of guilt, repentance, and desire to reform also arise from its action. It is a regulator of all the other faculties.

FIG. 90.

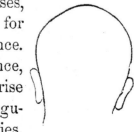

FIG. 91.

If Combativeness and Destructiveness be too active, Conscientiousness prescribes a limit to their indulgence; it permits defense, but no malicious aggression; if Acquisitiveness urge too keenly, it reminds us of the rights of others; if Benevolence tend toward profusion, this faculty issues the admonition, Be just before you are generous; if Ideality aspire to its high delights, when duty requires laborious exertions in an humble sphere, Conscientiousness supplies the curb, and bids the soaring spirit restrain its wing.

When this faculty is powerful, the individual is disposed to regulate his conduct by the nicest sentiments of justice; there is an earnestness, integrity, and directness in his manner which inspire us with confidence and give us a conviction of his sincerity. Such an individual desires to act justly from the love of justice, unbiased by fear, interest, or any sinister motive.

3. DEFICIENCY.—Small Conscientiousness leaves the propensities without adequate control. The feeling of justice being wanting, the mind does not furnish reasons to oppose to the influence of the baser inclinations. A deficiency of Conscientiousness in connection with large Secretiveness, especially when the latter is aided by Ideality and Wonder, produces a tendency to magnifying so strong in some cases that the unfortunate victim of a bad organization finds it quite difficult to overcome it.

4. ILLUSTRATIVE EXAMPLES.—The sentiment of truth is found by the English judges to be so low in the Africans, the Hindoos, and the aboriginal Americans, that such individuals are not received as witnesses in the colonial courts; and it is a curious fact, that a defect in the organ of Conscientiousness is a reigning feature in the skulls of these nations.

5. CULTIVATION.—A constant effort to keep a sense of right and wrong uppermost in our minds in all our transactions, and to make everything subservient to justice and moral principle, will induce activity and development in the organ, and make doing right more and more easy and pleasant. Our motto should be: "Let justice be done though the heavens fall."

6. RESTRAINT.—There is seldom great need to restrain this faculty, but sometimes it makes one in whom it is largely developed and morbidly active censorious, and too exacting

and fault-finding in respect to others, and liable to an uncalled-for sense of guilt and unworthiness in regard to himself. These perverted manifestations should be met by cultivating Benevolence, Self-Esteem, and Firmness, and by correcting intellectually the false estimates of sentiment and feeling.

XIX. HOPE. (16.)

Now the God of hope fill you with all joy and peace in believing, that ye may abound in hope.

1. LOCATION.—The organ of Hope is situated on the side of the top-head (16, fig. 23), on a perpendicular line drawn

LARGE.   NOT SO LARGE.

FIG. 92.—BESSIE INGLIS.*   FIG. 93.—EDWARD THOMSON, D.D.†

upward from the front part of the ear, and between Marvelousness and Conscientiousness.

2. PHYSIOGNOMICAL SIGN.—Hope elevates the center of the eyebrow, opens the eyes wide, and turns them upward. It gives an open and pleasant expression to the whole countenance.

3. FUNCTION.—In persons with large Hope, "the wish is father to the thought." With large Approbativeness, they expect to rise to distinction; with large Acquisitiveness, they think they shall become rich. "The sentiment of Hope,"

---

* An English authoress and a very popular public reader.
† A Bishop of the Methodist Episcopal Church, eminent as a writer and a preacher.

Spurzheim truly says, "is indeed necessary to the happiness of mankind in almost every situation. It often produces more satisfaction than even the success of our projects. Its activity, however, varies greatly in different individuals; while some easily despair, others are always elated and find everything for the best; constant hope sustains them in the midst of difficulties; the first plan for accomplishing any object having failed, only stimulates them to form new ones, which they confidently expect will succeed. Those who are everlastingly scheming, or building castles in the air, possess this faculty in a high degree. It seems to induce a belief in the possibility of whatever the other faculties desire, without producing conviction; for this results from reflection."

This sentiment is not confined to the business of this life, but, passing the limits of the present existence, inspires expectations of a future state, and a belief, hope, and trust in the immortality of the soul.

4. EXCESS AND DEFICIENCY.—Hope, like any other faculty, may be too strong or too weak. In the former case it induces us to expect things which are unreasonable, not founded on probability, or altogether impossible. When too feeble, on the contrary, especially if Cautiousness be large, it is apt to produce lowness of spirits, melancholy, and even despair.

5. CULTIVATION.—Lively youthful society, and the companionship of those who are cheerful and buoyant, has a tendency to promote Hope and develop the organ in those who are naturally too easily discouraged and apt to look on the dark side. Such ones should remember, too, that "every cloud has a silver lining," and that though "grief may endure for a night," "joy cometh with the morning." *Nil desperandum*—never despair.

6. RESTRAINT.—To hold in check excessive expectation, cool judgment must be kept always on guard to correct the over-estimates of this sentiment. In business, persons in whom Hope is too large or active, should adopt and strictly adhere to the cash principle, both in buying and in selling, as there is always a great liability to buy too much, and sell without sufficient security for the payment.

XX. SPIRITUALITY. (17.)

We through the Spirit wait for the hope of righteousness by faith.

1. LOCATION.—The organ of Spirituality (17, fig. 23) is situated immediately above Ideality, in the lateral parts of the anterior region of the top-head.

LARGE.   NOT LARGE.

FIG. 94.—P. N. LYNCH, D.D.*

FIG. 95.—H. W. BELLOWS, D.D.†

2. PHYSIOGNOMICAL SIGN.—Large and active Spirituality gives a singularly elevated expression of countenance. The eyelids are lifted and the eyes often turned obliquely upward. When the excitement of the organ results in the feeling of wonder, the expression becomes like that of fig. 96.

FIG. 96.—WONDER.

3. FUNCTION.—The function of this organ is to give a perception of spiritual things, faith in the unseen, and an intuitive knowledge of what is true and good, with a prophetic insight and an internal consciousness of immortality and a supersenuous existence.

4. PERVERSION.—Perverted Spirituality leads to super-

* Dr. Lynch, Roman Catholic Bishop of Charleston, S. C., holds a high position in his church. He is noted for his learning, kindness of heart, and spiritual-mindedness.
† Dr. Bellows is a distinguished Unitarian minister of New York.

stition, fear of ghosts, credulity, and excessive love of the wonderful. There are many disposed to believe in dreams, sorcery, amulets, magic, astrology, in the mystic influence of spirits and angels, in the power of the devil, in second-sight, and in miracles and incomprehensible representations of all sorts. Some also are disposed to have visions, and to see ghosts, demons, and phantoms. This sentiment gains credence to the true and also to the false prophet, aids superstition, but is also essential to the belief in the doctrines of refined religion. It is more or less active, not only in different individuals, but also in whole nations; its functions are often disordered, constituting one form of insanity called demonomania.

5. ILLUSTRATIVE EXAMPLES.—A gentleman who moved in the best society in Paris asked Dr. Gall to examine his head. The doctor's first remark was, "You sometimes see visions, and believe in apparitions." The gentleman started from his chair in astonishment, and said that he *had* frequent visions; but that never, up to this moment, had he spoken on the subject to any human being, through fear of being set down as absurdly credulous.

Spirituality was largely developed in Joan of Arc, Cromwell, Tasso, Swedenborg, Stilling, Wesley, Burns, Scott, Hawthorne, and Laura Bridgeman, and correct portraits of them show a marked fullness in the region assigned to its organ.

6. CULTIVATION.—To cultivate this faculty, the attention should be frequently directed to that class of subjects upon which it is legitimately exercised—the Deity, a future existence, intuitive perceptions, premonitions, etc. Meditations on divine things, the reading of religious works, and attendance upon religious meetings will aid in its development, if right use be made of such opportunities. The mind should be kept open to the intuitive perception of truth, and all supersensual impressions and premonitions be heeded.

7. RESTRAINT.—When it becomes necessary to hold in check the too active manifestations of Spirituality, the restraining organs of Cautiousness, Self-Esteem, and Firmness must be called to the support of reason, and the mind with-

drawn from the constant contemplation of the spiritual and fixed upon the real, tangible things of this life. Strict attention to practical matters, and a resolute performance of the common duties of life will help to give a healthy tone to the mind.

XXI. VENERATION. (18.)

Humble yourselves in the sight of the Lord, and he shall lift you up.

1. LOCATION.—The organ of Veneration is situated in the middle of the coronal region (18, fig. 23), between Benevolence and Firmness. Fig. 99 shows it large, and fig. 100 small.

LARGE.　　　　　　　　　　　　　SMALL.

FIG. 97.—DR. PUSEY.*　　　　FIG. 98.—GEO. EDWARDS.†

2. PHYSIOGNOMICAL SIGN.—Sir Charles Bell says, "When rapt in devotional feelings, when all outward impressions are unheeded, the eyes are raised by an action neither taught nor acquired. Instinctively we bow the body and

FIG. 99.—LARGE.

FIG. 100.—SMALL.

---

* Rev. Edward B. Pusey, D.D., is a distinguished "high church" Episcopalian clergyman, noted as a leader of the ritualistic party in the English Church.

† An English naturalist, in whom Veneration is somewhat wanting.

raise the eyes in prayer, as though the visible heavens were the seat of God. In the language of the poet—

Prayer is the upward glancing of the eye,
When none but God is near.

'I will lift up mine eyes unto the hills,' the Psalmist says, 'from whence cometh my help.'"

3. NATURAL LANGUAGE.—The natural language of this faculty carries the head upward in the direction of the organ. The voice is soft, subdued, reposing, and adoring. The greatest difference is perceptible in the tones and manner of prayer of clergymen in whom the organ is large, compared with those in whom it is small; there is a soft breathing fervor of devotion in the former, and a cold reasoning formality in the latter. One reaches the head, the other touches the heart.

4. FUNCTION.—The faculty of Veneration produces reverence in general, and especially for religion and things sacred; adoration of a Supreme Being; a disposition to pray and observe religious rites and respect for whatever is perceived to be great and good. It is the source of natural religion, and of that tendency to worship a superior Power which manifests itself in all well-organized men. The faculty, however, produces merely an emotion, and does not form ideas of the object to which adoration should be directed.

5. PERVERSION.—This faculty, when unenlightened, may lead to every kind of religious absurdity, as worshiping beasts and stocks and stones. Many African negroes, American Indians, and even Hindoos, have but a moderate intellectual development compared with Europeans, and their superstitions are more gross. Socrates did not assent to the popular religious errors of the Greeks, and in the ancient busts of him he is represented with a splendid forehead. Veneration is large also in negroes, who are prone to superstition.

Nothing is more common in the hospitals for the insane, says Pinel, than cases of alienation produced by devotional feelings excessively exalted, by conscientious scruples carried to prejudicial excesses, or by religious terror. As this kind of insanity, Dr. Gall says, is often present without derangement of the other faculties, physicians ought to have inferred that it is connected with disease of a particular part of the brain.

6. CULTIVATION.—Attendance on religious worship, daily family devotions, and association with persons religiously disposed, and especially those whose character is such as to command great respect, will do much to develop reverential feelings. Respect to all superiors should be cultivated, and the mind often led to the contemplation of the greatness and goodness of God.

7. RESTRAINT.—In those rare cases where there is danger of this sentiment running into the forms of fanaticism and religious monomania, measures should be taken to withdraw the mind from the constant contemplation of subjects on which the mind is warped, and to counteract the perverted tendency by enlisting interest in worldly matters and by the exercise of the reasoning faculties in relation to it. It should be remembered, in such cases, that worship is not the only business of life, but that while on the earth we have duties connected with the earth to perform, and which we are not at liberty to neglect. A *balanced* mind is the best.

XXII. BENEVOLENCE. (19.)

Be ye kind one to another, tender-hearted, forgiving one another.

1. LOCATION.—The organ of Benevolence is situated in the middle of the fore part of the top-head. Its location is marked with its proper number (19) in our diagram (fig. 23). On the skull, its place is just forward of the fontanel, or what is commonly called the opening of the head. The fontanel is at the meeting of the coronal and sagittal sutures. In the young child it is cartilaginous; but from the time of birth it begins to contract, and is generally completely ossified and closed between the second and third years. When large, it gives great elevation to the fore part of the top-head, as represented in fig. 103. Fig. 104 shows it small.

2. PHYSIOGNOMICAL SIGN.—The action of the muscular fibers, which, passing down from the middle of the forehead

over the phrenological organ of the faculty, are inserted near the root of the nose, elevates the inner extremities of the

LARGE.

FIG. 101.—S. H. WESTON, D.D.*

SMALL.

FIG. 102.—CHARLES FLEMING.†

brows, sometimes causing, when strong, short horizontal wrinkles in the center of the forehead, and indicates *active Benevolence*—kindness translated into deeds. Persons with this sign well developed will be found not merely sympathetic, but ready to take hold and *help* those in need of assistance. Men have more of this working Benevolence than women, and it is proper they should have, as their power to help is greater; but women are more sympathetic and more readily touched by pity.

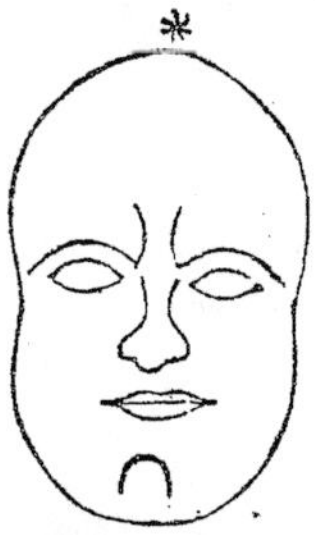

FIG. 103.

3. NATURAL LANGUAGE.—It should be observed, also, that the activity of this faculty relaxes the

FIG. 104.

features and gives an open, genial, benignant, and pleasing expression to the whole countenance. See the contrast in

---

* Dr. Weston is an Episcopal clergyman of New York, noted for his kind and sympathetic disposition.

† Mr. Fleming is thus described by the author of "The Autobiography of a Phrenologist:" "I can truly say that he was one of the worst characters I ever knew, and ignorant to a degree that perfectly amazed me. He had a small head, which swelled out above and behind the ears. His forehead was 'villainously low,' and retreating, and the vertex of the head was very high, but rapidly declined toward the forehead, and also sloped downward toward the parietal bones. His harshness and cruelty almost exceeded belief." *He* would not "spare the rod," but use it freely.

this respect, between the liberal, generous man and the pinched-up miser (figs. 105 and 106).

4. FUNCTION.—St. Paul gives a beautiful description of the genuine character of this sentiment in his account of Christian charity: "Charity," he says, "suffereth long and is kind; charity envieth not; charity vaunteth not itself, is not puffed up," etc. Christ also illustrates it in the parable of the good Samaritan. It gives kindness, sympathy, a desire to make others happy, and a self-sacrificing disposition. It produces liberality of sentiment toward all mankind, a disposition to love them, and to dwell on their virtues rather than their vices. A person in whom this feeling is strong, rarely complains of the ingratitude or heartlessness of others. His goodness provides its own reward.

FIG. 105.—A MISER.

FIG. 106.—A LIBERAL.

5. PERVERSION.—This sentiment, beautiful as it is in its proper action, is, like all others, liable to perversion and abuse. It requires to be directed by Conscientiousness and intellect and restrained by Firmness and Cautiousness, otherwise it produces abuses. Some men, for instance, give with an inconsiderate prodigality, which, while it soon deprives them of the means to exercise their Benevolence in that way, also fails to effect the degree of good that the same means judiciously applied might have accomplished. That individual is best fitted to mature wise plans of charity who has a large endowment of this sentiment combined with powerful intellectual faculties and a good degree of Cautiousness and Firmness.

6. ILLUSTRATIVE EXAMPLES.—Murderers generally have the forehead "villainously low" in the region of Benevolence. Caligula, Caracalla, Nero, Catherine de Medicis, Danton, Robespierre, and all individuals and tribes of men remarkable for cruelty, as the Caribs, the North American Indians, etc.,

are remarkable for the same characteristic. Foreheads remarkably lofty in the region assigned to the organ of Benevolence are, on the contrary, among the leading traits of persons distinguished for their benevolent feelings. Trajan, Marcus Aurelius, Henri Quatre, Father Mathew, Oberlin, Jeannin, Malesherbes, Beecher, and Howard may be referred to as illustrating this development.

7. CULTIVATION.—One in whom this sentiment is not sufficiently strong, should read and reflect upon the life of Christ, and of such men as Oberlin and Howard, and try to appreciate their self-sacrificing goodness. They should also strive to be less selfish and accustom themselves to deeds of active benevolence, giving according to their means as opportunity shall offer. The world is not so full of selfishness as such persons are apt to think, and they will find that those who are least selfish are most happy.

8. RESTRAINT.—There is no necessity, in general, to restrain this sentiment, but it needs the guidance of sound judgment, and should be subservient to Conscientiousness. "Be just before you are generous." But we may be both.

XXIII. CONSTRUCTIVENESS. (20.)

Skillful to work in gold, in silver, in brass, in iron, in stone, and in timber; in purple, in blue, in fine linen, and in crimson; also to grave any manner of graving.

1. LOCATION.—The organ of Constructiveness (20, fig. 23) is situated just forward of Acquisitiveness, the location of which has been already described. On the skull, its place is at the inferior and outer parts of the frontal bone immediately above the spheno-temporal sutures, and behind and above the outer angle of the orbit. Its development gives breadth to the head above the zygomatic arch. Fig. 109 shows it large, and fig. 110 small. "If the base of the brain be narrow, this organ," Mr. Combe says, "holds a situation a little higher than usual, and there will then frequently be found a slight depression at the external angle of the eye, between the zygomatic process and the organ in question."

2. FUNCTION.—By its means birds build nests, rabbits burrow, the beaver makes its hut, and man constructs whatever

his necessities, his comfort, his tastes, or his higher sentiments require, from the hovel and the tent to the palace and the temple. "It invents and produces fortifications, ships, the

LARGE. NOT SO LARGE.

FIG. 107.—JOHN SCOTT, D.D.* FIG. 108.—GEO. W. EATON, D.D., LL.D.†

engines of war, the implements of manufactures, instruments of all kinds, furniture, clothes, and toys; it is essential not only in every mechanical profession, but in all employments that in any way require manual nicety, as the arts of drawing, engraving, writing, carving, and sculpture.

3. PERVERSION.—Large Constructiveness not sufficiently controlled and guided by the higher intellectual faculties, sometimes leads to great waste of time and labor in attempts

 to invent perpetual motions or other impossible machines; with deficient Conscientiousness, it may employ itself in making counterfeit money, false keys, and other dis- honest contrivances.

FIG. 109. FIG. 110.

4. ILLUSTRATIVE EXAMPLES.— The organ of this faculty is seen to be largely developed in busts and portraits of Michael Angelo, Canova, Brunel, Whitney, Fulton, Franklin, Watt, Smeaton, Stephenson,

---

* A leading minister of the Pittsburg Conference of the Methodist Episcopal Church, and editor of the *Methodist Recorder*.

† Ex-President of Madison University, New York, and a Baptist minister of great earnestness and piety.

Howe, Morse, and artists, inventors, and builders. It is generally large in French, Italian, and American heads—and fairly so in the English.

IN THE ANIMALS.—Among the lower animals, it is clear that the ability to construct is not in proportion to the general intelligence; for the elephant, the dog, and the horse, though in sagacity approaching very closely to the more imperfect specimens of the human race, never attempt to construct anything, while the bee, the beaver, and the swallow, with far less general intelligence, rival the productions of their superiors. Their skulls make plain the reason why.

5. CULTIVATION.—The constant use of tools, however awkwardly at first, the study of the mechanic arts, writing, drawing, etc., will exercise this organ and promote its development.

6. RESTRAINT.—To restrain this faculty is not often necessary. If its action should lead to the pursuit of mechanical chimeras, or to become a mania, it must be kept within due bounds by the exercise of the judgment, or, if necessary, mechanical pursuits should be abandoned and some calling adopted which will bring other faculties more prominently into action.

XXIV. IDEALITY. (21.)

O Tyrus, thou hast said, I am of perfect beauty, thy borders are in the midst of the sea, thy builders have perfected thy beauty.

1. LOCATION.—The organ of Ideality is situated nearly along the temporal ridge of the frontal bone (21, fig. 23), between Mirthfulness and Sublimity, and directly above Constructiveness. It is here that the last fibers of the temporal muscle are inserted.

2. FUNCTION.—This faculty produces a perception and love of the beautiful, good taste, refinement, sense of propriety, and appreciation of art and poetry. It desires to elevate and endow with a splendid excellence every object presented to the mind. It stimulates the faculties which form ideas to create scenes in which every object is invested with the perfection which it delights to contemplate. It is particularly

valuable to man as a progressive being.   It inspires him with a ceaseless love of improvement, and prompts him to form and realize splendid conceptions.   When predominant, it gives a manner of feeling and of thinking befitting the regions of fancy rather than the abodes of men.   Hence those only on

LARGE.   NOT LARGE.

FIG. 111.—A. C. Cox, D.D.*   FIG. 112.—Barnas Sears, D.D.†

whom it is largely bestowed can possibly be poets; and hence the proverb, " *Poëta nascitur, non fit.*"

3. DEFICIENCY.—There are persons who can perceive no excellence in poetry, painting, or sculpture, and who value nothing merely for its beauty.   Such persons declaim against ornament in dress, furniture, architecture, etc., and deem the solid and the useful (in its restricted sense) as alone worthy of the attention of rational, immortal beings.   For such persons the varied loveliness of hill and dale, of sun and shade, of bird and flower is displayed in vain.   Wordsworth speaks of one of this sort when he says—

> A primrose by a river's brim,
> A yellow primrose was to him,
> And it was nothing more.

4. PERVERSION.—When permitted to take the ascendency

---

* Arthur Cleveland Cox, D.D., Protestant Episcopal Bishop of Western New York, is distinguished both as a preacher and as a poet. He is considered as the mouthpiece of High Church Episcopalianism in this country.

† Dr. Sears has an enviable reputation as a scholar and an author, as well as in the sphere of clerical duty and philanthropic effort. He is now general agent of the Peabody Southern Educational Fund.

over the other powers, and to seek its own gratification to the neglect of the serious duties of life,—or when cultivated to so great an excess as to produce a finical and sickly refinement, fastidiousness, and distaste for every-day life, it becomes a source of great evils.

5. ILLUSTRATIVE EXAMPLES.—If we pass in review the portraits and busts of the poets of all ages, we shall find the configuration of head produced by large Ideality common to them all; as in Pindar, Euripides, Sophocles, Heraclides, Plautus, Terence, Virgil, Tibullus, Ovid, Horace, Juvenal, Boccacio, Ariosto, Aretin, Tasso, Milton, Boileau, J. B. Rousseau, Pope, Young, Gorsset, Voltaire, Goethe, Klopstock, Wieland, Richter, Wordsworth, Tennyson, Bryant, Longfellow, etc. Dr. Bailly, in a letter, dated Rome, 30th May, 1822, addressed to Dr. Brayer, says: " You may tell Dr. Gall that I have a mask of Tasso, taken from nature, and that although part of the organ of poetry be cut off, nevertheless the lateral breadth of the cranium in this direction is enormous."

Shakspeare illustrates the poetical manifestation of Ideality, in connection with Sublimity, in the following lines:

" I have bedimmed
The noon-tide sun, call'd forth the mutinous winds,
And 'tween the green sea and the azured vault
Set roaring war ; to the dread rattling thunder
Have I giv'n fire, and rifted Jove's stout oak
With his own bolt; the strong based promontory
Have I made shake, and by the spurs pluck'd up
The pine and cedar."

6. CULTIVATION.—One who desires to cultivate this faculty should, in the first place, carefully avoid all low and vulgar habits, associates, and surroundings, and make it a point to keep good company, be scrupulously neat, and as tasteful as he knows how in dress, surround himself, if possible, with works of art, and practice the best style in conversation and manners. He should as an additional means study poetry, art, and general literature, and try to appreciate beauty in all its forms.

7. RESTRAINT.—Perfection is not one of the qualities of earthly things, and the fastidious and too imaginative must try to realize that air castles and ideal men and women are rather out of place in a rough practical world like this.

XXV. SUBLIMITY. (B.)

His pavilion round about him were dark waters and thick clouds of the skies; the Lord also thundered in the heavens, and the Highest gave his voice.

1. LOCATION.—The organ of Sublimity is situated on the side-head, directly above Acquisitiveness (B, fig. 23), and behind Ideality.

2. FUNCTION.—The function of Sublimity is to give perception of the grand and sublime in nature, art, and literature—to enable us to appreciate mountain scenery, the vastness of the ocean, the grandeur of a thunder-storm, the roar of artillery, the clash of armies, etc., or descriptions and pictures of such scenes. It is also an element in religious faith, and assists our conceptions of God and immortality. It co-operates with Ideality in the artist and the poet, and with Veneration and Spirituality in the religious worshiper.

FIG. 113.—WM. C. BRYANT.*

Sublimity is not recognized by the European phrenologists, generally, as a distinct faculty, but we believe it to be so, and consider its functions determined and its organ fully established.

3. CULTIVATION.—The contemplation of mountain scenery, the storm-tossed ocean, the roaring cataract, the fiery volcano, the reverberating thunder, and whatever else is grand, stupendous, or sublime, will call out this faculty and aid in the development of its organ; as will thoughts of the infinite and eternal, and of God the author of all.

4. RESTRAINT.—To restrain Sublimity is not often necessary, unless a perverted manifestation result in extravagance and bombast, which must be held in check by Ideality, Order, and the reflective faculties.

---

* The well-known American poet, author of "Thanatopsis" and other poems.

XXVI. IMITATION.   (22.)

Follow not that which is evil, but that which is good.

1. LOCATION.—The organ of Imitation is situated on the side of the top-head, between Ideality and Benevolence.

LARGE.   SMALL.

FIG. 114.—REV. DANIEL BALLOU.*   FIG. 115.—ROBERT COLLYER, D.D.†

When it is large, and Benevolence is only moderate, the anterior part of the top-head is nearly level; with Imitation and Benevolence both large, we have the handsomely curved outline shown in fig. 116; and when Benevolence is large and Imitation small, the form is like that represented in fig. 117.

2. FUNCTION.—This faculty gives one an aptitude to copy, take pattern, mimic, imitate anything

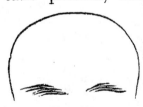

seen or heard—to become, for the time being, somebody else rather than our own proper self. It is essential to actors, ora-

FIG. 116.   FIG. 117.

tors, painters, sculptors, designers. If it be not well developed in them, their representations will be imperfect.

3. ILLUSTRATIVE EXAMPLES.—It is told of Garrick, the

---

* A Universalist clergyman of ability, benevolence, and high moral worth. An effective preacher.

† A Unitarian minister, noted for his fervid oratory, great kindness, active benevolence, and practical common sense.

great actor, that he possessed such an extraordinary talent for mimicry, that, at the court of Louis XV., having seen for a moment the king, the Duke d'Aumont, the Duke d'Orleans, Messrs. d'Aumont, Brissac, and Richelieu, Prince Soubise, and others, he carried off the manner of each of them in his recollection. He invited to supper some friends who had accompanied him to court, and said, "I have seen the court only for an instant, but I shall show you the correctness of my powers of observation and the extent of my memory;" and placing his friends in two files, he retired from the room, and, on his immediately returning, his friends exclaimed, "Ah! here is the king, Louis XV., to the life!" He imitated in succession all the other personages of the court, who were instantly recognized. He imitated not only their walk, gait, and figure, but also the expression of their countenances.

In children, Imitation is more active than in adults. Young persons are very apt to copy the behavior of those with whom they associate; and hence the necessity of setting a good example before them, even from the earliest years.

4. CULTIVATION.—Writing from copy, drawing, making patterns and models, attending dramatic exhibitions, taking part in private theatricals, and trying (on suitable occasions, of course) to mimic our friends and others we meet, will give exercise and development to this organ.

5. RESTRAINT.—A too strong tendency to mimic, copy, or plagiarize must be held in check by the exercise of Firmness, and the avoidance, so far as possible, of servile imitation of all sorts.

XXVII. MIRTHFULNESS. (23.)

A merry heart doeth good like a medicine

1. LOCATION.—The organ of Mirthfulness is situated on the side of the upper part of the forehead (23, fig. 23), between Causality and Ideality.

2. PHYSIOGNOMICAL SIGNS.—Mirthfulness shows itself on the face in a graceful turning upward of the corners of the mouth, as in fig. 120. The reader will need to make but a few careful observations to be convinced (if, indeed, any one

doubts it) that there is the relation of cause and effect between a disposition to make and enjoy " fun " and the upward curv-

LARGE.   SMALL.

FIG. 118.—ARTEMUS WARD.*   FIG. 119.--KANOSH, AN INDIAN CHIEF.

ing of the corners of the mouth.   See portraits of Cervantes, Rabelais, Sterne, Piron, Neal, and others noted for their large development of Mirthfulness.

3. FUNCTION.—The function of Mirthfulness is to enjoy sport and gayety, and appreciate the witty, the ludicrous, the droll, the comical, the incongruous, and the eccentric; and we take pleasure in saying that it is one of the distinguishing characteristics of man.   It is not permitted to the lower animals to laugh or comprehend the causes of laughter.

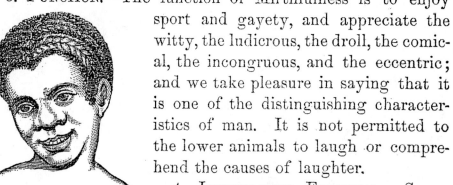

FIG. 120.—NEW HOLLAND WOMAN.

4. ILLUSTRATVE EXAMPLE. — Sometimes Benevolence is exercised in conjunction with Mirthfulness; sometimes Benevolence and Ideality join with Mirthfulness; sometimes Approbativeness; sometimes Secretiveness and Amativeness; sometimes all together, as when the

* Mr. Charles F. Browne, better known as " Artemus Ward," was one of the most noted of American humorists. Mirthfulness is seen to be very well developed. The contrast between his head and that of the Indian Chief is very striking.

Irish hod-carrier rescued the lady's parasol which was being blown away, and handing it to her said, "Och, if you were half as strong as you are handsome, it never would have got away from you." She replied, "I do not know which most to thank you for, your kindness or your compliment." He responded, "Niver mind; a single glance at your beautiful bright eyes pays me for both," and he again bent himself to his work. The wit of this consists in embracing an opportunity to say a brilliant, pleasant thing without being rude, and we admire it more than we laugh at it.

5. CULTIVATION.—The facetious aspects of things and subjects should be contemplated, and the idea that dignity and self-respect require perpetual seriousness must be resolutely combated. The company of mirthful people should be sought, for nothing is more contagious than genuine jollity. There is a time to laugh as well as a time to weep, and laughter is promotive of health and longevity. The injunction to "laugh and grow fat!" is not without a physiological reason, nor is the Shaksperian adage, that "a light heart lives long," a mere poetical flourish.

> " Jog on, jog on the footpath way
> And merrily hent the style-a;
> A merry heart goes all the day,—
> Your sad tires in a mile-a."

6. RESTRAINT.—It is the abuse of this faculty that we should strive to avoid, by cultivating sobriety and reverence. Benevolence also should be called in to aid us, showing that we often give great pain by our disposition to "make fun" at the expense of others.

XXVIII. INDIVIDUALITY. (24.)

Come, behold the works of the Lord.

1. LOCATION.—The organ of Individuality is situated in the center of the lower part of the forehead (24, fig. 23) immediately above the top of the nose. When large, it produces breadth, projection, and descent between the eyebrows at that part (fig. 121). When small, the eyebrows approach closely to each other and lie in a nearly horizontal line.

2. PHYSIOGNOMICAL SIGN.—The faculty is represented

facially by the projection and breadth between the eyebrows and the downward curving of the latter at their inner corners.

3. FUNCTION.—This faculty imparts the desire and ability to know objects as mere existences, without regard to their modes of action or the purposes to which they may be subservient. Individuals in whom it is large will observe and

LARGE.   SMALL.

FIG. 121.—JOHN STUART MILL.*   FIG. 122.—PRINCESS ALICE.†

examine an object with intense delight, without the least consideration to what it may be applied—a quality of mind which is almost incomprehensible to persons in whom this organ is small and Causality large. It prompts to observation, and is a great element in a genius for those sciences which consist in a knowledge of specific existences, such as natural history. It leads to giving a specific form to all the ideas entertained by the mind. It also gives the tendency to personify nations and phenomena, or to ascribe existence to mere abstractions of the mind, such as ignorance, folly, or wisdom.

4. DEFICIENCY.—When the organ is deficient, the individual fails to observe the things which are around him. He may

* A distinguished member of the English Parliament, a political economist, author of "A System of Logic," "Principles of Political Economy," "On Liberty," etc.

† Daughter of Queen Victoria of England.

visit a house and come away without knowing what is in it; or walk through the country and observe nothing. The external senses may be perfect, but owing to the feebleness of Individuality, they may not be called into action for the purpose of obtaining knowledge.

5. ILLUSTRATIVE EXAMPLES.—To the artist this organ is of great importance. It enables him to give body and substance to the conceptions of his other faculties, and confers on him a capacity for attending to detail. In the pictures of an artist in whose head Individuality is deficient, there is an abstractness of conception and a vagueness of expression that greatly detract from their effect. In the works of an individual in whom these organs are large, every object appears full of substance and reality; and if he paint portraits, the spectator will be so impressed with their individuality, that he will be apt to fancy himself acquainted with the original.

The organ was large in Shakspeare, Sheridan, and Sir Walter Scott. It is not so large in the German as Causality; it is larger in the English, and still larger in the French and Americans.

6. CULTIVATION.—Natural history—especially botany—anatomy, mineralogy, and chemistry are departments of knowledge particularly fitted to develop this faculty. It is also exercised in the study of Phrenology and Physiognomy.

7. RESTRAINT.—To restrain is seldom, if ever, necessary. Reflection may, however, be set as a guard upon Individuality, if observation become obtrusive.

XXIX. FORM.   (25.)

Show them the form of the house, the fashion thereof, and all the forms thereof.

1. LOCATION.—The organ of this faculty is situated in the internal angle of the orbit (25, fig. 23), and if large, pushes the eyeball toward the external angle, a little outward and downward.

2. PHYSIOGNOMICAL SIGN.—The phrenological organ and the physiognomical sign may be considered one in this case. It gives breadth between the eyes, as in the accompanying portrait of the celebrated Rubens, the artist (fig. 125).

3. FUNCTION.—It is this faculty which enables us to remember, and with the aid of Constructiveness to reproduce,

LARGE.

MODERATE.

FIG. 123.—REV. W. H. PENDLETON.*

FIG. 124.—REV. SIDNEY A. COREY.†

the forms of persons and things—to make patterns, models,
pictures, statues, etc., and to describe persons, places, and
objects of all sorts. It disposes us also to give figure to every
being and conception of our minds, as to God, to death, to
hope. It is essential to painters, sculptors, and architects,
and very important to the phre-
nologist and physiognomist.

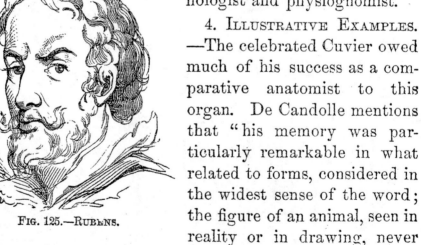

FIG. 125.—RUBENS.

4. ILLUSTRATIVE EXAMPLES.
—The celebrated Cuvier owed
much of his success as a comparative anatomist to this
organ. De Candolle mentions
that "his memory was par-
ticularly remarkable in what
related to forms, considered in
the widest sense of the word;
the figure of an animal, seen in
reality or in drawing, never
left his mind, and served him as a point of comparison for
all similar objects." This organ, and also the organs lying

* A Baptist minister, distinguished as an orator, and an advocate of the American
Bible Union. See how broad between, and how full the eye !
† A Baptist minister, noted as an eloquent and earnest preacher and lecturer.

along the superciliary ridge, were largely developed in his head.

Mr. Audubon says of the late Mr. Bewick, the most eminent wood-engraver whom England has produced: "His eyes were placed farther apart than those of any man I have ever seen."

5. CULTIVATION.—The best way to cultivate the organ of Form is to study such sciences as Phrenology, Physiognomy, botany, etc., and accustom one's self to constant observation of the configuration of everything presented to the eye.

6. RESTRAINT.—To restrain is not necessary.

XXX. SIZE.   (26.)

To measure Jerusalem, to see what is the breadth thereof and the length thereof.

LARGE.   NOT LARGE.

FIG. 126.—EDWARD R. AMES, D.D.*   FIG. 127.—RICHARD FULLER, D.D.†

1. LOCATION.—The organ of Size is placed at the internal extremity of the arch of the eyebrows (26, fig. 23), on each side of Individuality.

2. FUNCTION.—The faculty of Size, as its name implies, gives the power of determining the magnitude of objects, ability to measure by the eye and appreciate proportion, and to detect any departure from it. It is important to every one, but particularly so to geometricians, architects, carpen-

---

* Edward Raymond Ames, D.D., a bishop of the Methodist Episcopal Church, is noted for his devotion and for business sagacity in the affairs of his denomination.

† An eminent Baptist clergyman of Baltimore, much respected and loved by his people.

ters, machinists, and artists.   In union with Locality it gives conceptions of perspective.

3. CULTIVATION.—This organ may be exercised by constant attempts to estimate the length, breadth, and other dimensions of objects, verifying observation by measurement.   The same studies recommended for the cultivation of Form will be useful in this case also, as they involve size and proportion as well as configuration.

4. RESTRAINT.—To restrain is not necessary.

XXXI. WEIGHT.   (27.)

Who weighed the mountains in scales and the hills in a balance.

<table>
<tr><td align="center">LARGE.</td><td align="center">NOT LARGE.</td></tr>
</table>

FIG. 128.—ISAAC FERRIS, D.D., LL.D.*   FIG. 129.—RICH. S. STORRS, JR., D.D.†

1. LOCATION.—The organ of Weight is located on the superciliary ridge, about one third of its extent from the root of the nose (27, fig. 23).   When large, it sometimes depresses the eyebrow at that point, as may be seen in our likeness of Brunel, the distinguished English engineer (fig. 130).

2. FUNCTION.—The faculty of Weight gives a perception of the laws of gravity, motion, etc., and ability to apply them.

---

* An eminent minister of the Reformed Church and Chancellor of the University of New York.

† Dr. Storrs, an eloquent preacher of the Congregationalist denomination, is also well known as a writer and lecturer.

Persons in whom Individuality, Size, Weight, and Locality are large, have generally a talent for engineering and those branches of mechanics which consist in the application of forces; they delight in steam-engines, water-wheels, and turning-lathes. The same combination occurs in persons distinguished for successful execution of difficult feats in skating, in which the regulation of equilibrium is an important element.

3. ILLUSTRATIVE EXAMPLES.— Mr. Simpson published in the Edinburgh *Phrenological Journal* (vol. ii. p. 412) an interesting and ingenious essay on this organ, in which he enumerates a great number of examples in proof of its functions. It is large, says he, in Dr. Chalmers, Dr. Brewster, Sir James Hall, Sir George Mackenzie, Professor Leslie, and in Mr. Jardine and Mr. Stephenson, two very eminent engineers.

FIG. 130.—BRUNEL.

Mr. Richard Edmonson, of Manchester, England, mentions that a great number of observations have led him to the conviction that this organ gives the perception of perpendicularity. Workmen who easily detect deviations from the perpendicular possess it large; while those who constantly find it necessary to resort to the plumb-line have it small, and *vice versa*.

Brunel, the great engineer of the Thames Tunnel, and his son, builder of the Great Eastern (fig. 130), possessed a remarkable development of Weight, while the organ of Color was totally wanting.

4. CULTIVATION. — Skating, practicing gymnastic feats, balancing a pole, riding on a horse, walking, climbing, sailing, gunnery, etc., exercise and develop Weight.

5. RESTRAINT.—If one be prone to attempt dangerous feats of climbing, walking on narrow places, etc., he should cultivate Cautiousness and hold Weight in check.

XXXII. COLOR. (28.)

Though thou clothest thyself with crimson, and deckest thee with ornaments of gold, and rentest thy face with painting, in vain shalt thou make thyself fair.

1. LOCATION.—The place of the organ of Color (28, fig. 23) is the middle of the eyebrow, at the most elevated part of the superciliary ridge.

2. PHYSIOGNOMICAL SIGN.—The form of the eyebrow is

FULL.   MODERATE.

FIG. 131.—ISAAC WESTCOTT, D.D.*   FIG. 132.—CHARLES HODGE.†

greatly modified by the development of this organ. The ordinary indication of its full development is the regular arching of the brow, as seen in fig. 131; but sometimes the brow is pushed forward and made very prominent at that point. When large, it also gives a peculiar appearance of fullness to the upper eyelid.

3. FUNCTION.—Its function is to distinguish all the shades of color, and the relations of harmony or of discord between them. When large, the faculty of Color gives great delight in contemplating colors and good taste in their use and combination in dress, painting, etc. Those in whom the organ is deficient, on the contrary, experience little interest in coloring,

---

* Dr. Westcott is a Baptist minister of great piety and zeal, and a very effective preacher. He is pastor of the Bloomingdale Baptist Church, New York.

† A prominent Presbyterian minister, editor of the *Biblical Repertory*, and an author of note in his denomination.

and are almost insensible to difference of shades, hues, and tints.

4. DEFICIENCY.—Certain persons are almost destitute of the power of distinguishing colors. Dr. Spurzheim mentions a family, all the individuals of which distinguish only black and white. Dr. Unzer, of Altona, could not perceive green and blue; and inability to distinguish between these colors is very common. To many, also, green and red look the same. This defect is called color-blindness.

5. ILLUSTRATIVE EXAMPLES.—The organ of Color is generally more developed in woman than in man; hence it happens that the eyebrows of women are more finely arched; and this explains why they are more frequently lovers of flowers and fond of a variety of colors in dress. Among great painters, this organ is seen to be very large in those most distinguished as colorists; for instance, Corregio, Titian, Claude Lorraine, Rubens (fig. 125), Rembrandt, Poussin, and Raphael.

6. CULTIVATION.—Observing and classifying or arranging colors, painting, cultivating flowers, etc., will exercise and aid in the development of this organ.

7. RESTRAINT.—To restrain is not necessary.

XXXIII. ORDER. (29.)

Let all things be done decently and in order.

1. LOCATION.—The organ of Order is situated over the outer corner of the eye (29, fig. 23), between Color and Calculation.

2. FUNCTION.—The function of this organ is well indicated by its name. It gives method and order to physical objects, and is, perhaps, a co-worker with the reflective faculties in the conception of system, generalization, and classification.

3. ILLUSTRATIVE EXAMPLES.—Dr. Spurzheim mentions that the Sauvage de l'Aveyron, at Paris, though an idiot, could not bear to see a chair or any object out of its place; and that as soon as anything was deranged, he, without being excited to it, directly replaced it. He likewise saw in Edinburgh a girl who in many respects was idiotic, but in whom

the love of order was very active. She avoided her brother's apartment in consequence of the confusion that prevailed in it. It is usually large in Quaker ladies, of whom Lucretia Mott is an example.

4. CULTIVATION.—Any business that requires system and

LARGE.   SMALL.

FIG. 133.—HENRY C. CAREY.*   FIG. 134.—JAMES P. BECKWOURTH.†

orderly arrangement, as well as studies involving the contemplation, a regular arrangement of objects will help to develop Order.

5. RESTRAINT.—Where there is a morbid action of this organ, making the subject painfully susceptible to the influence of disorder and lack of methodical arrangement, an effort must be made to withdraw the mind from the contemplation of such matters. It should be considered how impossible it is to have everything exactly to one's mind in this respect, and that we only waste our time and mar our temper in the attempt to reduce everything to the regular arrangement we love. Avoid becoming "more nice than wise."

XXXIV. CALCULATION.   (30.)

The very hairs of your head are all numbered.

1. LOCATION.—The organ of Calculation is situated at the

---

* A distinguished American author and political economist.

† A noted hunter, trapper, and guide of the Rocky Mountains. He died in 1867.

outer angle of the eye (30, fig. 23). When large, it swells the frontal bone at that particular spot.

2. PHYSIOGNOMICAL SIGN.—In individuals endowed with great calculating powers, the external angle of the eyebrow is either much pressed down or much elevated, the configura-

LARGE.   SMALL.

FIG. 135.—DR. HIND.*   FIG. 136.—GEORGE COMBE.†

tion in both cases resulting from the great development of the part of the brain situated behind the outer angle of the orbit, which forms a ridge, above or below which the eyebrow naturally slides. The portraits and busts of great calculators, like Newton, Euler, Kaestner, Herschel, Buxton, Colborn, Safford, etc., all present either one or the other of these external signs.

3. FUNCTION.—Whatever concerns unity and plurality belongs to this faculty; hence its end is calculation in general. The recollection of the numbers of houses, or of pages where we have read passages, depends upon this faculty. It gives ability to reckon in the head, or facility in mental arithmetic.

4. ILLUSTRATIVE EXAMPLES.—Dr. Spurzheim mentions that "certain races of negroes make five the extent of their enumeration, that is, they count only as far as five by simple

---

* An English astronomer distinguished for his ability as a calculator.

† Mr. Combe was so deficient in this faculty of Calculation that he was never able to master the multiplication table. See his lectures on Phrenology.

5*

terms; all their numbers after five are compound, whereas ours are not so till they have passed the number ten; while our terms, six, seven, etc., are simple, they say five-one, five-two, five-three, etc. Negroes in general," he continues, " do not excel in arithmetic and numbers; and, accordingly, their heads are very narrow in the seat of the organ of Number."

Among the most remarkable examples of the extraordinary development of Calculation, Jedediah Buxton and George Bidder, of England, and Zerah Colburn and Truman H. Safford, of the United States, may here be mentioned.

5. CULTIVATION.—The study of arithmetic and algebra, and the practice of calculation in its various forms, and especially mental computations, exercise and develop this faculty; as also the habit of charging the mind with the memory of the numbers of houses in a street, the pages of a book, etc.

6. RESTRAINT.—To restrain is not necessary.

XXXV. LOCALITY.   (31.)

We are journeying to the place of which the Lord said, I will give it you; come with us.

1. LOCATION.—The organ of Locality is situated in the forehead, on each side of Eventuality and over the inner corner of the eyebrows (31, fig. 23).

2. PHYSIOGNOMICAL SIGN.—A marked prominence above the inner corner of the eyebrows, on each side of the mesial line, as in Captain Cook (fig. 139), indicates large Locality.

3. FUNCTION.—The faculty of Locality gives the ability to form conceptions of place and to find places, delight in scenery, memory of the location of objects, love of travel, etc.

4. ILLUSTRATIVE EXAMPLES.—Locality is large in the busts and portraits of all eminent navigators and travelers, such as Columbus, Cook, Mungo Park, and Sir Samuel Baker; also in great astronomers and geographers, as Kepler, Galileo, Tycho Brahe, and Newton. In Tasso the poet, also, it appears to be very large, and he manifested the faculty in a high degree.

In the mask of Sir Walter Scott the organ is large.   Readers similarly endowed are almost as much delighted with his descriptions of scenery as by a tour made by themselves amid

LARGE.   NOT LARGE.

FIG. 137.—O. B. FROTHINGHAM, D.D.*   FIG. 138.—JAMES F. CLARKE, D.D.†

the mountain glens; while those in whom the organ is small, are quite uninterested by his most splendid poetical landscapes. This author wrote so pictorially, that he almost saves an artist, who means to illustrate his pages, the trouble of invention. The organ is more developed in men than in women, and the manifestations correspond.

FIG. 139.—CAPTAIN COOK.

5. CULTIVATION.—Traveling, the study of geography, and a persevering exercise of the memory in reference to places, roads, landmarks, the location of the phrenological organs, etc., will promote the activity and development of this organ.

6. RESTRAINT.—A too strong disposition to rove, or a restless desire for a continual change of place, must be met by

* Dr. Frothingham is a Unitarian minister of New York, and a writer of great ability on theological subjects. He is one of the leaders of the rationalistic party in the Unitarian denomination.

† A preacher and writer of great talent, and minister of the Church of the Disciples (Unitarian) in Boston. He is known as a reformer and a philanthropist.

the cultivation of Continuity and Firmness, and a resolute determination to settle down and establish a permanent home.

XXXVI. EVENTUALITY.   (32.)

Remember the days of old, consider the years of many generations.

LARGE.   MODERATE.

FIG. 140.—S. H. TYNG, D.D.*   FIG. 141.—SAMUEL OSGOOD, D.D.†

1. LOCATION.—The organ of this faculty is situated in the center of the forehead (32, fig. 23), to which when large it gives a rounded fullness, as in fig. 142. Fig. 143 shows it small. Taking the root of the nose as the starting-point, we first come to Individuality, which lies between the eyebrows. The next organ is Eventuality, just above the eyebrows.

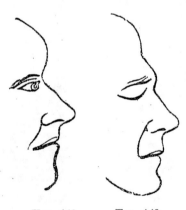

FIG. 142.   FIG. 143.

2. FUNCTION.—The function of Eventuality is to impart memory of facts, recollection of circumstances, news, occurrences, and passing events—whatever has been said, heard, seen, or in any way once known. It seems to perceive the impressions which

---

* Stephen H. Tyng, D.D., is a prominent clergyman of the Protestant Episcopal Church, and pastor of St. George's Church, New York. He is regarded by many as one of the best extemporaneous pulpit orators in the city.

† Rev. Dr. Osgood is pastor of the Church of the Messiah (Second Unitarian), New York, and is distinguished both as a writer and as a preacher.

are the immediate functions of the external senses, to change these into notions, conceptions, or ideas, and to be essential to attention in general. Its sphere of activity is very great, and expressed by the *verbs* in their infinitive mood. It desires to know everything by experience, and consequently excites all the other organs to activity; it would hear, see, smell, taste, and touch; is fond of general instruction, and inclines to the pursuit of practical knowledge.

3. CULTIVATION.—Reading history, mythology, the newspapers of the day, etc., always charging the memory with the events and occurrences related; writing down or verbally relating the incidents of every-day life, and telling stories and anecdotes, will give exercise to the organ and promote development.

4. RESTRAINT.—To restrain is not necessary.

XXXVII. TIME. (33.)

To everything there is a season; and a time to every purpose under the heaven.

LARGE. NOT LARGE.

FIG. 144.—OLE BORNEMANN BULL.* FIG. 145.—T. B. HAYWARD.†

1. LOCATION.—The organ of this faculty is situated just above the middle of the eyebrow (33, fig. 23), and between Locality and Tune.

---

* Ole Bull is well known the world over as a violinist of great ability. He is a Norwegian by birth.

† Rev. T. B. Hayward is a minister of the New Church (Swedenborgian), and much respected and esteemed by all who know him.

2. FUNCTION.—This organ imparts recollection and intuitive knowledge of the lapse of time; memory of dates; ability to keep time in music; also to perceive those minuter divisions, and their harmonious relations, which constitute rhythm. Persons who have it large are invariably accurate dancers, and generally fond of the exercise.

3. ILLUSTRATIVE EXAMPLES.—Individuals are occasionally met with who estimate the lapse of time so accurately that they are able to tell the hour without having recourse to a timepiece. An illiterate Highlander, who was long in the service of Sir G. S. Mackenzie as a plowman, could tell the hour of the day with great exactness, and also the time of high water, although he resided seven miles from the sea. Sir George had not become acquainted with Phrenology at the period of this man's death. The lower animals seems to be endowed with the power of perceiving and appreciating intervals of time. Mr. Southey, in his *Omniana*, relates two instances of dogs who had acquired such a knowledge of time as would enable them to count the days of the week. He says: "My grandfather had one which trudged two miles *every Saturday* to cater for himself in the shambles. I know another more extraordinary and well-authenticated example. A dog which had belonged to an Irishman, and was sold by him in England, would never touch a morsel of food *upon Friday*. This may or may not be true. We ourselves do not believe it. The same faculty of recollecting intervals of time exists, though in a more limited extent, in the horse.

4. CULTIVATION.—Regular habits in respect to time, as in rising, retiring, taking meals, etc., and the practice of music, dancing, and rhythmic gymnastic exercises tend to promote the activity of this organ.

5. RESTRAINT.—To restrain is unnecessary.

XXXVIII. TUNE. (34.)

Praise the Lord with harp; sing unto him with the psaltery and an instrument of ten strings. Sing unto him a new song.

1. LOCATION.—The organ of Tune is situated on the side of the forehead just above the outer corner of the eyebrow

and next to Time (34, fig. 23). A great development of the organ enlarges the lateral parts of the forehead; but its appearance varies according to the direction and form of the convolutions. Dr. Spurzheim observes, that, in Glück and others, this organ had a pyramidal form; in Mozart, Viotti, Zumsteg, Dussek, Crescentini, and others, the external and

LARGE.   NOT LARGE.

FIG. 146.—MLLE. DE KATOW.*   FIG. 147.—WILLIAM COLLIER, D.D.†

lateral portions of the forehead are enlarged, but rounded. Great practice is necessary to be able to observe this organ successfully; and beginners should place together one person possessing a genius for music, and another who can scarcely distinguish between any two notes, and mark the difference of their heads. The superior development of the former will be perceptible at a glance.

The heads of Italians and Germans, in general, are broader and fuller at the situation of this organ than those of Spaniards, Frenchmen, and Englishmen in general; and musical talent is more common in the former than in the latter.

2. FUNCTION.—The faculty of Tune gives a perception of melody, the harmony of sounds, and the ability to learn and remember tunes; other faculties are required to compose. Tune is only one ingredient in a genius for music. Time is

---

* A celebrated Russian violinist. See how full in the temples!

† A minister of the Methodist Protestant Church and a leader in the denomination. He is noted for zeal and earnestness.

requisite to give a just perception of intervals; Ideality, to communicate elevation and refinement; and Secretiveness and Imitation, to produce expression; while Constructiveness, Form, Weight, and Individuality are necessary to supply mechanical expertness—qualities all indispensable to a successful composer or performer.

3. CULTIVATION.—Singing and the practice of vocal and instrumental music, attending concerts, and the constant effort to appreciate music will lead to an increased activity and consequent development of the organ of Tune.

4. RESTRAINT.—Restraint is seldom called for, but should there be an excessive fondness for music, interfering with other studies or pursuits, or with the common duties of life, one must resolutely hold it in check by the exercise of the restraining organs, such as Conscientiousness, Firmness, and the reflective intellect.

XXXIX. LANGUAGE.   (35.)

Keep thy tongue from evil, and thy lips from speaking guile.

1. LOCATION.—The organ of Language is situated on the back part of the orbitary plates, the bones which form the roof of the eyes and support the anterior lobes of the brain.

2. PHYSIOGNOMICAL SIGN.—A large development of Language is indicated by prominent eyes. Sometimes the eyes not only project, but are also depressed, when the under eyelid presents a sort of sack or roll or appears swollen. Both of these signs are conspicuous in fig. 148.

3. FUNCTION.—This faculty gives verbal memory and capacity for learning arbitrary signs of all kinds; and persons who have it large readily remember words, and learn by heart with great facility. When Language is very large and the general intellect only moderate, it is surprising what a volume of words can be poured forth to express a few ideas, and sometimes no idea at all. This class of persons have great pleasure in hearing themselves talk, and are rendered uncomfortable if not allowed to indulge in their favorite occupation. If they write, their style is like their speaking,

destitute of condensation—they scribble whole pages about nothing.

4. ILLUSTRATIVE EXAMPLES.—This, like all other organs, seems composed of different parts. Some persons are apt to forget proper names, while they recollect words denoting the qualities of external objects. Disease or accident has entailed

LARGE.

ONLY FULL.

FIG. 148.—WM. R. WILLIAMS.*

FIG. 149.—ROBERT TURNBULL, D.D.†

this peculiarity in several instances. "One Lereard, of Marseilles," mentioned by Dr. Spurzheim, "having received a blow from a foil on the eyebrow, lost the memory of proper names entirely; he sometimes forgot the names of his intimate friends, and even of his father, as he stated in a letter written to Dr. Gall for advice." It is large in Charles Dickens, and small in General U. S. Grant.

We frequently meet with men of great talent only moderately endowed with Language, and others whose mental powers are very common-place who have this organ large. Many persons who are largely endowed with this faculty, and who have an excellent verbal memory, and learn by heart with great readiness, yet make little progress in learning the science of a language.

---

* Dr. Williams is pastor of the Fifty-fourth Street Baptist Church, New York, and is distinguished for his eloquence, learning, talent, authorship, and piety.

† A Scotchman by birth, and now pastor of the largest Baptist church in Hartford, Conn. He is also an author of merit.

5. CULTIVATION.—The constant practice of talking and writing, the study of languages, and the committing to memory of any arbitrary signs, are all adapted to promote the development of this faculty.

6. RESTRAINT.—Where Language is very large and active, it sometimes leads to verbosity, garrulity, and circumlocution, in which case there must be a systematic effort to check this tendency by a severe lopping off of redundancies in writing and a constant watchfulness over one's self in speaking.

XL. CAUSALITY.   (36.)

And Paul reasoned with them out of the Scriptures.   [The why and wherefore Faculty.]

LARGE.   NOT SO LARGE.

FIG. 150.—W. F. MORGAN, D.D.*   FIG. 151.—W. B. HAYDEN.†

1. LOCATION.—Causality is situated in the upper part of the forehead (36, fig. 23), on each side of Comparison, which occupies the center.   The two together, when both are large, give great fullness to that portion of the forehead, as seen in fig. 20.

2. FUNCTION.—The faculty of Causality gives the perception of the relation between cause and effect, " the why and wherefore."   Comparison seizes the general relations between

---

* William F. Morgan, D.D., is rector of St. Thomas' Church (Episcopalian) in New York, and is greatly respected and esteemed by all who know him.

† Rev. W. B. Hayden is a preacher of note in the Swedenborgian denomination, and the author of several works on subjects connected with New Church doctrines.

objects, but Causality ascends beyond juxtaposition and relations; it penetrates the manner in which effects and their causes are connected together, seizes the action of one body on another, and traces the result of that action. It impresses us with an irresistible conviction, that every phenomenon or change in nature is caused by something, and hence, by successive steps, leads us to the great Cause of all. It is also creative, producing originality and forethought, and ability to adapt means to ends.

3. ILLUSTRATIVE EXAMPLES.—Dr. Gall speaks of a cast molded on the head of Kant, the great metaphysical philosopher, after his death, in which he found an extraordinary prominence in the region assigned to Causality. (See fig. 20.) Afterward he became acquainted with Fichte, in whose head he found the region still more largely developed than in Kant.

As examples of large Causality, we may mention Plato, Socrates, Bacon, Montaigne, Galileo, Descartes, Leibnitz, Sir Isaac Newton, Franklin, Cuvier, Gall, Napoleon, Dupuytren, Fourier, Brunel, and Webster.

4. CULTIVATION.—The study of philosophy in all its branches, and especially Phrenology in its theoretical aspects; planning; contriving ways and means; meditating on the laws of nature; and trying to trace out the connection between observed phenomena and their causes, all serve to exercise Causality and increase its power.

5. RESTRAINT.—To restrain this faculty is seldom necessary. If too active, divert the mind by strict attention to practical affairs, cultivating the Perceptives.

XLI. COMPARISON. (37.)

The invisible things of him from the creation of the world are clearly seen, being understood by the things that are made.

1. LOCATION.—The organ of Comparison is situated in the upper part of the forehead on the middle line between the two sides, and generally just below the roots of the hair, the bottom being about the center of the forehead (37, fig. 23). It is prominent in the portrait of Linnæus, whose pursuits necessitated the constant exercise of the faculty.

2. FUNCTION.—Comparison gives ability to perceive differences and resemblances; to reason inductively; to analyze,

LARGE.   SMALL.

FIG. 152.—M. J. SPALDING, D.D.*

FIG. 153.—JOHN MCCLOSKEY, D.D.†

classify, compare, and draw inferences; and to judge correctly of the congruousness of objects or ideas. It seems also to exert a harmonizing influence over the action of all the other faculties.

3. ILLUSTRATIVE EXAMPLES. —Among nations, it is very large in the French and in the Irish. Thomas Moore may be instanced as one of the best examples of its manifestation in literary composition. "The harp that once through Tara's halls," illustrates his use of Comparison as a figure of

FIG. 154.—LINNÆUS.

speech. Another short poem—"Though fate, my girl, may bid us part"—is almost entirely made up of a description and

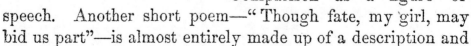

* Dr. Spalding is Archbishop of Baltimore and Primate of the Roman Catholic Church in the United States. His "History of the Reformation" is one of the standard works of his church.

† Dr. McCloskey, second Archbishop of New York, is considered one of the most polished pulpit orators in the Catholic Church, and he is noted for his kindness of heart and active benevolence.

comparison of conditions. The following often-quoted lines are likewise in point:

> "When I remember all
>   The friends so linked together,
> I've seen around me fall,
>   Like leaves in wintry weather;
> I feel like one who treads alone
>   Some banquet hall deserted,
> Whose lights are fled, whose garlands dead,
>   And all but he departed."

Comparison was large in the heads of Curran, Burke, Pitt, Chalmers, Franklin, Roscoe, Hume, Jeffrey, Patrick Henry, Clay, John Quincy Adams, and Webster.

The teachings of the Bible are addressed to this faculty in an eminent degree, being replete with analogies and comparisons; as "Unto what is the kingdom of God like, and whereunto shall I resemble it? It is like a grain of mustard seed," etc. "It is like leaven," etc.

4. CULTIVATION.—Studying logic, mental philosophy (phrenologically, of course), chemistry, botany, etc., or the constant exercise of one's analytical powers in any branch of study or business, may be made subservient to the development of this faculty.

5. RESTRAINT.—To restrain is not necessary.

XLII. HUMAN NATURE. (C.)

Behold, I know your thoughts, and the devices which ye wrongfully imagine against me.

1. LOCATION.—The organ of Human Nature is situated on the median line of the forehead, between Comparison and Benevolence (C, fig. 23).

2. FUNCTION.—The function of this organ is to furnish us with an intuitive knowledge of character, or to enable us to perceive the state of mind or feeling possessed by others, so that we may successfully adapt ourselves to them and operate upon their feelings. It gives sagacity, and is possessed in a very remarkable degree by our North American Indians. It was large in Napoleon and in old Hayes, the great rogue-catcher and detective of New York, as it is also in Gen. Grant.

3. CULTIVATION.—No better means can be made use of to improve this faculty than to make human nature a study, using Phrenology and Physiognomy as guides in its prosecution. Observe every one you meet, and note the expression,

LARGE.   MODERATE.

FIG. 155.—THEO. L. CUYLER.*   FIG. 156.—JOS. T. DURYEA.†

tones, and actions of each, and try to read them as you might an open book.

4. RESTRAINT.—If too suspicious, by reason of over-large Cautiousness and large or perverted Human Nature, one must cultivate Benevolence, Hope, and Conscientiousness, and try to take a kinder, more lenient, cheerful, and juster view of his fellow-men.

XLIII. AGREEABLENESS.   (D.)

A soft answer turneth away wrath, but grievous words stir up anger.

1. LOCATION.—The organ of Agreeableness is situated in the upper edge of the forehead (D, fig. 23). It lies directly over the inner angle of the eye and about two inches above the ridge of the eyebrow. It is apt to be marked by a depression in the American head; but is prominent in the French, who are said to be the most polite.

---

* Rev. Theodore L. Cuyler is pastor of the Lafayette Avenue Presbyterian Church in Brooklyn. He is one of the most popular preachers in the United States.

† Rev. Joseph T. Duryea, lately one of the pastors of the Collegiate Reformed Church in New York, now of Brooklyn, is a young man of brilliant powers and of great promise.

2. FUNCTION.—It imparts the ability to make one's self acceptable to others, and to adopt a persuasive and conciliatory mode of address and pleasant manners. One who has it large can utter even the most unwelcome truths without giving offense; and with large Imitation and Benevolence,

LARGE.

SMALL.

FIG. 157.—SCHUYLER COLFAX.*   FIG. 158.—FRANK P. BLAIR, JR.†

to which it is closely allied in location, is sure to be a general favorite, especially if the social organs be large.

3. CULTIVATION.—The study and constant practice of the art of politeness, which has its foundation in this organ in conjunction with Benevolence and Conscientiousness, will tend to arouse the spirit of Agreeableness. By acting in such a way as to make ourselves, so far as possible, agreeable to those around us, we shall in time come to feel agreeable, and shall develop the organ of that feeling. [See our handbook, "How to Behave,"‡ for lessons in politeness, and the study of a courteous deportment.]

4. RESTRAINT.—To restrain is not necessary.

---

* An American politician and statesman of fine ability and strong personal influence.
† A general in the Union Army during the American Civil War; not noted for suavity of manners.
‡ "How to Behave," A Pocket Manual of Republican Etiquette and Guide to Correct Personal Habits, with Rules for Debating Societies and Deliberative Assemblies. Price, 75 cents; or, in connection with "How to Write, How to Talk, and How to Do Business," complete in one volume, $2 25.

V.

THE ART OF CHARACTER READING.

I. PHYSIOLOGICAL CONDITIONS.

FIG. 159.—ANDREW JACKSON.

IN character reading, as in everything else, it is important that we begin in the right place—at the beginning—and that, having begun rightly, we proceed step by step according to the natural sequence of the points to be considered. "Order is heaven's first law," and by means of method we make simple and easy what at first sight seems complicated and difficult.

1. SIZE.—Size, you will remember, other things being equal, is the measure of power. Having the living subject before you, commence by considering his or her size—the size of the person as a whole. How does it compare with the average development of the race, nation, and sex to which the subject belongs. Having settled this point in your mind, you have the first element of the combination which is to determine your estimate of character.

2. QUALITY.—Having determined the size, your next inquiry should be, "What is the Quality?" Quality is mainly a matter of temperament. What, then, is the temperament of the subject? We have described the Temperaments, and shall take it for granted that you know how to distinguish them; but, to make the matter still plainer, if possible, we will restate and illustrate in a somewhat different form, look-

ing at the subject in its physiognomical as well as its physiological and phrenological aspects.

Each temperament has a configuration peculiar to itself; so

that the general outlines of the person, or of any part of it, will indicate to which the subject belongs. Take the head (including the face) as an example. Observe its configuration as seen in front and in profile.

3. THE VITAL TEMPERAMENT. —We will suppose, for instance, that the subject before you has a face and head which, in the front view, present a nearly circular outline, like fig. 160. The profile will show the same tendency to

FIG. 160.—THE ENGLISH GIRL.

roundness as in fig. 161; and this will be the character of the whole physical system—the body and limbs being plump and full, and the whole figure broad and stout rather than long and slender.

Now, you may at once conclude that your subject has a predominance of the Vital Temperament, and this fact will furnish the key to his or her character.

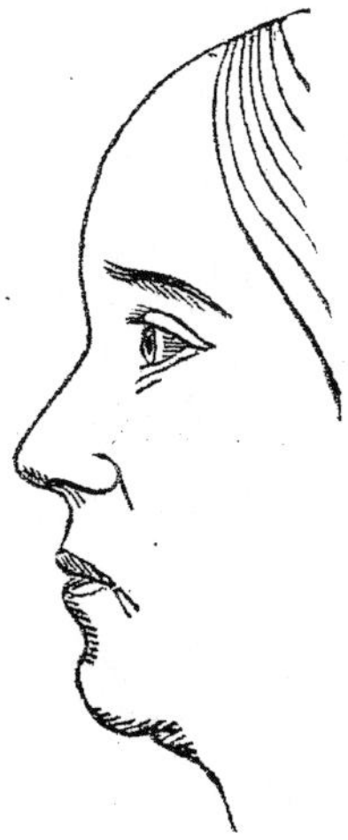

There will be great vigor, a good digestion, love of fresh air and exercise, and a fondness for good living and physical enjoyments generally, with a disinclination to hard and protracted labor.

Mentally, you may look for ardor, impulsiveness, enthusiasm, and versatility, if not fickleness. There will be more diligence than persistence, and more brilliancy than depth. There may be a quick and violent temper, but it will

FIG. 161.—PROFILE.

be easily calmed, and in general the disposition will be cheerful, amiable, and genial.

4. THE MOTIVE TEMPERAMENT.—Perhaps your next sub-

6

ject will have a face like figs. 159 and 162, in which length is the predominant characteristic. The profile will present strong angular lines, as in fig. 163, in place of the curves which prevail in the previous illustration. The figure will be

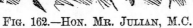

FIG. 162.—HON. MR. JULIAN, M.C.   FIG. 163.—PROFILE.

found to be tall and striking, with a manifest tendency to angularity, as in the features.

In this case you have the Motive Temperament before you, and may infer density and firmness of texture in all the organs, and great strength and endurance in the physical system, with energy, capacity for work, and a strongly-marked character, in which executiveness, love of power, stability, persistence, and directness are noticeable traits. There may be, though not necessarily, an objectionable degree of hardness and coarseness; but we shall generally find a degree of firmness and constancy which may be relied on in business, in friendship, or in love. This temperament and form of face are less common among women than among men, and the characteristics we have named are of course subject to the modifications superinduced by sex and age.

5. THE MENTAL TEMPERAMENT.—A third form of face is shown in fig. 164. It may be called the pyriform or pear-shaped face, of which the profile is less rounded than in fig. 161, less angular than in fig. 163, and more delicate than

either, as in fig. 165. As it is the expansion of the superior parts of the face, including the forehead, which gives the pyriform shape to the whole in the front view, you may without looking farther set down your subject who presents this form as having a predominance of the Mental Temperament. You

FIG. 164.—RACHEL.   FIG. 165.—PROFILE.

will find the figure in this case slender and delicate rather than elegant or striking. The indications are great mental activity, a lively imagination, fine sensibilities, refinement, delicacy, taste, and literary or artistic talent.

Of course these forms and the temperaments they indicate occur in all degrees of development and in combinations innumerable, and are modified by the state of the health and other conditions already noted. You will learn in time to attribute to each its proper strength and influence. See what is said on Balance of Temperaments (Chap. II., Sec. II.), also High and Low Quality (Chap. II., Sec. III.).

In connection with Temperament, Breathing Power, Circulation, Digestion, Activity, Excitability, and General Health, must be noted by means of the indications we have given in Chap. II.

Having proceeded thus far, you have a good general idea of the capacity and tendencies of the person before you—the outlines, as it were, of the character.

II. THE GROUPS OF ORGANS.

You should next seek to estimate the power of the brain, as a whole. You have already taken into account the element of size in the person, as a whole, and have considered the brain in its influence upon temperament. Get now its absolute size by measurement,* and then proceed to ascertain the relative development of its different parts or regions. Which predominates? the Region of Propensity, the Region of Intellect, or the Spiritual Region?

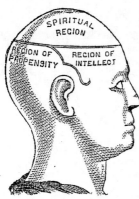

FIG. 166.—THREE REGIONS.

If Intellect be the leading development, the forehead and whole anterior compartment of the cranium, as marked on the diagram (fig. 166), will be deep and broad, as in fig. 167. Here the posterior compartment or Region of Propensity is short and narrow, and the Superior or Spiritual Region (seat of the Moral Sentiments) only moderately developed. If your subject have a forehead like this, you will infer that he is both an observer and a thinker of more than ordinary capacity.

If the lower part of the forehead predominate, as in fig. 169, perception will be found in the ascendant; and if the upper portion be largest, as in fig. 168, there will be more thoughtfulness or reflection and less observation—more philosophy and less science—more of the theoretical than of the practical.

The predominance of the propensities gives breadth to the base of the brain between and behind the ears, as in fig. 170, and length to the posterior lobe, as in fig. 171. From the lateral development you will infer appetite, energy, economy,

---

* In measuring the head as here suggested, pass the tape around it horizontally about an inch above the eyebrows, or so that it will pass over the organs of Individuality and Parental Love. This will give some idea of the size of the head; but the fact that some heads are round, others long, some low, and others high, so modifies these measurements that they do not convey any very correct notion of the actual quantity of brain. These measurements range somewhat as follows in adults:

7 or Very Large, 23¾ inches and upward; 6 or Large, from 22¾ to 23¾; 5 or Full, from 22 to 22¾; 4 or Average, from 21½ to 22; 3 or Moderate, from 20¾ to 21½; 2 or Small, from 20 to 20¾; 1 Below, 20. Female heads are half an inch to an inch below these measurements, corresponding with their bodies.

policy—a disposition to preserve, provide for, and defend one's self. The extent backward from the ear indicates the power of the social element, and gives the fraternal, affectionate, loving, domestic, and patriotic disposition

Development obliquely upward from the ear, or in the superior part of the posterior region, giving height and breadth to that portion of the head (of which also fig. 171 affords an illustration), imparts prudence, aspiration, dignity, pride, self-reliance, and love of distinction, power, and position. If the coronal region, or top-head, pre-

INTELLECTUAL.

FIG. 167.—WILKIE COLLINS.*

THOUGHTFUL.

FIG. 168.—HEPWORTH DIXON.†

OBSERVING.

FIG. 169.—A LOWLANDER.

dominate, as in fig. 172, in which it will be seen that the

---

* An English novelist and miscellaneous writer, noted for his skill in the management of the plot in his fictions. "After Dark," "The Dead Secret," and "The Woman in White" are among his most popular works.

† An English journalist and author, best known here through his "New America."

height from the opening of the ear to the apex of the head is very great, you may assume that the subject has a strong

EXECUTIVE.

SOCIAL.

FIG. 170.—GENERAL JOSEPH HOOKER.* FIG. 171.—THEODOSIA BURR ALLSTON.†

natural tendency toward a moral and religious life—to manifest faith, hope, and charity—to reverence God and his laws, and to aspire after purity and holiness.

SPIRITUALLY MINDED.

FIG. 172.—BENJ. SZOLD.‡

Having ascertained which of the groups of organs, as a whole, predominate, your next step should be to determine the controlling organ in that group. "If it be Conscientiousness in the moral group, and that is the controlling group of the brain, then everything must be squared according to the rule of rectitude. If Benevolence is the controlling organ in that group, then everything must be governed according to the spirit of kindness and sympathy. If Veneration be the strongest, then there is a tendency to think of God and to reverence his authority; if Conscientiousness lead the person to be honest, it is for God's sake;

---

* Known in the Union Army, in the American Civil War, as "fighting Joe Hooker."
† Daughter of Aaron Burr.
‡ Rev. Benjamin Szold is a Jewish Rabbi of Baltimore, but by birth a Hungarian, and is distinguished for piety and learning.

if through Benevolence he become a benefactor, it is for God's sake; his Spirituality begets a yearning for the life to come, because God is the light thereof; Hope fixes its aspiration upon the Father of all, and thus he inclines to walk with God and have his conversation in heaven. This, at least, will be the form of his piety and the tendency of his moral life.

"In the selfish group, with Acquisitiveness predominating, energy, skill, and executive force will back up that element, and money-making, though it may be honestly done, will seem to be the great drift of the person's life."

As the predominant group determines the general tendencies of the mind, so the strongest organ in that group influences the action of all the rest. In this way, if the faculty which inspires ambition be strong, the talent, skill, energy, enterprise, prudence, policy, friendship, affection, all incline toward and sustain ambition.

A perfectly balanced brain will seldom, if ever, be found; but supposing one to be in equilibrium, then the course of action which a person thus endowed would pursue, would be determined by the paramount external influence. Being equally fitted for business, law, medicine, mechanism, teaching, literature, and art, he would become what circumstances should render most desirable at the time. You will meet with approximations to this perfect balance of the elements of character, and the individuals in whom it occurs will be capable of succeeding in almost any branch of human effort.

Having thus completed your general observations, you will be prepared to examine the individual organs for the purpose of ascertaining the size of each, observing at the same time the corresponding physiognomical sign, where such a sign has been ascertained to exist; but in comparing the one with the other, it should be understood that while the brain (subject always to the conditions we have noted) measures the absolute power of the mind, the face is rather an index of its habitual activity, and that the two sets of indications, taken either collectively or individually, are not necessarily equal; in other words, there may be *latent* power—mental *capacity* not manifested in the character or shown in the face.

If, therefore, the sign of a faculty be large in the face, and its phrenological organ at the same time be moderate or small, there will be more activity than endurance or continuance in its characteristic manifestation; while, on the other hand, if the phrenological sign show more development than the physiognomical, there will be more endurance than activity. In the first case there will be a higher degree of manifestation than the brain, considered by itself, would warrant us in counting upon. In the second there would be less, a certain amount of power continually remaining latent; and this principle accounts for a large share of the misconception which exists in regard to both Phrenology and Physiognomy.*

In seeking to determine the size of the organs, you must not be guided merely by the undulations on the surface of the head. Phrenology is not " bumpology." You must not look for hills, hollows, and protuberances (though you will sometimes find them), but judge the length of brain fibers from the *medulla oblongata*—the center of the brain†—to the surface, where the organs are located in a manner analogous to the estimation of the size of a wagon wheel by the length of its spokes.

We have pointed out the location of all the organs in Chap. IV., and the student who has studied that chapter carefully in connection with the symbolical head and the phrenological bust, which every one should possess, will, after the necessary practice, experience little difficulty in finding them. Some further directions in regard to a few important points, however, may be useful.

III. HOW TO FIND THE ORGANS.

The locations of the perceptive organs and most of the others lying at the base of the brain are readily determined, by means of our diagrams (figs. 22 and 23) and descriptions; the eyes, the eyebrows, the ears, or the occipital protuberance,

---

* See "New Physiognomy; or, Signs of Character as manifested through Temperament and External Forms, and especially in the Human Face Divine." With more than a thousand engravings. By S. R. Wells, New York.

‡ See Description of the Skull and the Brain in our Introduction.

as the case may be, furnishing a convenient point of departure from which each may be reached with little chance for error. The exact situations of those lying farther from these fixed points are less easily determined by the beginner.

Drawing a line perpendicularly upward from the opening of the ear, you first cross Destructiveness, which lies above and partly behind the ear. When large, there will be great width of brain between the ears, and a swelling out of the organ, just over the orifice of the ear, say the size of one half of a common peach pit; when small, the head will be narrow between the ears, with no protuberance at the point designated. Next above this, and three quarters of an inch from the top of the ear, you come upon the fore part of Secretiveness. Extending this line upward, you pass over Sublimity and Conscientiousness, and at the top of the head strike the fore part of Firmness, which, when large, gives a fullness to the crown. Taking this as another fixed point, you can readily determine the location of the other organs, on the median line, and each side of it. Between Self-Esteem and Inhabitiveness, on this central line, is Concentrativeness, which, being generally small in American heads, is usually marked by a depression at that point, and is thus easy to find.

To find Cautiousness, another important point to fix correctly in the mind, draw a line perpendicularly upward from the back part of the ear, and just where the head begins to round off to form the top, you will come upon that organ. It is generally well developed in the heads of our countrymen, and often causes quite a prominence at that point. Forward of Cautiousness, and in a line with it, are Sublimity, Ideality, and Mirthfulness.

Between Firmness and Benevolence is Veneration, in the center of the top-head. When this middle part rounds out and rises above the parts next before and behind it, Veneration is larger than Firmness and Benevolence. Below Veneration are the two organs of Hope and Spirituality, the latter of which is unfortunately marked by a depression in many Protestant heads.

Above Alimentiveness, and the fore part of Destructiveness, is Acquisitiveness, and forward of that, Constructiveness.

A horizontal line drawn backward from the outer angle of the eye strikes at the center of the back-head the upper part of the organ of Parental Love. An inch or a little less below this point is the occipital protuberance, which denotes by its degree of development the power of endurance, and activity of the muscular system. It is large in great walkers—pedestrians, and in foxhounds, horses, etc. On each side of this, and just below, is the organ of Amativeness, giving thickness to the neck below and between the ears.

With these points fixed in the mind, the student will be enabled to carry out for himself the plan we have indicated for finding the organs; but he must bear in mind the fact, that there are slight modifications in the position of the organs on each head; and he must therefore learn to distinguish the *form* of each and its *appearance* when developed in different proportions to the others.

We have referred to our diagrams, symbolical head, and bust, but these can only show the situation of the organs on some particular head, taken as a model, and it is impossible by means of them to convey more information than we have thus conveyed. The different appearances in all the varieties of relative size must be discovered by inspecting numbers of heads and comparing one with another.*

When one organ is very largely developed, it encroaches on the space usually occupied by the neighboring organs, the situations of which are thereby slightly altered. When this occurs, it may be distinguished by the greatest prominence being near the center of the large organ, and the swelling

---

* The student is often at first unable to perceive differences which, after a few months, become palpably manifest to him, and at the former obscurity of which he is not a little surprised. The following anecdote, related by Dr. Gall, is in point: The physician of the House of Correction at Grætz, in Styria, sent him a box filled with skulls. In unpacking them, he was so much struck with the extreme breadth of one of them at the anterior region of the temples, that he exclaimed, "Mon Dieu, quel crâne de voleur!"—My God, what a thievish skull! Yet the physician had been unable to discover the organ of Acquisitiveness in that skull. His letter to Dr. Gall, sent with the box, was found to contain this information: "The skull marked —— is that of N——, an incorrigible thief."

extending over a portion only of the other. In these cases the *shape* should be attended to; for the form of the organ is then easily recognized, and is a sure indication of the particular one which is largely developed. The observer should learn, by inspecting a skull, to distinguish the mastoid process behind the ear, as also bony excrescences sometimes formed by the sutures, and several bony prominences which occur in every head, from elevations produced by development of brain.

In regard to the employment of the scale (or any scale) for the numbering of the organs, it may be remarked that each examiner attaches to the terms Small, Moderate, Full, etc., shades of meaning perfectly known only to himself, and it is not reasonable to expect that the markings or statements of development made by different phrenologists will always perfectly agree. It must be borne in mind, too, that the numbers indicate merely the relative proportions of the organs to each other, on the same head, and not absolute size in relation to some fixed standard.* Besides, the shape of one's head—like his features—is constantly changing. If one improves by study or the practice of an art, or if, from inaction, one deteriorates, it will soon tell on both brain and character, altering the shape of the head.†

---

* It is one object to prove Phrenology to be true, and another to teach a beginner how to observe organs. For the first purpose, we do not in general compare an organ in one head with the same organ in another; because it is the predominance of particular organs in the *same head* that gives ascendency to particular faculties in the individuals; and, therefore, *improving Phrenology*, we usually compare the different organs of the same head. But in learning to observe, it is useful to contrast the same organ in different heads, in order to become familiar with its appearance in different sizes and combinations. With this view, it is proper to begin with the larger organs; and two persons of opposite dispositions in the particular points to be compared, ought to be placed in juxtaposition, and their heads observed. Thus, if we take the organ of Cautiousness, we should examine its development in those whom we know to be remarkable for timidity, doubt, and hesitation; and we should contrast its appearance with that which it presents in individuals remarkable for precipitancy, and into whose minds doubt or fear rarely enters: or a person who is passionately fond of children may be compared, in regard to the organ of Philoprogenitiveness, with another who regards them as an intolerable annoyance.—*Combe.*

† If the student desire to find the truth, he will consider first the general principles, developed in the present work, and the presumptions for and against them, arising from admitted facts in mental philosophy and physiology. He will next proceed to make observations in nature, in the forms, situations, appearances, and functions of the organs.

VI.
PRACTICAL APPLICATION.

I. CUI BONO?

IF self-knowledge be, as wise men in all ages have considered it, the most important and useful of all learning, then Phrenology, which furnishes the key to this knowledge, is the most important and useful of all sciences. It enables us to measure our own capacity, to ascertain our strong and our weak points, to learn what sins most easily beset us, and what course to pursue to guard against them and promote virtue, purity, and holiness—how to cultivate the faculties which are deficient or inactive, and how to restrain or control excessive or perverted action. Knowing ourselves aright, we can set about the work of self-improvement understandingly and with the best prospects of full success.

Next to a knowledge of ourselves is that of our fellow-men, and especially of those with whom we live in close relations of love, friendship, or business, and with whom we are brought into daily and hourly contact. Much of our happiness and of our success in life depends upon the character of our intercourse with them. To make that intercourse pleasant and profitable we must understand their characters. Phrenology enables us to do this, and thus makes us masters of the situation.

II. PHRENOLOGY AND MATRIMONY.

The proper destiny of every well-organized man and woman is to love and marry, and it is in marriage, where the conditions are such as the laws of nature, written on our organization, demand, that the highest degree of usefulness and happiness is attainable. But men and women too often love "not wisely but too well," and marriage, if love lead to that, proves a terrible, irremediable *mistake*. Why is this? Because they neither know themselves or the persons of the other sex to whom they blindly give their hearts. Cupid is blind. Love between the sexes is a feeling, an impulse, a propensity. In its proper sphere it is, like all other faculties, good and conducive to human happiness and welfare; but it needs the guidance of intellect and the elevating and sanctifying influences of the moral sentiments. Phrenology, judiciously applied, enables the young man to judge whether the charmer who has attracted his attention and won his admiration by some grace of person or of mind, is fitted by organization to make him happy; and the young woman has in it a friendly counselor in her "affairs of the heart." Knowing her own physical and mental constitution, she will be able to determine to whom she may safely give her affections and her hand. He or she, then, who would love both wisely and well, should allow reason, instructed by science, to be his or her guide.

III. APPLICATION TO EDUCATION.

The parent and the teacher will find Phrenology an invaluable guide in the training of the young. What folly can be greater than that of applying the same sort of discipline and mode of culture to all children alike; yet the teacher or the parent who knows nothing of Phrenology is almost sure to fall into this error. On the other hand, those who have taken Phrenology as a guide, adapt their teachings to the peculiar mental organization of each pupil, and in governing him are not at a loss to what faculties to appeal when he needs to be restrained or brought back from any wrong course. They do not strive to suppress any faculty, knowing that all are God-given and bestowed for a good purpose; but they aim to educate and discipline them, bringing, if possible, the lower into due subordination to the higher. No one is well fitted to become a teacher or a parent who does not understand the science of the mind and the art of character reading.

IV. CHOICE OF A PURSUIT.

In choosing a pursuit, our science is of the utmost value. Some persons are fitted for one thing and some for another.

A few are found who can do almost anything—are nearly as well fitted for one branch of business as another. Phrenology enables us to decide what pursuit to choose for a child. We consult his organization and find out what his natural tendencies, tastes, and capacities are, and instead of making a poor preacher an indifferent lawyer, or a blundering doctor of a youth whom nature intended for a first-rate mechanic, engineer, or business man, we allow the boy's own natural predilections to be our guide in choosing a calling for him.

VI. THE PROFESSIONS.

The clergyman finds his usefulness greatly enhanced by a knowledge of Phrenology, as it enables him to understand the mental peculiarities of his parishioners, and to adapt his teachings and admonitions to individual cases, so that his appeals are understood and felt. To the physician it proves not less useful as a guide in the treatment of his various patients, no two of whom are organized exactly alike. In all cases he finds that the mind affects the body in one way or another, either promoting or retarding recovery, and that the mode and degree of its action depend upon the relative development of different parts of the brain. Fully comprehending these conditions, he is enabled to make the patient's mental activity an ally instead of an enemy in the curative process. The lawyer confessedly owes much of his success to a thorough knowledge of human nature, and in no way can he so well obtain this knowledge as through the medium of Phrenology and Physiognomy. The merchant may make use of it in choosing his clerks and other assistants, so as to secure honesty and business talent; the mechanic who understands Phrenology will not take for an apprentice a boy who is poorly developed in Constructiveness and Imitation or who has a weak constitution; and the farmer will look for a love of animals, an interest in plants, and a delight in the free, unconventional life of the country to adapt a young man to the profession of agriculture. The statesman, the military commander, the actor, the artist, and the mechanic, all need a knowledge of it, and may profit greatly by its teachings.

VII.

OBJECTIONS TO PHRENOLOGY.

THE truth of Phrenology having long since been demonstrated, all objections to it are futile, and hardly deserve to be cited in a work like this. Every truth must be consistent with all other truths. Truth is always safe. It is error that is dangerous and subversive of morality and religion. But as old objections to our science continue to be reiterated in certain quarters, and as some of our readers may not have seen the answers which have been made to them, and in which their utter groundlessness has been shown, we have decided to notice briefly a few of the more common and plausible of them.

1. NUMBER OF THE FACULTIES.—"Phrenologists do not agree in regard to the number of the faculties, and are constantly adding to them, showing that there is nothing fixed or certain about the system."

Answer.—The differences among phrenologists in reference to the number of faculties, are not greater but less than among the teachers of other systems of mental philosophy. In neither case does the circumstance invalidate the system taught. Phrenologists do not create faculties and organs; they simply discover and describe them. They are not responsible for their number. Our list of organs is increased by the discovery of new ones. The functions of certain portions of the brain yet remain unknown. Is the science of astronomy considered unsettled and untrustworthy because some astronomers "see stars" where others, with less development of the observing powers or inferior instruments, have found only blank space? or because they are constantly adding to the number of the known planets? In fact, is not the objection under notice slightly absurd?

2. THE ANATOMICAL OBJECTION. — "No phrenologist has ever observed the supposed lines of demarkation between the organs assumed to exist in the brain, or has ventured in the course of his dis-

sections to divide a hemisphere of the brain accurately into any such number of organs as have been mapped out on the surface of the skull."

Answer.—1. Were this objection literally true, it would not be relevant, because it is an admitted principle of physiology that, in the present state of our knowledge, the form and structure of an organ are not sufficient to convey an idea of its function. The most expert anatomists had looked frequently and long upon a bundle of nervous fibers, inclosed in a common sheath, without discovering that one set of them was the organ of voluntary motion, and another that of feeling; on the contrary, from their similarity of appearance, these nerves had, for ages, been regarded as possessing similar functions. Nevertheless, Sir C. Bell and Magendie have demonstrated, by experiment, that they possess the distinct functions of feeling and motion. It may therefore be proved by observation, that the different parts of the brain have distinct functions, although it were true that no difference of structure could be perceived; but—

2. It is not a fact that no difference of appearance is discoverable. It is easy to distinguish the anterior, the middle, and posterior lobes of the human brain from each other; and were they shown separately to a skillful phrenological anatomist, he would never take one for the other. The mental manifestations are so different, according as one or other of these lobes predominates in size, that there is, even in this case, ample room for establishing the fundamental proposition, that different faculties are connected with different parts of the brain. Further: many of the organs differ so decidedly in appearance, that they could be pointed out by it alone.

3. It is admitted that the organs of the brain are not perceived to be separated by strong lines of demarkation; but the *forms* of the organs are distinguishable and the mapping out is founded in nature, though originally the result of the observation of the external surface of the cranium.

3. IGNORANCE OF PHRENOLOGISTS.—"The teachers and disciples of Phrenology are ignorant of anatomy and physiology, and they delude only those equally uninstructed."

Answer.—This statement is untrue, and therefore the objection it is intended to embody falls to the ground. Drs. Gall and Spurzheim were admirable anatomists. The dissections of the brain made by the latter are acknowledged to have been the most satisfactory ever performed. The Messrs. Combe of Edinburgh, Drs. Vimont and Broussais of Paris, and Dr. Charles Caldwell of the United States, all advocates and teachers of Phrenology, were also anatomists of great skill and learning; and among the "uninstructed" ones who have been "deluded" by their teachings, we may name such men as Dr. Samuel George Morton, Professor of Anatomy, etc., and author of "Crania Americana;" Prof. John Elliotson, M.D., F.R.S.; Dr. Robert Hunter, Professor of Anatomy, etc.; Prof. John Bell, M.D.; J. V. C. Smith, M.D., Professor of Anatomy, and Editor of the Boston *Medical and Surgical Journal;* Nathan Allen, M.D., and John M. Carnochan, M.D., the most distinguished surgeon in the United States. We might increase this list indefinitely, but these names will suffice.

4. MATERIALISM, FATALISM, ETC.—"Phrenology leads to materialism and fatalism."

Answer.—If Phrenology be false, it can lead to nothing in the end but to the confusion of its supporters and to a merited oblivion; but if it be true, and if materialism follow as a logical deduction from its facts, then, of course, materialism is true, and Phrenology is no more responsible for its existence than chemistry or astronomy is. It simply makes it known.

But the materialist says that it is the medullary matter that thinks—in other words, that *the brain is the mind.* Now we teach no such doctrine, and Phrenology leads to no such conclusion. It declares that mind, in this mortal life and while linked to matter, is *manifested through the brain.* It has not necessarily anything to do with the question, What is the substance of the mind itself? It deals with mind as it is observed through its manifestations. If it be material, Phrenology has not made it so. If it be immaterial, Phrenology can at best only make the fact apparent. We always, as all who know anything about our teachings are well aware, draw a broad line of demarkation between the organ of the mind and the mind itself. The one must perish, the other we believe will survive and

> Flourish in immortal youth,
> Unhurt amid the war of elements,
> The wreck of matter, and the crash of worlds.

In regard to the asserted fatalistic tendencies of Phrenology, our reply must be mainly the same as in regard to the first part of the objector's statement. If man's constitution of body and brain determine unalterably his character and destiny, so that he can neither be better nor worse than he is, nor in any way different, Phrenology, although it may reveal this character and destiny, is no more responsible for it than theology is for the existence of evil. But while Phrenology finds mind in this life connected with matter, and subject, so far as its manifestations are concerned, to certain organic laws, it also recognizes within the limits of its organization, and as an element in the unalterable law of life, the freedom of the will, and a consequent personal responsibility.

We are not responsible for our being. We are born into this world, made dependent while here upon material organs for our ability to act, and rendered liable to the accidents which happen to matter, and to the final death of the body. In these arrangements we had no voice—no freedom to choose when or where we would be born, or how we would be endowed in the matter of body and brain, and therefore can have no responsibility, so far as they are concerned. But there has been bestowed upon us, or rather made a part of our mental constitution, *a sense of right and wrong*, and with it the power to choose between good and evil—to rise or to fall—to improve or to deteriorate, and here we are responsible, not for our faculties, but for the use we make of them.

As an additional evidence that Phrenology is in no way inimical to religion, we may here mention that it is now embraced and taught by many of the most prominent and truly pious clergymen of Europe and America, including Archbishop Whateley, Thomas Chalmers, D.D., Rev. Orville Dewey, Rev. John Pierrepont, E. H. Chapin, D.D., Rev. Henry Ward Beecher, and many others.

VIII.

THE TRADES AND PROFESSIONS.

I. A CLASSIFIED LIST.

I. THE MECHANIC ARTS.—Artificial Flower Maker—Baker—Basket Maker—Bookbinder—Blacksmith—Bricklayer—Butcher—Cabinet Maker—Carpenter—Carriage Maker—Carriage Ironer—Carriage Trimmer—Compositor — Cooper — Dentist — Dressmaker — Engineer — Finisher of Work — Founder — General Mechanic — Gold Beater—Harness Maker—Inventor—Jeweler—Locksmith—Machinist—Manufacturer—Miller—Milliner—Molder—Paper Box Maker — Painter — Penman — Picture-frame Maker — Printer—Shoemaker—Silversmith—Stone Cutter—Surgeon—Tailor—Tanner—Upholsterer—Watchmaker.

II. THE FINE ARTS. — Architect — Actor — Daguerrean—Designer — Draughtsman — Engraver — Florist — Historical Painter—Landscape Painter—Landscape Gardener—Modeler—Musician—Musical Composer—Poet—Portrait Painter—Sculptor.

III. LITERATURE.—Author—Dramatist—Editor, Literary, Commercial, Political, General—Historian—Journalist—Lecturer — Librarian — Novelist — Orator — Poet — Preacher — Reporter.

IV. SCIENCE.—Botanist—Chemist—Editor—Entomologist—Explorer (Scientific)—Engineer—Geographer—Geologist—Lecturer—Mineralogist—Naturalist — Navigator — Phrenologist—Physician—Surgeon—Surveyor—Zoologist.

V. EDUCATION.—Author (of Educational Books)—College Professor — Editor — Elocutionist — Governess — Lecturer—Phrenologist—Teacher.

VI. THE " PROFESSIONS."—Attorney—Author—Barrister—Clergyman — Counselor—Judge—Lawyer—Phrenologist—Physician—Preacher—Surgeon.

VII. COMMERCE. — Accountant — Agent — Auctioneer — Bookseller—Cattle Dealer—Commission Business—Clerk—Dry Goods—Fancy Goods—Grocer—Hardware—Lumber Dealer—Importer—Jobber,—Merchant—Publisher—Salesman—Stock Jobber.

VIII.—GENERAL BUSINESS. — Agent, General Business, Insurance, Express, Freight—Banker—Broker—Canvasser—Cashier—Collector—Conductor—Contractor—Conveyancer—Financier—Post Master—President of Bank, Railroad, Insurance Company—Real Estate Dealer—Superintendent.

IX. MISCELLANEOUS EMPLOYMENTS. — Diplomatist—Explorer—Farmer—Fisherman—Fruit Grower—Horseman—Horticulturist—Hotel Keeper—Livery Keeper—Lumberman—Policeman or Detective—Politician—Seaman—Soldier—Statesman—Stock Raiser—Undertaker—Watchman.

II. DEVELOPMENTS FOR PARTICULAR PURSUITS.

I. THE LAW.—Lawyers require the mental-vital temperament, to give them intensity of feeling and clearness of intellect; large Eventuality, to recall law cases and decisions; large Comparison, to compare different parts of the law and evidence—to criticise, cross-question, illustrate, and adduce similar cases; and large Language, to give freedom of speech. Phrenology will tell you how to acquire and use these powers and faculties to the best advantage. Try it.

II. STATESMANSHIP.—Statesmen require large and well-balanced intellects, to enable them to understand and see through great public measures and choose the best course, together with high moral heads, to make them DISINTERESTED, and seek the PEOPLE's good, not selfish ends.

III. MEDICINE.—Physicians require large Perceptive Faculties, so that they may study and apply a knowledge of Anatomy and Physiology with skill and success; full Destructiveness, lest they shrink from inflicting the pain requisite to cure; large Constructiveness, to give them skill in surgery; large Combativeness, to render them resolute and prompt; large Cautiousness, to render them judicious and safe; and a large head, to give them general power of mind. Phrenology will predict, in advance, whether or not a boy will succeed in this profession. The same is true of Dentistry.

IV. DIVINITY.—Clergymen require the mental temperament, to give them a decided predominance of MIND over their animal propensities; a large frontal and coronal region, the former to give them intellectual capacity, and the latter to impart high moral worth, aims, and feelings, elevation of character, and blamelessness of conduct; large Veneration, Hope, and Spirituality, to imbue them with the spirit of faith and devotion; large Benevolence and Adhesiveness, so that they may make all who know them LOVE them, and thus win each over to the paths of truth and righteousness. Clergymen will do well to consult Phrenology; it would enable them to account for many *seeming* mysteries, and give them power and influence to do great good. It is in the most perfect harmony with the highest Christianity.

V. JOURNALISM.—Editors also require a mental temperament, with large Individuality and Eventuality, to collect and disseminate incidents, facts, news, and give a PRACTICAL cast of mind; large Comparison, to enable them to illustrate, criticise, show up errors, and the like; full or large Combativeness, to render them spirited; large Language, to render them copious, free, spicy, and racy; and large Ideality, to give taste and elevated sentiments. An Editor who understands and *applies* Phrenology possesses a power which he may use with great effect. "He can take your measure."

VI. COMMERCE. — Merchants require Acquisitiveness, to impart a desire and tact for business; large Hope, to promote enterprise; full Cautiousness, to render them safe; large Perceptives, to give quick and correct judgment of the qualities of goods; good Calculation, to impart rapidity and correctness in casting accounts; large Approbativeness, to render them courteous and affable; and full Adhesiveness, to enable them to make friends of customers, and thus retain them. Why is *one* young man a better salesman than another? and why is one better worth a salary twice or thrice the amount than another? Phrenology answers this by pointing out the constitutional differences, and showing who is, and who is not, adapted to mercantile life. You had better consult Phrenology, and choose accordingly.

VII. THE MECHANIC ARTS. — Mechanics require strong constitutions, to give them muscular power and love of labor; large Constructiveness and Imitation, to enable them to use tools with dexterity; work after a pattern, and easily learn to do what they may see others do; and large Perceptive Faculties, to give the required judgment of matter and the fitness of things.

VIII. THE FINE ARTS.—Artists require the mental temperament, high organic quality and large Ideality to impart the necessary intellectual appreciation of the laws of beauty and the rules of art, taste, refinement, delicacy, imagination, and lofty aspirations; Constructiveness, to give skill in the use of the implements of art; Imitation, to enable them to copy well; and large perceptives to impart judgment of the forms and qualities of things.*

---

* Finally, while we do most confidently affirm that there is a marked difference in the natural capacities and aptitudes of men for particular callings; and that one will show great talent as an artist, mechanic, or merchant, another would excel in neither of these, but in something else; still it must be admitted that each of us, having the same number and kind of organs and faculties—differing only in quality, culture, and degree of development—it is possible for most of us to learn to do very nearly the same thing. Nor is it best to push a student in those studies in which he already *excels*, but rather in the studies most difficult, in order to develop deficient or inactive faculties. If one already manifests mechanical skill, turn his attention to art, philosophy, or invention. If one is naturally musical, and wanting in mathematics, let music be made second to mathematics, and so on through all the studies. The end desired is an even, harmonious, well-balanced character.

Part II.

A DELINEATION

OF THE

CHARACTER, PHYSIOLOGICAL DEVELOPMENT,

AND PRESENT CONDITION

OF

Dr A. T. Beckett

AS GIVEN BY

Nelson Sizer

[DATE.]

Feb 20 1883

EXPLANATION OF THE TABLE.

Opposite to the name of each organ or quality taken into account in a delineation of character, and in the column indicating its relative power, the examiner will place a figure, a dash, or a dot, to indicate the subject's development in respect to that organ or quality. The printed figures in the square thus marked refer to the pages in this work on which, under the name of the organ or quality standing in the margin opposite, will be found a description of the traits of character which the development is believed to denote. At the end of this description are other figures, indicating pages where directions for cultivating or restraining, as may be directed, the faculty in question.

When an organ is half way between two sizes, it is represented by two figures, as 5 to 6, or 3 to 4, etc., which is equivalent to $5\frac{1}{2}$ or $3\frac{1}{2}$. In these cases both paragraphs referred to may be read, and a medium between the two will be appropriate.

The sign $+$, *plus*, signifies about one third of a degree more, and $-$, *minus*, one third of a degree less, than the marks indicate, thus giving virtually a scale of twenty-one degrees.

AN EXPLANATORY NOTE.

☞ PLEASE READ THIS FIRST. ✍

In a *printed* delineation, we can only approximate to the real character. No two persons, even though they be twins, are exactly alike. The almost numberless combinations of which the temperaments and mental faculties (to say nothing of the ever-varying physiological conditions involved) are susceptible, result in phases and shades of character as numerous as the individuals of the human race. To bring these out in a fully satisfactory manner requires a *carefully written* analysis. We can give, as a general rule, in a chart like this, merely the simple elements. The subject should combine them for himself, considering well the temperaments, and the modifications which must result from the action of one faculty upon another, and especially the influence of the predominating group and the leading organ. (See p. 124 *et seq.* for further hints.")

Our aim here is to give as accurate a delineation of character as the circumstances will admit. Absolute correctness in every particular is not claimed, nor would it be possible in following the markings of the several organs and conditions as here set down; and due allowance, in every case, by examiner and examined, must therefore be made.

For a Full Explanation of this Table,

CONDITIONS.	7 Very Large.	6 Large.	5 Full.	4 Average.	3 Moderate.	2 Small.
Organic Quality.......	PAGE 149	149	149	150	150	150
Health	150	150	150	150	150	150
Vital Temperament	151	151	151	151	151	151
Breathing Power......	152	152	152	152	152	152
Circulatory Power.....	153	153	153	153	153	153
Digestive Power.......	153	153	153	153	154	154
Motive Temperament....	154	154	154	154	154	155
Mental Temperament ...	155	155	155	155	155	156
Activity............	156	156	156	156	156	156
Excitability........	156	156	156	156	157	157
Size of Brain, inches...	157	157	157	157	157	158
1. Amativeness.........	158	158	159	159	159	159
A. Conjugality..........	159	159	159	160	160	160
2. Parental Love........	160	160	160	160	160	161
3. Friendship	161	161	161	161	161	162
4. Inhabitiveness........	162	162	162	162	162	162
5. Continuity...........	162	163	163	163	163	163
E. Vitativeness..........	163	164	164	164	164	164
6. Combativeness.......	164	164	165	165	165	165
7. Destructiveness	165	166	166	166	166	166
8. Alimentiveness	166	166	166	167	167	167
9. Acquisitiveness.......	167	167	168	168	168	168
10. Secretiveness........	168	168	169	169	169	169
11. Cautiousness.........	169	169	169	170	170	170
12. Approbativeness	170	170	170	170	171	171
13. Self-Esteem..........	171	171	171	171	171	172
14. Firmness............	172	172	172	172	172	172

The Reader is Referred to Page 144.

CONDITIONS.	7 Very Large.	6 Large.	5 Full.	4 Average.	3 Moderate.	2 Small.
15. Conscientiousness.....	PAGE 173	*(6)* 173	*(5)* 173	173	173	173
16. Hope................	174	174	174	*(4)* 174	174	174
17. Spirituality	175	175	*(5)* 175	*(4)* 175	175	175
18. Veneration..........	176	176	*(5)* 176	*(4)* 176	176	176
19. Benevolence	176	*(6)* 177	*(5)* 177	177	177	177
20. Constructiveness	177	*(6)* 177	178	178	178	178
21. Ideality.............	178	*(7)* 178	*(5)* 178	178	179	179
B. Sublimity	179	*(6)* 179	179	179	179	179
22. Imitation	180	180	180	*(4)* 180	180	180
23. Mirthfulness	180	180	*(5)* 181	181	181	181
24. Individuality........	181	*(6)* 181	181	181	181	182
25. Form...............	182	*(6)* 182	182	182	182	182
26. Size................	182	*(6)* 182	182	182	183	183
27. Weight.............	183	*(6)* 183	183	183	183	183
28. Color..............	183	*(6)* 184	184	184	184	184
29. Order..............	184	*(6)* 184	184	184	184	185
30. Calculation	185	*(6)* 185	*(5)* 185	185	185	185
31. Locality	185	*(6)* 186	186	186	186	186
32. Eventuality.........	186	*(6)* 186	*(5)* 186	186	186	186
33. Time...............	187	187	*(5)* 187	187	187	187
34. Tune...............	187	187	*(5)* 187	*(4)* 187	187	188
35. Language	188	*(6)* 188	188	188	188	188
36. Causality..........	189	189	*(5)* 189	189	189	189
37. Comparison	*(7)* 189	*(6)* 189	190	190	190	190
C. Human Nature.......	190	*(6)* 190	190	190	191	191
D. Agreeableness	191	191	*(5)* 191	191	191	191

ADAPTATION IN MARRIAGE.

WHEN a person has a perfect balance of temperament and a harmonious development of all the mental faculties and dispositions, a companion should be chosen whose development is similar; but as this is very rarely found, each person should seek to form a union with one who is properly contrasted so that the excess of one may be balanced and modified by a less development in the other.

The person for whom the foregoing Chart is marked should choose a companion having a constitution and mental qualities as indicated by the *marking* of this table

Vital Temperament..	Strong. ✓	Medium.	Moderate.
Motive Temperament.............	Strong. ✓	Medium.	Moderate.
Mental Temperament..............	Strong.	Medium.	✓ Moderate.
General Build or Form.............	Tall and Bony.	Medium.	Short and Plump. ✓
Size of Head........	Large.	✓ Medium.	Moderate.
Weight........	Heavy.	✓ Medium.	Light.
Full and Plump......	Decidedly. ✓	Medium.	Moderately.
Complexion..........	Dark Brunette. ✓	Medium.	Light, or Blonde.
Hair.............	Dark and Strong. ✓	Medium.	Light and Fine.
Eyes................	Dark. ✓	Medium.	Light, or Blue.
Social and Domestic.	Strong.	✓ Medium.	Moderate.
Energy of Character.	Strong.	✓ Medium.	Moderate.
Self-Reliance........	Strong.	✓ Medium.	Moderate.
Prudence and Policy.	Strong.	✓ Medium.	Moderate.
Regard for Praise and Public Opinion.....	Strong.	✓ Medium.	Moderate.
Economy and Love of Property..........	Strong.	✓ Medium.	Moderate.
Cheerfulness and Self-Control........	Strong. ✓	Medium.	Moderate.
Ingenuity, Skill, and Taste.........	Strong.	✓ Medium.	Moderate.
Practical Talent......	Strong.	✓ Medium.	Moderate.
Reasoning and Planning Talent........	Strong. ✓	Medium.	Moderate.
Conversational Power....	Strong. ✓	Medium.	Moderate.
Moral and Religious.	Very Strong. ✓	Full.	Medium.

DELINEATION OF CHARACTER.

I.

PHYSIOLOGICAL CONDITIONS.

I.—ORGANIC QUALITY.

(7.) Very Good.—You have a remarkably refined, sensitive, and delicate organization; are susceptible of exquisite enjoyment and intense suffering; and are greatly affected by extremes of heat and cold, especially the latter. You are adapted to fine and light work rather than to that which is coarse and heavy, have poetic and artistic tastes, lofty aspirations, tender sympathies, and a longing for congenial companionship. Being inclined to live too far above the common interests and pursuits of life, you fail to find full appreciation, and are subjected to much suffering by the rude contacts involved among the every-day realities of this life. Cultivate a more robust bodily condition—eat, drink, sleep, and grow fat—and try to live more in the real and less in the ideal world. [23.]*

(6.) Good.—You are fine-grained, high-toned, and delicately organized; susceptible, sensitive, and sympathetic; refined in your tastes, pleasures, and aspirations; and repelled by whatever is low, coarse, or gross. You are liable to extremes in feeling and acting; are likely to be either very good or very bad; suffer keenly, enjoy deeply, and are generally either greatly exalted or greatly depressed; have exquisite tastes; love the beautiful, and desire, if you do not always seek, the good and the true. [23.]

(5.) Full.—Yours is neither a coarse nor an over-wrought organization. Your tendencies, so far as your constitution affects them, are upward rather than downward, and your tastes elevating rather than degrading. You must avoid all those habits which minister to the animal passions and clog mental manifestation, and strive to elevate yourself far above the gross and groveling multitude. [23.]

---

* These figures, and others similarly introduced in [brackets] throughout this part of the work, refer to pages in the first part—"How to Read Character"—where additional information or explanatory remarks may be found.

(4.) AVERAGE.—You are rather deficient in quality or delicacy in your organization; plain in your tastes; practical in your views; not very poetical or sentimental; and better fitted for the matter-of-fact routine of every-day life than for the higher walks of literature and art. You must cultivate the Mental Temperament, and be careful to contract no debasing habits, as one error, in a person of your organization, is likely to lead to others and to final ruin. [23.]

(3.) MODERATE.—Your organic quality is below the average and your mental manifestations sluggish and weak. You are better adapted to manual labor than to study, and should not attempt any of the more delicate mechanical trades. You must try to make up, by the assiduous cultivation of your intellectual and moral powers, for your lack of natural organic endowments. Avoid, by all means, drinking, smoking, and low company. [23.]

(2.) POOR.—Yours is a coarse-grained structure, and all your appetites, tastes, and desires are of the plainer, coarser kind. There is the most urgent need in your case to restrain the passions; to put yourself in the way of moral and religious influences; and to cultivate the intellectual faculties, so far as you are able. [23.]

II.—STATE OF THE HEALTH.

(7.) VERY GOOD.—You are full of life; vigorous, strong, buoyant, and hearty in the highest degree, and enjoy exquisite pleasure in the mere sense of animal existence. [24.]

(6.) GOOD.—All your bones, muscles, and nerves are apparently in good working order, and you enjoy the exercise of every organ of body and brain. You should now manifest your greatest efficiency in both physical and mental action; find study and work alike easy and pleasant; and be able to endure toil, exposure, and hardship with impunity. [24.]

(5.) FULL.—You have a full share of vigor and vital stamina; can work with efficiency and endure considerable hardship; but have no life-force to waste in unnecessary and fruitless effort. [24.]

(4.) AVERAGE.—You have a fair degree of health, but are liable to ailments, and must live regularly, pay strict attention to the laws of your being, and be careful not to overwork yourself, and thus break down your constitution. [24.]

(3.) MODERATE.—You are deficient in vitality; are easily fatigued; often ailing, and seldom capable of any great degree of physical or mental exertion. You must avoid overdoing, and make the restoration of your health your first object. Stop all unnecessary drafts upon your remaining stock of vitality, and seek, by means of rest, sleep, and recreation, to increase it. Drinking, smoking, chewing, late hours, and all kinds of dissipation, must be entirely avoided. [24.]

(2.) POOR.—You have but a small amount of health left, and must make use of every means within your reach for its improvement. Try to arouse yourself to combat your ailments. Pluck is as essential in meeting the attacks of disease as in opposing a human foe. A strong will has saved many a life. "Courage and Hope"—let that be your motto. [24.]

III.—THE VITAL TEMPERAMENT.

(7.) VERY LARGELY DEVELOPED.—This temperament is characterized by rotundity. You are plump, stout, full-chested, and fond of fresh air and the luxuries of life; but you like play better than hard work. In mental character there is a tendency to impulsiveness, enthusiasm, versatility, practicality, and to take a matter-of-fact view of things. Your fondness for good living, jovial company, sports and amusements, render you liable to fall into habits of intemperance, against which you must be continually on your guard. If you find yourself inclined to an uncomfortable obesity, your remedy must be *work*, and a spare diet. Keep both body and mind actively engaged, and avoid indolence and the indulgences of the table as your greatest foes. By a rigid adherence to a low and moderate diet, and by vigorous manual labor, you may greatly modify and improve your temperament. [20.]

(6.) LARGELY DEVELOPED.—You are well-proportioned, full-chested, and amply supplied with the oil of life. All your joints are thoroughly lubricated, and your mental machinery works without friction. You are likely to manifest a good degree of business talent, and to be not averse to doing your share of necessary work, when there is profit in it. You have great need to exercise all your moral sense, caution, and will-power in avoiding and resisting the temptations to excess in eating, drinking, and indulging the propensities, which so easily beset you. Occasional *fasting*, rather than *feasting*, should be practiced. [20.]

(5.) FULL.—You possess a fair share of the vital element, and partake of the characteristics noted in (6) and (7) in a proportionate degree. You need to increase rather than diminish this element. Every sort of dissipation should be avoided, and regular hours, with plenty of sleep, secured. [20.]

(4.) AVERAGE.—Your vitality is sufficient to give the functions of body and brain a fair share of energy, and to sustain life and health if carefully husbanded; but you should seek to increase it by a diet and habits promotive of alimentation and nutrition. Alternate exercise and rest; sleep as much as nature seems to demand; seek recreation; take life more easy; eat plain but nutritious food; enjoy all of life; "laugh and grow fat." [20.]

(3.) WEAKLY DEVELOPED.—Your constitution is deficient in the vital element, and you are languid and inefficient in consequence. You require much rest and sleep, and must be very careful not to overwork either body or mind [see previous section (4)], and assiduously make use of all available means to increase your vitality. [20.]

(2.) VERY FEEBLY DEVELOPED.—You have barely enough vitality to keep your bodily and mental functions in operation. You must make use of the very small stock you now possess, as capital to be used for the purpose of increasing it, as directed in previous sections. You must "stop the leaks," and give the reservoir time to fill up; live on the interest, instead of consuming both interest and principal, and thus becoming so far impoverished that there shall be no hope of recovery. [20.]

IV.—BREATHING POWER.

(7.) VERY GOOD.—Your respiratory organs are admirably developed, and their functions well-nigh perfectly performed. You breathe freely and deeply, moving the abdominal muscles as well as the lungs, and filling your chest at every inspiration. The effects of this functional power and activity may be observed in your warm hands and feet, elastic motions, and buoyant spirits. [25.]

(6.) GOOD.—You have a well-developed chest and excellent breathing power, indicated as in (7), only in a slightly lower degree. [25.]

(5.) FULL.—You are above the average in breathing power generally, but if your habits be sedentary, you will need to resort to artificial means to expand the lungs and to keep up the circulation. [25.]

(4.) AVERAGE.—Your breathing power is only medium, but you have a fair share of warmth, and can keep your feet and hands warm by proper exercise. You should take the measures recommended on p. 26 (foot note) for expanding the chest. [25.]

(3.) MODERATE.—You breathe too little to thoroughly vitalize the blood, seldom filling the lungs, moving the chest but little, and the abdominal muscles scarcely at all; are liable to colds, which have a tendency to settle on the lungs; have cold feet and hands and blue veins near the surface. You must cultivate breathing power, and expand the chest. This can be done with great certainty, but you must begin carefully and avoid fatigue in your exercises. [25, 26 (note).]

(2.) WEAK.—You are very deficient in the development of the respiratory organs, liable to colds and coughs, and predisposed to consumption; but while your lungs remain sound, you may hope to ward off disease and greatly improve your breathing power and general health by right living and the necessary physical culture. In addition to the chest-expanding exercise [26 (note)], you must live much in the open air; keep your rooms well ventilated; sit, stand, and walk erect, bathe the chest frequently with cold water, rubbing it briskly with the naked hands, to bring the blood to the surface. Go into the mountains, or take a sea voyage. [25.]

V.—CIRCULATION.

(7.) VERY GOOD.—You have an excellent circulation; a strong, steady pulse; perspire freely; and are able to withstand great cold and heat without discomfort. [26.]

(6.) GOOD.—Your circulation is generally good, and your lower extremities seldom cold. You suffer little from clear cold weather and do not readily contract disease. [26.]

(5.) FULL.—You have a fair circulation, but need bodily exercise to keep the extremities warm in cold weather, and should promote this function by active employments or recreations. [26.]

(4.) AVERAGE.—Your circulation is not remarkably good, and you sometimes feel chilly or have cold feet and hands. Promote the uniform movement of the vital fluid by brisk exercise, especially in cold weather. [26.]

(3.) MODERATE.—Your circulation is rather poor. You are very liable to cold feet and hands, headache, palpitation of the heart, and a dry skin; can not withstand extremes of heat and cold, and need to exercise briskly and practice breathing fully and deeply, as recommended in previous section. [26 (note).]

(2.) WEAK.—You have a weak and very unequal circulation; suffer greatly from changes of temperature; are often chilly, even in warm weather; are troubled with headache, pressure on the brain, and very cold extremities. The Turkish bath, if accessible, will benefit you; also tepid foot-baths, brisk and hard rubbing of the hands and feet, walking, and the breathing exercise. Horse-back riding is one of the very best exercises to promote and equalize the circulation. Skating, rowing, climbing the hills, etc., are also useful, *when taken with proper care.* [26 (note).]

VI.—DIGESTION.

(7.) VERY GOOD.—Your digestion is almost perfect, and you can eat with impunity any sort of food suitable, under any circumstances, to be received into the human stomach. [26.]

(6.) GOOD.—Your digestive power is strong and your relish for food excellent. Plain substantial aliment suits you best, and you are able to make whatever you take into your stomach contribute to the nourishment of the system. [26.]

(5.) FULL.—You have good digestion, but not so strong that it may not be easily injured by improper food and wrong habits of eating. You must avoid heavy meals and indigestible articles of diet. Regulate the quantity of food taken by the judgment, rather than by the appetite. [26.]

(4.) AVERAGE.—You have only a fair degree of digestive power, and must be careful not to impair it by overeating, by the use of condiments, stimulants, etc. [26.]

7*

(3) and (2.) MODERATE OR WEAK.—You are predisposed to dyspepsia; often have a poor appetite; suffer from indigestion, and, as a result, are apt to be irritable, peevish, dispirited, and gloomy. The improvement of your digestive function should be your first object and study. Eat plain and easily digested but nutritious food; let the quantity be moderate; masticate thoroughly; talk, laugh, and enjoy at your meals, or at least try to be in a cheerful, thankful, happy mood; avoid a hurried feeling or an anxious state of mind; take plenty of exercise in the open air; have your rooms well ventilated; practice full, deep breathing and other chest-expanding exercises, as indirect but important helps to the stomach; and observe strictly all the laws of health. Correct this dyspeptic tendency by *recreation* rather than by *stimulation*. [26.]

VII.—THE MOTIVE TEMPERAMENT.

(7.) VERY STRONGLY DEVELOPED.—The bony frame-work of your structure is strongly marked, and encased with only muscle enough to bind all firmly together; but what flesh you have is dense, tough, compact, and wiry. There is a tendency to angularity in your configuration. You love active, muscular work, and are endowed with great physical power and capacity for severe and prolonged exertion of both body and mind. In character you are energetic, efficient, determined, and persistent. You are adapted to active life, and to such enterprises as will give your energy, steadfastness, and perseverance full and free scope. See also (6.) [18.]

(6.) STRONG.—Your configuration and character are like those described in (7), in a somewhat lower degree. You have strong feelings and passions, but are also endowed with a powerful will and strong common sense with which to hold them in check. The restraining and regulating powers of the mind—Firmness, Self-Esteem, Conscientiousness, and Cautiousness—must be kept in constant activity to keep your strong propensities within their proper sphere, for when they are bad, persons of your constitution are often *very* bad. You are capable of great things, but need strong self-government and restraint. [18.]

(5.) FULL.—You have a good share of motive power, and are vigorous, determined, and efficient. You are not afraid of work, or, for that matter, of anything else. Your tastes and abilities fit you for active life. See (6) and (7.) [18.]

(4.) AVERAGE.—You are not deficient in motive power, but can not endure a long-continued strain upon either muscle or brain. You can work hard, but are not particularly fond of severe labor, preferring light or sedentary employments, and should cultivate muscular power and love of activity by such recreations and exercises as tend to develop bone and sinew. [18.]

(3.) MODERATELY DEVELOPED.—You are deficient in the motive

element of the constitution, lack strength for continuous exertion, and prefer sitting or lounging about to activity of any kind. Cultivate muscular power. [18.]

(2.) WEAK.—You are poorly endowed with muscular force, and the propelling and governing powers connected with the motive temperament. You must give much attention to the cultivation of the motive apparatus. Walking, running, rowing, swimming, skating, and gymnastics are all good exercises, but must be adapted to your weak condition, and increased as you gain strength. Make yourself comfortably tired, but do not exhaust your small stock of energy and strength by too much exertion. [18.]

VIII.—THE MENTAL TEMPERAMENT.

(7.) VERY LARGELY DEVELOPED.—You are delicate in structure, with small bones, a moderate development of muscle, finely cut features, and a high organic condition generally. Brain predominates over body, and your mental states have a powerful influence over your physical condition. You are refined in your tastes; quick and delicate in your perceptions; rapid in your mental operations; emotional, sympathetic, aspiring, earnest, eager, and easily excited. You are admirably adapted, so far as constitutional qualities are concerned, to literary or artistic pursuits. If a mechanic, a manufacturer, or a merchant, one of the lighter and more elegant branches in these departments would suit you best. See next section (6). [21.]

(6.) A LARGE DEVELOPMENT.—You are characterized as set forth in (7), only in a lower degree; are more inclined to mental than to animal enjoyments; fond of literature and art; ambitious, clear-headed, discriminating, quick-witted, intellectually efficient, rather brilliant, and calculated to lead in the higher walks of literature, art, or science, provided you have had the necessary mental culture. Stimulants of all kinds should be avoided, as well as too strong or long continued mental excitements. [21.]

(5.) FULLY DEVELOPED.—You are well endowed mentally, and calculated (with proper culture) to speak and write effectively, and to wield considerable influence in the realms of thought; being less sensitive and delicately organized than those in whom there is a larger proportional development of this temperament, you are better fitted to come into contact with people of all classes, and to control them by means of your superior mental development, backed by the vigor imparted by a larger measure of vital and motive power. [21.]

(4.) AVERAGE.—You have a fair degree of mental activity, and, with the advantages of education, are capable of attaining a position in intellectual society; but you are better adapted to manual labor, mechanism, or to business than to the learned professions, so-called. [21.]

(3.) MODERATELY DEVELOPED.—You have no real love for literature or art, are not fond of study, and would be apt to fall asleep over a good book. You should cultivate a taste for reading. [21.]

(2.) POORLY DEVELOPED.—You are dull in perception, and slow to comprehend even simple truths. Your judgment is poor, and you need the direction of minds more highly endowed. You should get sound advice, and follow it. [21.]

IX.—ACTIVITY.

(7.) VERY GREAT.—You are very agile, lithe-limbed, and quick-motioned, and your mental operations are equally rapid and facile. You are always wide-awake, eager, knowing, and brilliant. You are liable to overwork yourself and become prematurely exhausted. [27.]

(6.) GREAT.—Yours is a restless, active, lively organization. You speak rapidly, comprehend quickly, and decide at once on the course to be pursued, and are in danger of excessive action, and consequent early exhaustion of the vital powers. [27.]

(5) and (4.) FULL OR AVERAGE.—You have a fair degree of activity, but are likely to be sufficiently deliberate to weigh the *pros* and *cons* before deciding how to act; are not lazy, but prefer light work to heavy, and play to either. [27.]

(3.) MODERATE.—You are rather slow and deliberate in your movements, are seldom or never in a hurry, and always take plenty of time to consider. Your mental operations are slow, and you are apt to see the point of a joke, if at all, after the laugh is over. Wake up! [27.]

(2.) SMALL.—You are too slow to be of much service to yourself or anybody else—decidedly inert. Try to cultivate activity by pushing about. You should have some one " after you with a sharp stick." [27.]

X.—EXCITABILITY.

(7.) VERY GREAT.—You are remarkably impressible, very easily excited, subject to extremes of feeling; greatly exalted at one moment and much depressed the next; driven now this way and then that by constantly changing impulses; and very much disposed to exaggerate everything, whether good or bad. Your need is to restrain this excitability, first, by avoiding all stimulating food and drink, and all unnatural or violent mental excitements; and, second, by cultivating a calm, quiet, enjoyable frame of mind. Repose is the proper antidote of too great activity. [27.]

(6.) GREAT.—You are constituted as described in (7), only in a somewhat lower degree—too susceptible to external influences for your own welfare or that of your friends. [27.]

(5.) FULL.—You are sufficiently susceptible to exciting causes, but not readily carried away by any sudden impulse; are self-possessed, and act coolly and with forethought. [27.]

(4.) AVERAGE.—You are very cool, deliberate, and placid, and allow external influences to sway you but little; act from judgment and not from impulse, and are very equable in disposition. [27.]

(3.) MODERATE.—You are rather dull, and can with difficulty be aroused by external causes; rather cold and passionless, and show little spirit in anything. You may with advantage put yourself in the way of social excitements, and profit by mixing much with wide awake people. [27.]

(2.) LOW.—Yours is a torpid sort of existence. You seem to be half asleep, and might almost as well be quite so. Try to arouse yourself, and seek society and the excitements of busy, active life. [27.]

XI.—SIZE OF BRAIN.

(7.) VERY LARGE.—If your organic quality be good and your activity sufficient, you should manifest extraordinary mental power; and if there be also a proper balance between the various groups of faculties, you are capable of taking a place in the first ranks, among the intellectual giants of the age. Such a mind, backed up by adequate physical stamina, will overcome all obstacles, and achieve greatness in spite of all difficulties. You may not have had your full powers called out, but the capacity is here. [14.]

(6.) LARGE.—Yours is a mind of great reach and power, and you can, if you will, make yourself widely felt in society. You are capable of managing extensive enterprises, taking broad views of things, and of drawing correct conclusions from ascertained facts. If you are a scholar, you should be widely known and admired in the sphere of letters, and exert great influence wherever the supremacy of mind is acknowledged. Much, however, depends upon the tendencies impressed upon your character by the predominating group of organs, and your power may be a blessing or it may be a curse to yourself and to the world, according to the manner in which it is used. [14.]

(5.) FULL.—With the proper physiological conditions [14, *et seq*.], you are capable of accomplishing much, and attaining a high position in the direction of the leading faculties, acquiring an excellent education, and manifesting talent of a high order, but have not that commanding and all-conquering genius which can bend everything to its will. [14.]

(4.) AVERAGE.—With activity largely developed, and good bodily conditions, you are capable of manifesting good talent, and of succeeding well in a business for which you are specially fitted. Out of this sphere your abilities would be commonplace and your success small. You are quick of perception, but neither original nor profound. [14.]

(3.) MODERATE.—You have sufficient brain, if conjoined with good organic quality and a fair share of activity, to give you a moderate degree of ability in practical matters, but little planning or directing talent. You will do best when working under the direction of persons better endowed than yourself with mental power. Strive to improve your intellect by means of reading, study, and the conversation of intelligent persons. [14.]

(2.) Small.—You are weak in mind and need the guidance of other intellects in every undertaking ; are incapable of managing any business. [14.]

II.

MENTAL FACULTIES.

XII.—AMATIVENESS.

(7.) Very Large.—You possess in a pre-eminent degree the desire to love and to be loved ; are irresistibly attracted by the opposite sex ; and are capable of exerting a similar power over them. You are winning in your manners ; very gentle and sympathetic, conforming to the tastes and wishes of the one beloved ; are devoted in your attentions ; yearn continually for the caresses and endearments of affection, and are made utterly miserable by coldness and indifference on the part of the beloved one. See (6.) [38.] With deficient coronal development, a low organic quality, or an inflamed state of the vital fluids, you would be very liable to the perversion of the procreative function, and to excesses ruinous to body and soul. If restraint be necessary, see I., 7. *Restrain.* [40.]

(6.) Large.—You are as described in (7), but in a lower degree ; are very fond of personal beauty, and seek in the other sex good bodily development and a warm heart as well as intellectual capacity and moral worth. The love-element is a very influential one in your organization, and will affect powerfully, for good or for evil, your destiny in life,—for the fire that warms may also consume. Rightly controlled, and made subservient to moral principle, it will be a source of strength and happiness—a blessing to yourself and to others ; perverted, it may lead to speedy and irretrievable ruin. Let your prayer be, " Lead us not into temptation !" If you are happily married, you are fortunate ; if not, you should seek in matrimony, where alone it can be found, the satisfaction of your loving and yearning heart. *Restrain.* [40.]

(5.) FULL.—You love the opposite sex with much tenderness; are somewhat ardent, but can control your desires; are very attentive toward those you love, honoring the other sex in a high degree and giving your confidence and esteem with your love. You are well calculated to enjoy the marriage relation. [37, *et seq.*]

(4.) AVERAGE.—You may be warm and loving at times, but, in general, manifest only a fair degree of attachment to the other sex; can enjoy the marriage relation, but need to have your love called out and cherished by a loving companion; are likely to be refined and faithful in your affections and to honor as well as love your mate, if worthy and devoted to your happiness and welfare. [37, *et seq.*]

(3.) MODERATE.—You are rather cold and indifferent toward the other sex, manifesting more friendship and respect than love; but esteem and friendship may lead to warmer feelings toward a truly congenial companion; so that while you might not find it disagreeable to live unmarried, you are capable, under favorable circumstances, of being happier in the conjugal relation. With large Ideality, you would manifest more admiration than affection for the opposite sex. *Cultivate.* [39.]

(2.) SMALL.—You are very indifferent toward the other sex, and have neither the desire nor the ability to win their love. *Cultivate.* [39.]

(1.) VERY SMALL.—You are almost entirely destitute of the love-element. *Cultivate.* [39.]

XIII.—CONJUGALITY.

(7.) VERY LARGE.—All your love must, as a necessity of your nature, be concentrated upon one person of the opposite sex, who will be to you the embodiment of all that is good and lovely, and whose faults you will be ever ready to conceal or overlook; and you will require the same exclusive attachment in the chosen one. If fully satisfied in this respect, you will enjoy the marriage relation very highly. If still heart-free, you should be very careful to bestow your affections where they will be fully reciprocated, for any failure in this respect would be likely to affect very seriously your destiny in life. *Restrain.* [41.]

(6.) LARGE.—You will require and seek but one intimate personal companion or mate, and are liable to be made very miserable by disappointment in love. Where you truly love you must possess, and you should know no such word as "fail" in your "affairs of the heart." Being well mated, you will find your highest happiness in the society of the one you have chosen, all of whose virtues and attractions you will fully appreciate. You will tolerate almost anything in him or her except infidelity to the marriage relation. *Restrain.* [41.]

(5.) FULL.—You can love cordially and faithfully any person of the other sex upon whom your affections may be placed; but, if love be interrupted, can change and become equally absorbed in a new love. You would not die of a broken heart were the beloved object removed by death or otherwise placed beyond your reach. [40, *et seq.*]

(4.) AVERAGE.—You are inclined to a single love and to union for life to a chosen one; but can readily change the object of your affections, and, with Adhesiveness small and Conscientiousness moderate, may be coquettish. *Cultivate.* [41.]

(3.) AVERAGE.—You are not particularly inclined to fickleness in love, and are disposed, under favorable circumstances, to union for life, but are liable to be led astray by new faces and to allow an old love to be supplanted by new ones. *Cultivate.* [41.]

(2.) SMALL.—You are inclined to the promiscuous society of the other sex and have little respect for the conjugal relation. *Cultivate.* [41.]

(1.) VERY SMALL.—You manifest none of this faculty and experience little of the feeling it imparts. *Cultivate.* [41.]

XIV.—PARENTAL LOVE.

(7.) VERY LARGE.—Your love for children and pets is intense, and as a parent you would idolize your offspring and probably spoil them by pampering and hurtful indulgence, or by allowing them to rule instead of yielding obedience. If you have children, you suffer continual anxiety on their account, especially when absent from them, and the death of one of them would be a blow almost too great to bear. *Restrain.* [44.]

(6.) LARGE.—As a parent, you would be tender and indulgent, perhaps, to a fault, unless restrained by high moral considerations, and are too apt to overlook the faults and imperfections of your young favorites, whether your own children or those of your friends. You are passionately fond of the society of the young, who are equally fond of you, and you will have groups of children clustering around you whenever you go among them. You must keep this faculty strictly under the control of moral principle, or it will lead to harm rather than good to the little ones you love so well. *Restrain.* [44.]

(5.) FULL.—You are capable of loving your own children well, and will do and sacrifice much for them, but will not be over-indulgent, and will feel no very strong attraction toward children generally, or toward animal pets. *Cultivate.* [43.]

(4.) AVERAGE.—You will love your own children, but will care little for those of others. If Benevolence be large, you will be tender toward the helpless infant, but will like children better as they grow older. *Cultivate.* [43.]

(3.) MODERATE.—You are rather indifferent even toward your own children, if you have any, and cold toward all others; can bear little from them, and are not calculated to win their affections. You care nothing for pets. *Cultivate.* [43.]

(2.) Small.—You are inclined to be cold and indifferent toward your own children, and to manifest a positive dislike for all others. You need to bring your Benevolence, Adhesiveness, and Conscientiousness to bear in your dealings with them as well as to assiduously cultivate Parental Love. [43.]

(1.) Very Small.—You will manifest little or no love for children, but will be guided in your treatment of them by other faculties. *Cultivate.* [43.]

XV.—FRIENDSHIP.

(7.) Very Large.—You are exceedingly warm-hearted, affectionate, and devoted; are ready to make any sacrifice for your friends; are blind to their defects and faults, and too much wrapped up in them for your own welfare or peace of mind. You should remember that even in friendship there may be an abnormal or perverted action—a mania, as it were—and keep your heart free from idolatry. Even your friends are human and have their weaknesses. *Restrain.* [46.]

(6.) Large.—You are very social, warm-hearted, and affectionate, enjoy the society of your friends in a high degree; cling to those you love through all changes of time and circumstance. Once a friend, you are one forever—in adversity as in prosperity—to aid, encourage, sympathize with, and console while living and to mourn when departed. You must be very careful in the choice of your friends, for you are liable to suffer much from the unworthiness and ingratitude of those to whom you may become attached. You are hospitable, and delight to entertain your friends at the social board; are very popular among those who know you; are generally beloved, and have few enemies. *Restrain.* [46.]

(5.) Full.—You are friendly and companionable with those whom you deem worthy, but are not disposed to sacrifice too much in their behalf; are hospitable; cordial in your intercourse with those around you, and disposed to make friends; but your attachments are not always lasting, and you do not bind others to you by very strong bonds of affection; neither are you likely to make many enemies. [44.]

(4.) Average.—You can make friends, and are capable of considerable affection for them under favorable circumstances, but will not be likely to mourn greatly over their absence. With large Acquisitiveness, you will be apt to place business before friends, and make use of them to promote your interests, rather than to sacrifice your interests in their behalf. *Cultivate.* [46.]

(3.) Moderate.—You form but few attachments, and manifest but a moderate degree of affection for any one. If you make friends, it is more likely to be through some other good qualities you may possess than through your social nature; and while you may be greatly respected and esteemed, you are not likely to be so generally loved. *Cultivate.* [46.]

(2.) SMALL.—You do not like society, and are cold and indifferent toward those around you; have neither the desire nor the ability to make friends, and possess little faith in friendship. *Cultivate.* [46.]

(1.) VERY SMALL.—You seem to be utterly incapable of feeling friendship, or awakening it in others. *Cultivate.* [46.]

XVI.—INHABITIVENESS.

(7.) VERY LARGE.—Your love of home and country is very strong indeed, and you are liable to the most terrible feeling of homesickness when absent from them. You prefer poverty and the humblest position in life at home to wealth and station abroad, and would willingly die for "the old flag," which is to you the symbol of all that is dearest on earth. *Restrain.* [47.]

(6.) LARGE.—You are very strongly attached to home; love your native land with a pure devotion; leave your place of abode with great reluctance, and are homesick and miserable if compelled to remain long away from it. You would not like the life of a Methodist itinerant, who changes his house so often. You become strongly attached to any place where you may reside; desire above almost everything else a *home* of your own, and when you have one, can scarcely be persuaded to leave it for a day. To you,

Be it ever so humble, there's no place like home!

Restrain. [47.]

(5.) FULL.—You manifest considerable attachment to home and country; prefer to live in one place, and surround yourself with the comforts of domestic life; feel some regret in leaving the place of your birth, or of long residence, but can easily change if circumstances require it; and are not likely to get homesick even if compelled to remain absent for a long time. [46.]

(4.) AVERAGE.—You have some love for home, but can change your place of abode without much regret, and are not inclined to expend much time or money in improvements, or in surrounding yourself with home comforts. You are never homesick, and if Locality be full or large, are fond of traveling. *Cultivate.* [47.]

(3) or (2.) MODERATE OR SMALL.—You care little for home or country; are cosmopolitan in your tastes, and indifferent about places. You like to travel, and, with Continuity small, enjoy constant change of scene. *Cultivate.* [47.]

(1.) VERY SMALL.—You have no local attachments; can "pull up stakes" and pack off on short notice. You rather prefer to live the life of a vagabond. *Cultivate.* [47.]

XVII.—CONTINUITY.

(7.) VERY LARGE.—You have great application, and can attend to but one thing at a time, and must stick to anything you have commenced till you finish it; are apt to be tedious and prolix, and to exhaust the patience of your hearers or readers, as well as the subject of discourse. All sudden changes are distasteful to you, and there is a tendency to a monotonous sameness in everything you do. *Restrain.* [49.]

(6.) LARGE.—You have great capacity for following out a train of thought and concentrating all your faculties upon one subject, and are noted for thoroughness in your studies, or in working out the details of any plan you have to execute. When you have commenced any piece of work, you wish to finish it before commencing anything else, and are annoyed by interruption or change of programme. In talking or writing you are liable, unless you take pains to guard yourself against it, to become prolix and tedious; tell long stories; are sometimes absent-minded; very persistent and steady in any course of action determined upon, and have no patience with fickleness or sudden changes of plan. *Restrain.* [49.]

(5.) FULL.—You like to carry out to completion anything you have commenced, but are not greatly annoyed by interruption, and can lay down one thing and take up another without much disadvantage. Are tolerably thorough and patient; can concentrate your thoughts when occasion requires it, and follow out a subject in all its details, but are not inclined to be tedious or "long-winded." [47.]

(4.) AVERAGE.—You can concentrate your thoughts upon one thing, and dwell upon it till fully elaborated, or you can readily divert your attention to other matters; prefer to do one thing at a time, but can have several irons in the fire at once, and attend to them all; are capable of consecutive thinking, but never tedious, and generally talk or write to the point. [47.]

(3.) MODERATE.—You love variety; change readily from one thing to another; commence many things that you never finish; think clearly, perhaps, but not always consecutively; lack connectedness and application, and should aim at more fixedness of mind and steadiness of character. *Cultivate.* [48.]

(2.) SMALL.—You are inclined to be very rambling and incoherent; very ready to begin, but having too little perseverance to finish; fly rapidly from one thing to another, and no one ever knows where to find you, or in what mood to receive you. You talk about several things at once, and the listener is seldom much wiser for the information you seek to impart. You should have been a butterfly. *Cultivate.* [48.]

(1.) VERY SMALL.—You are made up of change and restlessness, and are never the same two minutes at a time. *Cultivate.* [48.]

XVIII.—VITATIVENESS.

(7) VERY LARGE.—You have an astonishingly tenacious hold upon life; resist disease with the utmost determination, and will die at last

only after a protracted struggle. Your dread of the final change to which all mortals are subject is too great, and you should learn to look at it through the medium of religious faith rather than that of animal instinct. *Restrain.* [50.]

(6.) LARGE.—You cling to life with great tenacity, and shrink from death as if it were annihilation. Your power to resist disease is such that you will "never say die," and will recover under circumstances which would preclude hope in the case of any one less largely endowed with Vitativeness. You will not be likely to "die before your time," unless by accident; but should learn to fear death less, through faith in the LIFE TO COME. *Restrain.* [50.]

(5.) FULL.—You love life, and are disposed to cling to it with tenacity; can resist disease with considerable power; but have no great dread of death, especially if Hope and Spirituality be full or large, and if your Christian philosophy be correct on this subject. [49.]

(4.) AVERAGE.—Your love of life is fair, and you are not disposed to yield unresistingly to the encroachments of disease, but have less power to resist sickness and death than one more largely developed in the region of Vitativeness. *Cultivate.* [50.]

(3.) MODERATE.—Your hold of life is not very strong; you care comparatively little for existence, for its own sake, but like to live on account of family or friends, or with a view to do good in the world, and will yield without any great or prolonged resistance to the attacks of disease. *Cultivate.* [50.]

(2.) SMALL.—You have little dread of death; no great power to resist disease, and care to live rather for the sake of others than from any love of life for its own sake. You would be likely to soon sink under the attacks of any serious disease. *Cultivate.* [50.]

(1.) VERY SMALL.—You have little if any desire to live merely for the sake of life itself, but value existence only as an opportunity to gratify the other faculties. You should try to appreciate more fully the value of life and health, and your duty in regard to their preservation and enjoyment. *Cultivate.* [50.]

XIX.—COMBATIVENESS.

(7.) VERY LARGE.—You are remarkably energetic, determined, and courageous; ready to grapple with anything, fight against any odds, or to face danger or death in any form; let no difficulties discourage or baffle you; love hazardous enterprises; prefer a rough, daring life; and, if Cautiousness be only moderate, have more valor than discretion. With a lack of moral restraint, or intemperate habits and low associates, you would be quarrelsome, desperate, and dangerous. *Restrain.* [53.]

(6.) LARGE.—You are resolute, brave, determined; fond of argument; with large Approbativeness, quick to resent an insult; always ready to resist any encroachment upon your rights; high-tempered; fond of opposition; energetic in carrying out your plans; delight in opposing obstacles; are spirited and cool in times of danger; never lose your presence of mind; and if unfavorably organized in other respects, or with bad habits and coarse and low-bred companions, may be pugnacious and quarrelsome. Under the control of the intellect and the moral sentiments, your energy and propelling power may be turned to good account, and made a blessing to yourself and the world. *Restrain.* [53.]

(5.) FULL.—You manifest a disposition similar to that described in (6), in a somewhat lower degree; do not lack courage, energy, or relish for argument, but are not naturally contentious or quarrelsome. You may consider yourself happily endowed in respect to this element of character. [50.]

(4.) AVERAGE.—Your manifestation of courage and energy will depend in a measure upon circumstances. You can be aroused to the manifestation of a good degree of combative spirit, and with large Conscientiousness, Firmness, Self-Esteem, and Approbativeness to back up Combativeness, may stand your ground resolutely and strike boldly in a good cause; but with these organs moderate or small, and Cautiousness large, would be at times irresolute, or even cowardly. *Cultivate.* [53.]

(3.) MODERATE.—You are rather inefficient and too little disposed to assert and maintain your rights; give way too readily to opposition; avoid argument and contention and show little resentment; shrink too much from rough and disagreeable contacts; and will surrender much for the sake of peace. *Cultivate.* [53.]

(2.) SMALL.—You lack self-defense; are too gentle; can not say "no;" and are deficient in energy and spirit. *Cultivate.* [50.]

(1.) VERY SMALL.—You are almost destitute of courage and energy. *Cultivate.* [53.]

XX.—DESTRUCTIVENESS.*

(7.) VERY LARGE.—You are very executive, can do two days' work in one, and are exceedingly resolute; if perverted, you are prone to anger, and when greatly provoked may give way to ungovernable rage; and become stern, harsh, and violent; feel and manifest the most terrible indignation; take pleasure in destroying and exterminating whatever seems to be inimical to your wishes or stands in the way of your plans; have extraordinary executive ability; will bear down all opposition; can endure pain heroically, or, if need be, inflict it upon others without compunction if not with positive pleasure. Your powerful executiveness must be kept strictly under the control of

---

* We prefer the term EXECUTIVENESS to that of Destructiveness.

reason and moral principle, or it may at times manifest itself in acts of violence, cruelty, and revenge. *Restrain.* [57.]

(6.) LARGE.—When angry you are inclined to be very bitter, severe, and cutting, and to use the most forcible language to express your indignation; are apt to be unsparing and, with small Benevolence, merciless; manifest great energy and executive power; take pleasure in breaking, pulling down, uprooting, and destroying; could assist in cutting off an arm or a leg without faltering, or submit one of your own limbs unflinchingly to the surgeon, if necessary; are not averse to killing animals; are fond of flesh meat; and probably like your steaks "rare." You need the restraining influences of large Benevolence, Conscientiousness, and Cautiousness to keep your anger and your disposition to punish and destroy within proper bounds. *Restrain.* [57.]

(5.) FULL.—You can be forcible, determined, and indignant when aroused, but are not disposed to be vindictive, cruel, or unforgiving. Your anger is more likely to expend itself in sarcasm and bitter invectives than in acts of violence, but you may resort to force if too much provoked; will manifest a good degree of fortitude and energy in business; and can endure or inflict pain if necessary, but rather shrink from it. [54.]

(4.) AVERAGE.—Your manifestations are similar to those described in (5), only in a lower degree. *Cultivate.* [56.]

(3.) MODERATE.—You are not very forcible, executive, or severe; your anger is not deep and you threaten more than you execute; you shrink from pain and inflict it upon others very reluctantly; are likely to be more beloved than feared. *Cultivate.* [56.]

(2.) SMALL.—You are too tender-hearted; very deficient in energy; can neither bear suffering with fortitude nor inflict even necessary pain without great compunction. *Cultivate.* [56.]

(1.) VERY SMALL.—You are almost destitute of this faculty. *Cultivate.* [56.]

XXI.—ALIMENTIVENESS.

(7.) VERY LARGE.—You enjoy your food very greatly; are inclined to epicurean habits; find it difficult to control your appetite; live to eat rather than eat to live; are in danger of eating more than nature requires, and of ruining your digestive powers by gormandizing. *Restrain.* [58.]

(6.) LARGE.—Your appetite is generally excellent; you fully appreciate the good things of the table; are in danger of over-eating rather than eating too little; give your meals a too important place in your thoughts and in your arrangements; and should guard yourself against excesses. *Restrain.* [58.]

(5.) FULL.—You have a good appetite when in health, and eat

heartily of whatever is set before you; enjoy the pleasures of the table, but do not set a too high value upon them; and you can control your love for food and drink, making them subservient to their higher purposes. [58.]

(4.) AVERAGE.—You enjoy your food well, but can easily control appetite, and are seldom disposed to over-eat. [58.]

(3.) MODERATE.—You are inclined to be dainty; have no very great love for the luxuries of the table, but are particular in regard to the quality and preparation of your food. You eat to live, and not for the pleasure of eating. [58.]

(2.) SMALL.—You have no great relish for food, and care little what you eat, provided it will sustain life. *Cultivate.* [58.]

(1.) VERY SMALL.—You have little or no appetite. *Cultivate.* [58.]

XXII.—BIBATIVENESS.

(7.) VERY LARGE.—You are exceedingly fond of water; love bathing, swimming, sailing, etc.; and with a perverted appetite might easily contract the habit of drinking intoxicating liquors to excess, this being the form in which a perversion of this faculty is apt to manifest itself. You should beware of the " social glass." *Restrain.* [59.]

(6.) LARGE.—You are often thirsty, and experience great pleasure in drinking; also enjoy washing, bathing, swimming, etc. [59.]

(5.) FULL.—You enjoy water both internally and externally in a fair degree. [59.]

(4) and (3.) AVERAGE OR MODERATE.—You are not fond of water; are rather averse to bathing; dislike swimming, sailing, etc., and shrink from a sea voyage as something fearful. *Cultivate.* [59.]

(2.) SMALL —You care little for liquids in any form; prefer solid food; do not like to bathe; and avoid going into or upon the water if possible. *Cultivate.* [59.]

(1.) VERY SMALL.—You have an instinctive aversion to water. *Cultivate.* [59.]

XXIII.—ACQUISITIVENESS.

(7.) VERY LARGE.—Your desire for accumulation is excessive; you love money with a devotion approaching to idolatry; are close-fisted; make hard bargains; are meanly economical; place the possession of property above everything else; are penurious, avaricious, and miserly, and can be restrained from taking dishonest advantages to secure the coveted gain only by a good development of Conscientiousness; with this you will be honest, but close and exacting. *Restrain.* [62.]

(6.) LARGE.—You have the disposition and ability to turn everything to a good account; are industrious, economical, and close; buy cheaply and sell at the highest price; have great love for wealth, and a strong tendency to accumulate, but, with large Benevolence, spend freely where your sympathies may be enlisted. You are liable, unless you hold this strong propensity in check, to become penurious and miserly as you grow older. Conscientiousness, Benevolence, and Adhesiveness should be constantly called into action with Acquisitiveness, so that everything shall be honestly got and liberally expended, for the benefit of the world in general and of your friends and neighbors in particular. *Restrain.* [62.]

(5.) FULL.—You are industrious in acquiring; take good care of what you get; value property for its uses; are saving, but not avaricious or close; ready to help your friends, but not willing to impoverish yourself, and are not likely to spend quite so fast as you earn. [59.]

(4.) AVERAGE.—You have a fair appreciation of the value of property, and considerable desire to accumulate, but will be governed in your expenditures by other faculties, and may keep yourself poor by living up to the limits of your income. Cautiousness should be called to the aid of Acquisitiveness, so that provision be made for the future. *Cultivate.* [61.]

(3.) MODERATE.—You may seek property with considerable zeal and interest, but will value it merely as a means, not as an end; will be economical when your necessities require it, but are apt to disregard small expenses, and are very likely to spend about as fast as you earn. Your money-making talent is but moderate, and you have no love for "buying, selling, and getting gain" for its own sake. *Cultivate.* [61.]

(2.) SMALL.—You hold your money too loosely; have more talent for spending than for getting; are liable to contract habits of extravagance, and to live beyond your means. *Cultivate.* [61.]

(1.) VERY SMALL.—You are wasteful, extravagant, and idle, and will probably always be poor. *Cultivate.* [61.]

XXIV.—SECRETIVENESS.

(7.) VERY LARGE.—Your ability to restrain your feelings, to evade scrutiny, and to conceal your plans and intentions is very great. You are reserved, politic, guarded, shrewd, enigmatical, and mysterious; so much so, perhaps, that your most intimate friends are never sure that they really understand or know you. With small Conscientiousness you would be tricky, deceptive, double-dealing, and untrustworthy, and might, with large Acquisitiveness and small Cautiousness, both cheat and falsify. *Restrain.* [64.]

(6.) LARGE.—You are reserved in the expression of your sentiments; keep your plans and designs to yourself; are very discreet; delight in concealment; are fond of surprising your friends; incline to practice strategy; prefer indirect approaches to a straightforward course; and, even when your purposes are entirely honest and commendable, may often resort to cunning devices to accomplish them. Your character and intentions are too carefully covered up, and you subject yourself to suspicion where there is no better ground for it than the uncertainty by which you delight to surround yourself and your affairs. With Acquisitiveness large, you will get, and try to keep, all the property you can. *Restrain.* [64.]

(5.) FULL.—You can keep a secret; have a good degree of self-government; can conceal your emotions if necessary; keep your plans well hidden; and are discreet, but not disposed to be cunning, sly, or hypocritical. [62.]

(4.) AVERAGE.—You have no great degree of reserve; are inclined to be outspoken and frank, but can keep your own counsel and restrain the manifestation of your feelings, except under violent excitement, when you are liable to give your emotions or opinions full expression. [62.]

(3.) MODERATE.—You are inclined to pursue an open and direct course; to express your sentiments fully on proper occasions; possess little reserve, and are liable, in unguarded moments, to imprudence in speech if not in conduct. You are sincere and frank, and generally express your thoughts and emotions in a clear, unequivocal manner. Your friends know just what you are, see both your virtues and your faults, and will find you neither better nor worse than you seem. [62.]

(2.) SMALL.—You are open, spontaneous, and transparent; have little power or disposition to conceal your feelings, and generally speak out exactly what you think. Policy, cunning, evasion, equivocation, strategem, and indirection have no place in your nature; but you are open and above-board in everything. You have hardly enough policy, restraint, or self-government for your own good. *Cultivate.* [64.]

(1.) VERY SMALL.—You disclose everything; can not keep a secret; and tell all you know, if not more. *Cultivate.* [64.]

XXV. CAUTIOUSNESS.

(7.) VERY LARGE.—You are too cautious, watchful, anxious, and easily worried; are in perpetual fear of evils and accidents; dare not advance lest you should go wrong; are timid, afraid to take responsibilities or to run risks; procrastinating, cowardly, and easily thrown into a panic. You are made miserable by groundless fears, and should try to make use of your reason in combating them. *Restrain.* [67.]

(6.) LARGE.—You are careful, prudent, watchful, anxious, and apt to procrastinate; are slow in coming to a decision; try to be always on the safe side; are judicious in making plans, but apt to be more slow and cautious in carrying them out than is consistent with the highest success, and lose many a good opportunity through fear to take a little risk. You are apt to be over-solicitous about the health or welfare of children or friends, and to give yourself unnecessary pain in view of evils which may never come. *Restrain.* [67.]

(5.) FULL.—You are generally careful, prudent, and deliberate; are

8

not inclined to procrastinate, but take proper time to consider; are watchful rather than suspicious; are judiciously cautious, but not timid. Under excitement you might act rashly; but are generally safe, and work with well-laid plans. [65.]

(4.) AVERAGE.—You are capable of being prudent and careful, but with an excitable temperament may be rash and unreliable, acting rather from impulse than from judgment; are inclined to act rather hastily, and may sometimes get into trouble by a lack of due deliberation. *Cultivate.* [66.]

(3.) MODERATE.—You are rather careless and imprudent; liable to suffer from want of forethought; meet with many accidents; take too many risks; undertake enterprises without counting the cost; are afraid of nothing; and are apt to " get into hot water." *Cultivate.* [66.]

(2.) SMALL.—You do not know what fear is; are rash, reckless, and liable to rush headlong into difficulties. *Cultivate.* [66.]

(1.) VERY SMALL.—You are as described in (2), only in a lower degree. **Have no prudence.** *Cultivate.* [66.]

XXVI.—APPROBATIVENESS.

(7.) VERY LARGE.—You are exceedingly sensitive to praise or blame; care too much for public opinion; are mortified by censure and greatly elated by words of commendation; are ambitious of notoriety, distinction, or respectability; and are liable, if this faculty be not kept under good control, to be ostentatious and vain. You are obsequious where courtesy only is required. *Restrain.* [69.]

(6.) LARGE.—You are fond of praise and easily wounded by a word of censure or criticism; are too anxious to please others, too ambitious to shine, and too much alive to the smiles or frowns of the public for your own peace of mind. You are polite and courteous in the extreme, and unless Conscientiousness be large may sometimes be false to truth and duty for the sake of being agreeable, or be guided too much in what you say and do by the consideration of what others may think or say of you. Self-Esteem and Conscientiousness should be exercised against your too great susceptibility to the influence of public opinion. No matter *what* " Mrs. Grundy " may say. *Restrain.* [69.]

(5.) FULL.—You have a good degree of respect for the opinions of others; value praise, but will not sacrifice self-respect or principle to gain it; can endure censure when administered in a proper spirit; like to appear well, but are not over-anxious about appearances; with large Cautiousness value character highly; are courteous but not obsequious; and have a fine degree of ambition. [67.]

(4.) AVERAGE.—You are not insensible to praise or blame, but are rather independent and careless of public opinion; you appreciate the commendation of your fellow-men, but are not much elated by praise or deeply wounded by censure. You are not given to flattery or insincere compliments; and are hardly enough disposed to practice the graces of courtesy or to assume a winning address. *Cultivate.* [69.]

(3.) MODERATE.—You have but little regard for popularity; are not very complaisant, and despise flattery and idle compliments. Censure does not disturb you, and you care little for praise. *Cultivate.* [69.]

(2.) SMALL.—You care little what others think or say of you; have no respect for etiquette, style, or fashion; are brusque and unpleasing in manners; and too independent to be popular or beloved; put too low an estimate on public opinion. *Cultivate.* [69.]

(1.) VERY SMALL.—You are indifferent alike to praise and censure, and care nothing for reputation. *Cultivate.* [69.]

XXVII.—SELF-ESTEEM.

(7.) VERY LARGE.—You are very dignified, haughty, imperious, domineering, proud, high-headed, and stiff-necked; place *self* above everything else; are ambitious and aspiring in the highest degree; and unless restrained by other strong faculties are liable to be self-conceited, supercilious, and repulsively pompous and overbearing. Veneration should be made, as far as possible, to off-set your self-sufficiency. Humble yourself before God, if not in the presence of man. What are you but a worm of the dust? *Restrain.* [72.]

(6.) LARGE.—You think quite highly enough of your own abilities; are very self-reliant; are proud and dignified; seldom ask advice, and never follow it when given; will not stoop even to conquer; aim high; are not satisfied with moderate success or with a small business; desire to surpass all others—to stand at the head of your class or profession; and with Hope full or large, "know no such word as fail." With large moral organs, you will command universal respect; but if governed by the propensities, will be egotistical, haughty, domineering, and rather feared and hated than esteemed. *Restrain.* [72.]

(5.) FULL.—You evince a good degree of self-respect, dignity, and aspiration, but are not proud, overbearing, or greedy of power; are disposed to listen to advice though you may seldom follow it; and prefer the place of a leader to that of a follower. Respecting yourself, you will secure the respect of your fellow-men. [69.]

(4.) AVERAGE.—Your manifestation of this faculty will depend mainly upon its combination with those that are larger, but you are inclined, in the main, to place about a fair estimate upon yourself and to act with a becoming degree of ambition, dignity, and self-reliance. *Cultivate.* [71.]

(3.) MODERATE.—You are rather humble than proud; underrate your own abilities and worth; lack dignity and self-assertion; allow your inferiors to take leading positions which of right belong to yourself; are apt to put yourself upon an equality with the unworthy, and to do trifling or mean things of which you are afterward ashamed;

lack dignity; and are too familiar with inferiors to be respected even by them. *Cultivate.* [71.]

(2.) SMALL.—You lack self-appreciation, dignity, and independence; are too humble; easily discouraged; have too poor an opinion of yourself to command the respect of the world. *Cultivate.* [71.]

(1.) VERY SMALL.—You seem to be nearly destitute of this faculty. *Cultivate.* [71.]

XXVIII.—FIRMNESS.

(7.) VERY LARGE.—You can not be driven, and are not easily persuaded; are sometimes disposed to be obstinate; have an unshaken stability of purpose; are very persevering, tenacious, and averse to change; and sometimes defeat your own purposes by too great self-will. One often gains a great deal by yielding a little. Try to be more pliant. *Restrain.* [74.]

(6.) LARGE.—With moral principles, you would be steadfast and reliable; can not be driven; are not easily convinced that you are wrong; generally carry your point by persistent effort; are very determined and positive; set in your way; sometimes willful, if not obstinate. With large Causality you may yield to reason, or with large Adhesiveness be persuaded by friends; but with Combativeness and Firmness well developed, adhere tenaciously to preconceived opinions, right or wrong, and never change a plan once adopted. *Restrain.* [74.]

(5.) FULL.—You manifest a good degree of stability, determination, and perseverance, but are not set in your way or obstinate, and can change your opinions or purposes when they are shown to be erroneous or impracticable. Under the influence of large Cautiousness, you may evince irresolution and procrastination; but with Conscientiousness well developed, can not be turned from what you think truth and right require of you. You are more easily persuaded than driven. *Cultivate.* [74.]

(4.) AVERAGE.—You have hardly enough stability and fixedness of purpose, and unless this faculty be supported by full or large Combativeness, Conscientiousness, or Causality, will be too easily influenced by those around you, and too ready to abandon your positions if attacked. *Cultivate.* [74.]

(3.) MODERATE.—You are too much inclined to change; too easily persuaded; lack steadfastness; are prone to say " I can't;" are often irresolute, and inclined to go with the current. *Cultivate.* [74.]

(2.) SMALL.—You are unstable and wavering; fitful, impulsive, and fickle; have no will of your own, and are liable to be constantly the victim of circumstances. *Cultivate.* [74.]

(1.) VERY SMALL.—You are a perfect weather vane, changing with the slightest variation of surrounding circumstances. Try to hold yourself at a point. *Cultivate.* [74.]

XXIX.—CONSCIENTIOUSNESS.

(7.) VERY LARGE.—You are governed by moral principle; are scrupulously exact in matters of right; perfectly honest; very ready to accuse yourself and to repent of any wrong; are inclined to be censorious; make too little allowance for the weakness and imperfection of human nature; are exacting of friends; set up a very high standard of morality, and are tormented by remorse if you go astray from the narrow path you have prescribed for yourself. You are liable, unless the faculty be controlled, to become morbidly sensitive in matters of conscience. *Restrain.* [76.]

(6.) LARGE.—You are disposed to be strictly honest and upright in all your dealings; hate whatever is unjust or contrary to your ideas of right; feel very guilty when conscious of having done wrong; are very severe in your reproofs of wrong-doing, but will forgive those who show repentance. You always consult duty before expediency; seek to know what is right, and then pursue it with singleness of heart; but with a false education may do conscientiously, and in the belief that it is right, what is really wrong; or with strong propensities may be led astray, but will quickly repent and seek to reform. You are perhaps inclined to be over-penitent and self-accusing as well as too exacting and censorious in regard to others. *Restrain.* [76.]

(5.) FULL.—You have strong feelings of justice and are honest and upright in all your intentions, but may yield to the influence of stronger faculties against your conscientious scruples. You give expediency some weight, but are never wholly satisfied with yourself unless walking in the path of rectitude. Duty is generally uppermost in your mind, but is not always the governing motive in your conduct. You do not always resist temptation, and often sin, but as often repent with sorrow and regret. *Cultivate.* [76.]

(4.) AVERAGE.—You are inclined to do what is right and to be guided by moral principle, but have not always the strength to resist the temptations held out by stronger faculties, and when you do wrong are inclined to justify yourself. You are too often governed in your conduct by expediency rather than by considerations of duty or moral right. With large propensities and moderate Self-Esteem, Veneration, and Spirituality, you may manifest much selfishness and but a weak sense of duty, honor, or honesty; but with these conditions reversed will be honorable and trustworthy under ordinary temptations. *Cultivate.* [76.]

(3.) MODERATE.—Your ideas of right and wrong are rather feeble, and you are inclined to allow interest rather than duty to rule; but may be restrained by Approbativeness or Cautiousness from dishonest or dishonorable actions. *Cultivate.* [76.]

(2.) SMALL.—You have few scruples of conscience, and do right as a matter of expediency or through fear of the consequences of an opposite course, rather than from moral principle; are governed by expediency. *Cultivate.* [76.]

(1.) VERY SMALL.—You are almost entirely destitute of moral principle. *Cultivate.* [76.]

XXX.—HOPE.

(7.) VERY LARGE.—Your expectations are almost unbounded. Everything desirable seems attainable; you build castles in the air; have many ships at sea, all of which you think sure to come in loaded with treasures; and, living in the future, which is always bright, you are generally joyous, sanguine, and happy. You are constantly disappointed; never realize half that you expect; and spend your life in a world of brilliant illusions. *Restrain.* [78.]

(6.) LARGE.—You are inclined to overrate the future; look on the bright side of things; overlook obstacles and evils; attempt much more than you can accomplish; console yourself when disappointed by the anticipation of better fortune next time; are a firm believer in " the good time coming;" are sanguine, buoyant, and joyous; never despair; " hope on, hope ever;" live in the future more than in the present; are liable to be led into extravagant expenditures and extensive speculations on the most delusive grounds and with disastrous results. *Restrain.* [78.]

(5.) FULL.—Your expectations are generally reasonable; you are sanguine and enterprising; often realize more than you expect. You are not much inclined to castle building, and " when your ships come home from sea " anticipate only ordinary cargoes; are neither desponding nor too much elated. [77.]

(4.) AVERAGE.—You are inclined to expect and to attempt too little rather than too much; get too easily discouraged by the obstacles you encounter, some of them imaginary; look on the dark side at times, and are disposed to be satisfied with the present instead of looking forward to the future; generally count the cost and make safe investments. *Cultivate.* [78.]

(3.) MODERATE.—You are very moderate in your expectations of the future; inclined to despondency; often look on the dark side; lack enterprise, and are afraid to attempt any great enterprise; make sure gains, but small ones; live in the present, and have more fear than hope for the future. *Cultivate.* [78.]

(2.) SMALL.—You expect little from the future but misfortune; see so many obstacles and discouragements ahead that you dare attempt very little; are very liable to become despondent and melancholy. *Cultivate.* [78.]

(1.) VERY SMALL.—You expect little or nothing that is desirable, and undertake nothing for fear of loss. *Cultivate.* [78.]

XXXI.—SPIRITUALITY.

(7.) VERY LARGE.—You have strong intuitive perceptions of what is right and best; have faith in spiritual monitions; and are most likely to take the true course when you allow yourself to be guided by what you internally feel to be the right way. A morbid or undue action of this faculty may lead you to become superstitious; to blindly believe in dreams, omens, fortune-telling, and false prophecies, or to induce religious fanaticism. It must be properly regulated, and made to act in harmony with reason, though it may transcend it. *Restrain.* [80.]

(6.) LARGE.—You have a large measure of faith; an internal consciousness of right, duty, truth, falsehood, and what is best; love to meditate on spiritual subjects—the immortality of the soul, the future life, the existence and perfections of God, and the destiny of man; enjoy spiritual communion, or the blending of soul with soul; and, if Veneration be large, find ecstatic happiness in fervent adoration of the Deity. In certain states of the physical system, one may be naturally clairvoyant; be forewarned in visions or in dreams; perceive the highest truths by intuition, and even possess prophetic gifts. One must carefully guard against the perversion of this noble and exalted faculty (see 7), and not allow our living faith to degenerate into superstition, or our piety to become mere fanaticism. *Restrain.* [80.]

(5.) FULL.—You are not lacking in the ground-work of faith; have a good share of spiritual feeling, and considerable intuitive inspiration; but do not always allow yourself to be guided by the premonitions which would lead you aright. You desire to believe in all truth, but are sometimes beset by doubts. *Cultivate.* [80.]

(4.) AVERAGE.—You are not destitute of the light within; have some spiritual monitions, and are not inclined to disregard the guidance of the internal sense; but your intuitions are not always sufficiently distinct to insure their full influence, or your belief in their authority so implicit as to make them very potential in your life. *Cultivate.* [80.]

(3.) MODERATE.—The spiritual part of your nature is not so influential as would be desirable; you have rather indistinct perceptions of spiritual things; lack faith; believe little that can not be logically proved; rely on evidence rather than on intuition; and would "*prove all things*" in order to "hold fast that which is good." *Cultivate.* [80.]

(2.) SMALL.—You have very weak perceptions of spiritual truths; must have proof before believing; are not guided by faith—a doubting Thomas; have no premonitions or warnings, and do not believe in them. *Cultivate.* [80.]

(1.) VERY SMALL.—You are nearly destitute of the spiritual sentiment—believe little or nothing; are skeptical in regard to a future life; ridicule the idea of revelations from Heaven, and treat premonitions and warnings with contempt. *Cultivate.* [80.]

XXXII.—VENERATION.

(7.) Very Large.—You are eminently respectful, deferential, and inclined to be religious, prayerful, and devoted to the worship of God; circumstances favoring, you would manifest extreme fervor in your petitions before the throne of Grace; evince great reverence for time-honored usages, forms, ceremonies, and institutions; and are profoundly respectful toward the aged, the good, or the great. *Restrain.* [83.]

(6.) Large.—You are, by organization, strongly inclined to worship; take great delight in religious exercises; are fervent in prayer; feel awed in the presence of the great; are very deferential toward the aged; naturally conservative in your views; reverence ancient forms and ceremonies; are inclined to adhere to long-established customs and to admire the "good old ways." You have need to beware of the perversion of this faculty, leading to religious bigotry, slavish fear, and the domination of a blind impulse. Carefully direct, if not *Restrain.* [83.]

(5.) Full.—You are not lacking in devotion, respect for superiors, reverence for age, or a fair degree of conservative feeling in reference to established institutions; but these emotions are greatly influenced by circumstances, and are strongly or weakly manifested accordingly as they are incited or restrained by other faculties. There may often be an internal conflict in you between the worldly and the spiritual. [81.]

(4.) Average.—You are inclined to worship when the devotional feeling is specially called out, but are apt to make religion subservient to business or to whatever else may be your dominant tendency. Acting with Conscientiousness and Benevolence, your Veneration will dispose you to make justice, mercy, and good works the basis of your religion, while the rites of worship will be esteemed less important. *Cultivate.* [83.]

(3.) Moderate.—If you are religious, it is probably because your education has been favorable to it, and were fortunate enough to have been brought up under religious influences; but your religion is one of works rather than of humility, submission, and faith. You have little respect for customs or institutions merely on account of their antiquity, and no reverence for creeds, rites, and ceremonies. *Cultivate.* [83.]

(2.) Small.—You experience little devotional feeling, and are deficient in reverence for age and respect for superiors. *Cultivate.* [83.]

(1.) Very Small.—You seem to be nearly destitute of reverence and respect, and have no devotional feeling. *Cultivate.* [83.]

XXXIII.—BENEVOLENCE.

(7.) Very Large.—You have a large, loving, kindly heart; are remarkably benevolent, charitable, and forgiving; have ready sympathies and an open purse; and with moderate or small Acquisitiveness may impoverish yourself to assist others, or with small Conscientiousness spend in charity the money which of right belongs to your creditors. "Be just before you are generous," and do not allow sympathy to overrule judgment. *Restrain.* [83.]

(6.) LARGE.—You are very tender, generous, and kind-hearted; ready to sympathize with suffering and to relieve want, to the extent of your means; prefer to suffer yourself rather than to see others suffer; are charitable, forgiving, and merciful; a "good Samaritan," and, in this respect, a true follower of Him who "went about doing good." [83.]

(5.) FULL.—You are kind and obliging; like to see others happy, and desire to make them so; but will not overtax yourself to relieve your neighbors of their burdens, and may allow selfish feeling to overrule your kindness. With Conscientiousness full or large, will "be just before you are generous." *Cultivate.* [83.]

(4.) AVERAGE.—You are kind to those you love, especially if Adhesiveness be large, and may practice general benevolence through the influence of Approbativeness or for selfish ends, but are not inclined to philanthropy. *Cultivate.* [83.]

(3.) MODERATE.—You are not inclined to be obliging, but manifest a feeling of indifference in regard to the comfort or welfare of those around you; are rather selfish and unsympathizing. *Cultivate.* [83.]

(2.) SMALL.—You care little for the sufferings of others, so long as you are yourself at ease. "It is not my affair," you say. You have no "sweet sympathy" in your soul. *Cultivate.* [83.]

(1.) VERY SMALL.—You are almost utterly selfish—have no generous or sympathetic feelings. *Cultivate.* [83.]

XXXIV.—CONSTRUCTIVENESS.

(7.) VERY LARGE.—You should manifest remarkable mechanical ingenuity, a passion for making things, and (with Causality large) great inventive talent. You take to tools naturally, and almost seem to be master of all trades without having learned them; you can make almost anything; and are constantly contriving "improvements;" you might devote yourself to mechanical invention with great benefit to the world, if not to yourself; but must beware of "perpetual motions," or of *monomania* on this subject. *Restrain.* [88.]

(6.) LARGE.—You have great taste and talent for mechanical pursuits; delight in building, repairing, and employing machinery; with large Imitation, can make anything after a pattern—anything, in fact, that you have seen made; and with large Causality, are strongly inclined to invent and to contrive new ways of doing things. As a writer, you would show great skill in the construction of your

8*

sentences, as well as in the arrangement of the subject-matter of your essay or book. [88.]

(5.) FULL.—You have a good degree of mechanical judgment and ingenuity; are interested in machinery and mechanical operations, and with practice would attain skill in the use of tools. [88.]

(4.) AVERAGE.—With the education of a mechanic—a thorough training in any particular trade—you may make a good workman, but manifest no special liking for the use of tools. *Cultivate.* [88.]

(3.) MODERATE.—You are rather awkward in the use of tools, and should not attempt anything requiring much mechanical skill. *Cultivate.* [88.]

(2.) SMALL.—You are deficient in constructive talent, and should not attempt to invent. *Cultivate.* [88.]

(1.) VERY SMALL.—You are very awkward in your attempts (if you ever make any) to use tools, and could scarcely build a rough hen-coop. *Cultivate.* [88.]

XXXV.—IDEALITY.

(7.) VERY LARGE.—You have the most exquisite taste, the highest degree of refinement, and intense love of the beautiful; live in an ideal world; set up a high standard in character and manners; have a most vivid imagination, and with the mental temperament and a good development of the reflective faculties, Constructiveness, Imitation, etc., are capable of achieving success in the highest walks of poetry or art. [90.] Your danger lies in the direction of extra fastidiousness and the tyrannical domination of the ideal, shutting you out from all participation in the interests and enjoyments of the real world around you. *Restrain.* [90.]

(6.) LARGE.—You are imaginative, refined, and tasteful; love poetry, art, and the beautiful in nature; have high ideas of propriety in expression and conduct; are graceful and polished in manners; have lofty aspirations; incline to strive after perfection in character and performance, and if otherwise well-endowed (see 7), possess a talent for the creation of the beautiful in poetry or art. [88.]

(5.) FULL.—You are not wanting in taste, refinement, or love of the beautiful; enjoy poetry and art; appreciate elegance and polished manners; and have elevated notions of the proprieties of life, but are not sentimental, fanciful, or over-fastidious. You love adornment and display, but are not disposed to sacrifice the useful to the ornamental. [88.]

(4.) AVERAGE.—You show more liking for the plain and substantial than for the ornamental; are a utilitarian; live in a real, every-day, matter-of-fact world; and never "soar into the blue," or wander enchanted in the realms of the ideal. You are rather plain in your manners, and in talking or writing make use of few figures of speech, preferring to say what need be said in the most direct and literal way. *Cultivate.* [90.]

(3.) MODERATE.—You are somewhat deficient in taste; rather "homespun" in manners; very plain in speech; and have little imagination. You are no lover of art, poetry, or the beautiful in nature, and your character is lacking in elevation and refinement. *Cultivate.* [90.]

(2.) SMALL.—You show a marked deficiency in taste, polish, and refinement, and are extremely utilitarian. *Cultivate.* [90.]

(1.) VERY SMALL.—You evince no taste and no appreciation of beauty. *Cultivate.* [90.]

XXXVI.—SUBLIMITY.

(7.) VERY LARGE.—You appreciate and admire in the highest degree the wild, the romantic, the grand, the sublime, the illimitable, the eternal, the infinite; have a real passion for mountain scenery, vast prospects, foaming breakers, and roaring waterfalls; enjoy with the greatest zest "the war of elements—thunder, lightning, tempest, the ocean in a storm, the surging rush of a swollen stream in a freshet—whatever is magnificent or awful;" love to contemplate the seemingly boundless expanse of ocean; the glory of the starry heavens; and above all (with Veneration full or large), the omnipotence of the Deity and the infinitude of His works. In writing or speaking, you are inclined to use high-sounding words and metaphorical expressions, and must guard yourself against verbal extravagance and bombast. In other respects there is no need to restrain. [91.]

(6.) LARGE.—Your manifestations are like those described in (7), except in a somewhat lower degree. With a good development of the intellectual organs, you will take comprehensive views of subjects, and give a wide scope to your thoughts and investigations. [91.]

(5.) FULL.—You enjoy the grand, the sublime, and the magnificent, and appreciate mountain scenery, the vastness of the ocean, and the awfulness of the tempest, but in a lower degree than (7) and (6), which see. [91.]

(4.) AVERAGE.—You manifest only a moderate degree of this element of character, under ordinary circumstances, but when the organ is powerfully excited, may enjoy sublimity and grandeur very highly. *Cultivate.* [91.]

(3.) MODERATE.—You are rather deficient in the manifestation of this faculty. *Cultivate.* [91.]

(2.) SMALL.—You care very little for the grand and sublime in any form. *Cultivate.* [91.]

(1.) VERY SMALL.—You are nearly destitute of this faculty. *Cultivate.* [91.]

XXXVII.—IMITATION.

(7.) VERY LARGE.—You are capable of becoming a consummate mimic; could make almost anything from pattern; have a taste and talent for acting and of representing life to the letter. It would be natural for you to make use of many gestures when speaking; impart great expression to your countenance when animated; and with large Mirthfulness can relate anecdotes to the very life, and keep a company in a roar of laughter by your droll personations. *Restrain.* [93.]

(6.) LARGE.—You have great ability to copy, make things after a pattern, mimic, and act a part in an assumed character; can readily adapt yourself to different circumstances, take on any mood you choose and act out its proper manifestations; can be anybody else just about as easily as your own proper self; are able to imitate the voice, gestures, mode of walking, expression, etc., of your friends and acquaintances to the life. [93.]

(5.) FULL.—You have good imitative powers, and can copy, mimic, or personate others very well when you try, but are not particularly inclined to assume a character or to follow an example unless stimulated thereto by more influential faculties. [92.]

(4.) AVERAGE.—You can copy tolerably well, when this faculty is excited and backed up by other organs, but have no strong inclination to mimic or imitate others. You prefer to be yourself rather than anybody else. [92.]

(3.) MODERATE.—Your imitative capacities are rather limited, and you manifest little inclination to take pattern from others, or to be a mere copyist; are disposed to strike out new paths; work on a plan of your own; and seek originality. [93.]

(2.) SMALL.—You have your own way of doing things, and seldom willingly copy anything or take pattern from anybody. *Cultivate.* [93.]

(1.) VERY SMALL.—You have little ability to copy anything, and manifest no disposition to do so. *Cultivate.* [93.]

XXXVIII.—MIRTHFULNESS.

(7.) VERY LARGE.—You should be remarkably witty, jovial, comical; and have a great love for jokes and the ludicrous. With Ideality only average, you are in danger of becoming too comical, if not clownish, descending to low, coarse jests, and of making fun on solemn or unsuitable occasions. *Restrain.* [95.]

(6.) LARGE.—You can fully appreciate a joke, and know how to make one; enjoy fun, and do your share in creating it; laugh heartily, and keep a company in good-humor by your mirthful sallies. With large Comparison and Combativeness, you would be capable of severe sarcasm. You should cultivate Ideality, to give your wit delicacy and refinement, otherwise your jokes may not always be in good taste. *Restrain.* [95.]

(5.) FULL.—Your capacity for appreciating wit and humor is good, and you have considerable ability for making fun; are witty, playful, and humorous, especially under the stimulus of jovial company, but are not remarkable for the manifestation of this faculty. [93.]

(4.) AVERAGE.—You may enjoy wit and humor and appreciate a joke under a powerful excitement of this faculty; but in general you are sober, serious, and sedate, and not inclined to encourage laughter or fun-making. *Cultivate.* [95.]

(3.) MODERATE.—You are rather too seriously inclined, as a general rule, but may occasionally manifest considerable playfulness and humor. If Combativeness and Approbativeness be full or large, you may not always take a joke so good-humoredly as you ought. It will do you good to cultivate good-humor and to laugh more. *Cultivate.* [95.]

(2.) SMALL.—You are rather slow to perceive the point of a joke, and are seldom able to turn back a witticism aimed at yourself; are not inclined to laugh, and perhaps think it foolish or wrong to be jovial or merry. *Cultivate.* [95.]

(1.) VERY SMALL.—You are quite too sober, and have few if any humorous conceptions—can not take a joke. *Cultivate.* [95.]

XXXIX.—INDIVIDUALITY.

(7.) VERY LARGE.—You have extraordinary powers of observation, and an insatiable desire to see everything and to know all about what ever comes under your observation. You are irresistibly impelled to individualize things, and are very minute and particular in your observation, taking account of particulars which would escape most persons altogether. You should carefully guard yourself against *obtrusiveness* in exercising your curiosity or passion for observation. Do not so far forget good manners as to "stare" impudently at any one. Try to *think* as well as to *look*. In other respects, there is no need to restrain. [95.]

(6.) LARGE.—You are a great practical observer of men and things; see everything; and take account of all the particulars. You are char acterized as (7), only in a lower degree. [95.]

(5.) FULL.—You are a good observer; keep your eyes open to some purpose; see clearly whatever is readily observable, but are not inclined to a very close scrutiny or to the scanning of minute details. You have a desire to see and examine things generally, but do not allow this faculty to assume a controlling influence in your character. [95.]

(4.) AVERAGE.—Your observation is confined mainly to the more conspicuous objects around you, or to such as interest other and larger faculties, and is rather general than particular. *Cultivate.* [97.]

(3.) MODERATE.—You have only ordinary observing powers, and, unless the faculty be specially stimulated, take but little notice of things, and are consequently vague in your descriptions of what you have seen. *Cultivate.* [97.]

(2.) SMALL.—Your observing powers are feeble. You use your eyes to so little purpose that they might almost as well be closed. Your notions of what you have seen are very vague. *Cultivate.* [97.]

(1.) VERY SMALL.—You seem to be literally one of those who, having eyes, see not." *Cultivate.* [97.]

XL.—FORM.

(7.) VERY LARGE.—You are remarkable for ability to observe and remember shapes and forms, and an excellent judge of configuration. You hardly ever forget a face or a picture that has attracted your attention. [97.]

(6.) LARGE.—Your memory of faces, forms, features, outlines, etc., is excellent, and you are a good judge of symmetry, proportion, and beauty of form. Can remember *names* by seeing them in writing. [97.]

(5.) FULL.—Your memory of faces and forms is good, but not remarkably tenacious. Your judgment of configuration and symmetry is fair. *Cultivate.* [99.]

(4.) AVERAGE.—You have a tolerable development of this faculty, and with practice may recollect countenances, shapes, and so forth, with considerable distinctness. *Cultivate.* [99.]

(3.) MODERATE.—Your memory of faces, forms, and shapes is neither very distinct nor very retentive, and your ability to recognize persons is poor. *Cultivate.* [99.]

(2.) SMALL.—You have a very feeble recollection of faces, and soon forget the appearance of things you have seen. *Cultivate.* [99.]

(1.) VERY SMALL.—You manifest little or none of this faculty. *Cultivate.* [99.]

XLI.—SIZE.

(7.) VERY LARGE.—You have great ability to judge of magnitude; can determine very closely by the eye alone the length, breadth, or height of an object; have an accurate eye for proportion, and detect at a glance any departure from perfect correctness in this respect. [99.]

(6.) LARGE.—You have an excellent eye for measuring angles, proportions, and dimensions; are a good judge of harmony between the different parts of a thing, and are annoyed by a want of proportion or a departure from accuracy in the lines of direction. [99.]

(5.) FULL.—You possess a good share of the ability to measure by the eye, but require practice to give you entire correctness in this particular. *Cultivate.* [100.]

(4.) AVERAGE.—You have only a fair share of this eye-measuring power, but with considerable practice may do tolerably well. *Cultivate.* [100.]

(3.) MODERATE.—You are not a good judge of size or proportion, and should not trust to the eye where correct measurements are required. *Cultivate.* [100.]

(2.) SMALL.—You have very vague ideas of length, breadth, height, etc., and a poor judgment of proportion. *Cultivate.* [100.]

(1.) VERY SMALL.—You manifest little or none of this faculty. *Cultivate.* [100.]

XLII.—WEIGHT.

(7.) VERY LARGE.—You have remarkable skill in balancing; are sure footed; seldom stumble or fall; possess wonderful skill in skating, swimming, sleight-of-hand, hurling, shooting, horseback-riding, etc.; and naturally assume easy and natural attitudes in standing, and a graceful gait in walking. Your perception of the laws of gravity and ability to maintain the equipoise of any body you can control are very great. With a little practice, you could perform wonderful feats in walking a tight-rope, balancing poles and other objects; or in riding, vaulting, etc. [100.]

(6.) LARGE.—You have nice intuitive perceptions of the laws of gravity, and great ability to apply them; are fond of exercises involving skill in balancing, such as riding, skating, shooting; have a steady hand and a sure foot; love to walk on narrow and dangerous places; assume natural attitudes; are annoyed by seeing anything out of plumb or unevenly balanced; and, with Constructiveness large, possess great natural ability to operate machinery. [100.]

(5.) FULL.—You have good command over your muscles, and with practice can balance well, but have no extraordinary perception of the laws of gravity. *Cultivate.* [101.]

(4.) AVERAGE.—You are described in (5), but in a somewhat lower degree; would require much practice to balance well. *Cultivate.* [101.]

(3.) MODERATE.—You have but little skill in balancing, and lack the nice appreciation of the laws of gravity which give ability to ride, skate, shoot, or hurl well; you should not attempt to walk on high and narrow places. *Cultivate.* [101.]

(2.) SMALL.—You can hardly walk a broad plank over a ditch; get dizzy on high places; are easily made sea-sick, and are not a good rider, skater, or marksman. *Cultivate.* [101.]

(1.) VERY SMALL.—You have barely sufficient appreciation of the laws of gravity and command over the muscles to stand erect. *Cultivate.* [101.]

XLIII.—COLOR.

(7.) VERY LARGE.—You have a passion for colors, and an instinctive perception of their harmonies; can arrange and blend all the shades, hues, and tints in painting or otherwise, with the greatest skill; as a painter, would excel in coloring. Inappropriate or inharmonious arrangements of colors give you pain. [102.]

(6.) LARGE.—You are as described in (7), only in a lower degree. [102.]

(5.) FULL.—You are a fair judge of colors and of fitness in their combination; but require practice to enable you to determine their finer shades and blendings. *Cultivate.* [103.]

(4.) AVERAGE.—You are as described in (5), but in a lower degree. *Cultivate.* [103.]

(3.) MODERATE.—You are naturally deficient in the discrimination of colors, and only glaring ones or strong contrasts attract your attention; with a good deal of practice, however, you might acquire a fair degree of skill in judging of the primitive colors and their more common combinations. *Cultivate.* [103.]

(2.) SMALL.—You are very deficient in perception of colors, and care little for them. *Cultivate.* [103.]

(1.) VERY SMALL.—You have no love for colors, and but a very weak perception of the distinction implied by the word. One who can not distinguish different colors may be pronounced idiotic in this particular, *i. e.*, he lacks the faculty. *Cultivate.* [103.]

XLIV.—ORDER.

(7.) VERY LARGE.—You are exceedingly systematic; very particular about having everything in its proper place; are tidy, precise, and formal to a fault, and unless this faculty be restrained, you will spend too much time in trying (in vain) to keep everything "just so," or to restore order where others are continually creating what to you seems confusion. You are liable to be "more nice than wise." *Restrain.* [104.]

(6.) LARGE.—You are inclined to be very regular, orderly, and systematic in all your arrangements; are sometimes too precise and formal; have a place for everything, and are annoyed by seeing anything out of place, or by any failure on the part of those around you to appreciate your methodical habits or to adhere to your strict rules of order. *Restrain.* [104.]

(5.) FULL.—You are systematic and orderly; like to see things in their places; are disposed to be tidy and careful in dress; but are not a slave to method, and when disorder can not be avoided, submit to it with a good grace. You are more orderly in theory than in practice, unless trained in some business in which method is particularly requisite. *Cultivate.* [104.]

(4.) AVERAGE.—You like order, and will make some effort to secure it; but often permit disorder to usurp its place. You are not disposed to be precise, formal, or "old-maidish." *Cultivate.* [104.]

(3.) MODERATE.—You are rather untidy and careless in dress and habits; seldom have a place for anything or anything in its place; leave your business at loose ends; and have a slip-shod, disjointed way of doing everything. *Cultivate.* [104.]

(2.) SMALL.—You have a very careless, unmethodical, and inaccurate way of doing things, and are inclined to be shiftless and slovenly in your habits. *Cultivate.* [104.]

(1.) VERY SMALL.—You have little appreciation of order, neatness, or system, and manifest no arranging power. *Cultivate.* [104.]

XLV.—CALCULATION.

(7.) VERY LARGE.—You have remarkable natural talent for computation; multiply and divide intuitively; seem to solve difficult problems in mathematics by instinct; and take intense delight in figures and statistics, and in the various applications and relations of numbers. [104.]

(6.) LARGE.—You excel in mental arithmetic, add, subtract, multiply, and divide with great facility; perceive very readily the value and relations of numbers; are fond of statistical information; and with full or large Locality and Causality may excel in the higher branches of mathematics. [104.]

(5.) FULL.—You succeed very well in the use of numbers, but are not remarkable for ability to calculate " in the head." *Cultivate.* [106.]

(4.) AVERAGE.—You require considerable study and practice to give you facility in arithmetical calculations, but with it can succeed very fairly. *Cultivate.* [106.]

(3.) MODERATE.—You remember numbers with difficulty, and are neither quick nor accurate in adding, subtracting, multiplying, or dividing. You think arithmetic a bore, and should not attempt to become a book-keeper or an accountant. *Cultivate.* [106.]

(2.) SMALL.—You are dull and slow in learning arithmetic, and, perhaps, like Mr. George Combe, have never been able to master the multiplication table. You have no taste for numbers, and a very poor memory of them. *Cultivate.* [106.]

(1.) VERY SMALL.—You have hardly the ability to count, much less to calculate, and are unfortunate in respect to this faculty. If you take a realizing sense of your deficiency, you will not venture on mathematical calculations. *Cultivate.* [106.]

XLVI.—LOCALITY.

(7.) VERY LARGE.—You have an insatiable love of traveling, and desire to see the world, and a remarkably retentive memory of the localities you visit; have an intuitive idea of both the relative and absolute position of places, and never lose your way either in the forests or in the streets of a strange city. You are inclined to be too roving and unsettled in your habits, and to spend all your time and money in traveling. *Restrain*. [107.]

(6.) LARGE.—You have a strong desire to travel and to see places; delight in books of travel; are deeply interested in the study of geography and astronomy; seldom forget any place you have once seen, and can find your way anywhere, as if by instinct. Would make a good explorer. [106.]

(5.) FULL.—Your memory of places is good, and you enjoy traveling and reading of travels; find your way quite well ordinarily, but are not remarkably endowed in this particular. *Cultivate*. [107.]

(4.) AVERAGE.—Your recollection of places is fair, but you have no great desire to travel or to see strange countries, and may sometimes lose your way. *Cultivate*. [107.]

(3.) MODERATE.—Your local memory is rather poor, and you prefer staying at home to traveling, and often become confused, "turned about," or lost in strange places. *Cultivate*. [107.]

(2.) SMALL.—You have a very poor memory of places, and find even familiar ones with difficulty. *Cultivate*. [107.]

(1.) VERY SMALL.—Your local instinct is so weak that you can hardly find your way home from any neighboring place. *Cultivate*. [107.]

XLVII.—EVENTUALITY.

(7.) VERY LARGE.—You should possess a wonderfully retentive memory of facts, incidents, and general knowledge; and have strong craving for information. You would be a great devourer of books, newspapers, and periodicals; and with large Language and Imitation, would excel in story-telling. [108.]

(6.) LARGE.—You ought to have a retentive memory of historical facts, incidents, stories, and general information; love to acquire knowledge; are fond of books, learn readily anything relating to history or biography. You are likely to be well informed on common subjects and, with fair opportunities, to be a good scholar. [108.]

(5.) FULL.—Your memory of facts and circumstances should be good, if properly cultivated, but may have become indifferent through neglect. You may, if the reflective faculties be large, remember principles better than facts. *Cultivate*. [109.]

(4.) AVERAGE.—You may recollect leading events, and facts in which you are particularly interested, but are rather deficient in memory of indifferent matters and the details of occurrences. *Cultivate*. [109.]

(3.) MODERATE.—You have a rather poor memory of events, and are particularly forgetful of details. You are a poor story-teller. *Cultivate*. [109.]

(2.) SMALL.—Your memory is treacherous and confused, and can not safely be relied upon for anything relating to facts, occurrences, or the circumstances of active life. *Cultivate.* [109.]

(1.) VERY SMALL.—Your memory is utterly untrustworthy. You forget almost everything relating to what has happened, no matter how recently. *Cultivate.* [109.]

XLVIII.—TIME.

(7.) VERY LARGE.—You seem to have an intuitive knowledge of the lapse of time; can keep time in music, tell the time of day almost as correctly without a time-piece as with one; and can wake at any pre-appointed hour of the night. [109.]

(6.) LARGE.—You are an excellent judge of time; can tell when any event of which you have a knowledge occurred; keep time in music very correctly; rarely forget appointments; and should be an accurate chronologist. [109.]

(5.) FULL.—You can keep time in music and, with practice, can carry in your head the time of day, but are not remarkably endowed in this particular. *Cultivate.* [110.]

(4.) AVERAGE.—Your memory of dates is fair, but you require practice to give you accuracy in keeping time in music. *Cultivate.* [110.]

(3.) MODERATE.—You have a rather defective notion of time, and not a good memory of dates. *Cultivate.* [110.]

(2.) SMALL.—You have a confused and indistinct idea of time, and are apt to forget appointments. *Cultivate.* [110.]

(1.) VERY SMALL.—You are nearly destitute of this faculty. *Cultivate.* [110.]

XLIX.—TUNE.

(7.) VERY LARGE.—You are passionately fond of music; have extraordinary musical taste and talent; and with a good development of Imitation, Constructiveness, Ideality, and Time, and a fine organization, may become an expert performer, or, with large Ideality, Causality, and Comparison, a composer. [110.]

[6.] LARGE.—You are constituted as described in (7), except in a somewhat lower degree; have a fine ear for music, and enjoy if you do not readily learn anything you hear. [110.]

(5.) FULL.—You have good musical taste; are very fond of music; and with practice can become a performer. *Cultivate.* [112.]

(4.) AVERAGE.—You have fair musical ability, but considerable practice would be required to give you proficiency in music. You have more love for the "concord of sweet sounds" than power to produce it. *Cultivate.* [112.]

(3.) MODERATE.—You are not particularly fond of music, but are capable of acquiring some taste for the simpler kinds, and with practice may learn to sing. *Cultivate.* [112.]

(2.) SMALL.—You have very little taste or love for music, and less ability to produce it. *Cultivate.* [112.]

(1.) VERY SMALL.—You manifest little or none of this faculty. *Cultivate.* [112.]*

L.—LANGUAGE.

(7.) VERY LARGE.—You have great copiousness of expression, a passion for talking or writing; are capable of becoming very fluent and correct in the use of language; generally put the right word in the right place; have a remarkable verbal memory; readily make quotations; learn languages with facility by hearing them spoken; are very liable, unless this faculty be restrained, or balanced by reason, to be tediously verbose. *Restrain.* [114.]

(6.) LARGE.—You are fluent and copious in the use of words, both in writing and speaking; can learn to talk well, and would love to talk; can learn foreign languages easily; and have an excellent memory of words. You can tell all you know, and generally make use of correct if not elegant language; are rather inclined to verbosity than to barrenness of expression, and to talk too much rather than too little. *Restrain.* [114.]

(5.) FULL.—You have a good command of language; express yourself with considerable ease and fluency, but are not remarkable for copiousness, and are seldom verbose or redundant. With practice you might make a good speaker, but can do better with the pen than with the tongue. *Cultivate.* [114.]

(4.) AVERAGE.—You are not very fluent in the use of language; say what you desire to say in few words; are not very fond of talking; with practice may write well, but not rapidly. *Cultivate.* [114.]

(3.) MODERATE.—You find some difficulty in expressing your ideas, your vocabulary being small and your memory and command of words poor. With constant practice, you may write effectively, but your style will be rather dry and barren. As a speaker, you would not be likely to succeed. You may learn foreign languages, but will speak them with difficulty, if at all. *Cultivate.* [114.]

(2.) SMALL.—You speak with difficulty; often hesitate for words; and are apt to blunder in the construction of your sentences. *Cultivate.* [114.]

(1.) VERY SMALL.—Your memory of words is exceedingly poor, and your power of expression almost entirely lacking. *Cultivate.* [114.]

---

* The Friends, or Quakers—many of them—are opposed to music, on the ground that it is used as a sensuous gratification; a disturbing element; opposed to simple, silent devotion. *We* regard Tune as a faculty of the human mind, created for a useful purpose, and not to be ignored or suppressed because of its abuse, any more than that of the appetite, or of Veneration itself, which is sometimes exercised on idols, images, and gods of wood and stone. The *right* use of all the faculties will be acceptable to Him who created them.

LI.—CAUSALITY.

(7.) Very Large.—You should be noted for originality, planning capacity, intuitive perception of the relations of cause and effect, and great reasoning power and comprehension. You are naturally a thinker and a philosopher, and are in danger of becoming an impracticable theorist. *Restrain.* [115.]

(6.) Large.—You have excellent reasoning power; uncommon capacity for contriving ways and means; can generally trace effects back to their causes, or predicate results; are good at making plans; have a strong desire to know the "why" and "wherefore" of everything; are not satisfied with a superficial knowledge, but desire to go to the bottom of every subject; are liable to be abstruse and more theoretical than practical. *Restrain.* [115.]

(5.) Full.—Your capacity to plan, invent, originate, and adapt means to ends is good, and with activity well developed and Comparison and the perceptives large, may manifest a good degree of reasoning power; but with these conditions reversed, you will plan better than you will execute. You like to know why things are as they are, but are not disposed to push your investigations too closely. [114.]

(4.) Average.—Your planning and reasoning ability depends greatly upon the influence of other and larger organs, but in general it is only fair. *Cultivate.* [115.]

(3.) Moderate.—You are rather deficient in the ability to discern and apply principles, and possess no great originality or planning capacity. *Cultivate.* [115.]

(2.) Small.—You are decidedly deficient in reasoning power and ability to contrive, plan, and adapt means to ends. *Cultivate.* [115.]

(1.) Very Small.—You are almost utterly destitute of originality. *Cultivate.* [115.]

LII.—COMPARISON.

(7.) Very Large.—You possess remarkable powers of analysis; ability to reason from analogy and to discover new truths by induction; can clearly trace out relations between the known and the unknown which escape common investigators, and with Individuality, Eventuality, and Causality well developed, will manifest great capacity for making discoveries and a passion for analytical investigations most useful to the phrenologist. [115.]

(6.) Large.—Your capacity for inductive reasoning is excellent; you manifest great ability in tracing the connection between known facts and phenomena and the laws or principles which govern them; a disposition to analyze, resolve combinations into elements, dissect, criticise, compare, and classify; to observe similarities and dissimilarities; to trace analogies; to explain by illustration; and in speaking, to

LI.—CAUSALITY.

(7.) VERY LARGE.—You should be noted for originality, planning capacity, intuitive perception of the relations of cause and effect, and great reasoning power and comprehension. You are naturally a thinker and a philosopher, and are in danger of becoming an impracticable theorist. *Restrain.* [115.]

(6.) LARGE.—You have excellent reasoning power; uncommon capacity for contriving ways and means; can generally trace effects back to their causes, or predicate results; are good at making plans; have a strong desire to know the "why" and "wherefore" of everything; are not satisfied with a superficial knowledge, but desire to go to the bottom of every subject; are liable to be abstruse and more theoretical than practical. *Restrain.* [115.]

(5.) FULL.—Your capacity to plan, invent, originate, and adapt means to ends is good, and with activity well developed and Comparison and the perceptives large, may manifest a good degree of reasoning power; but with these conditions reversed, you will plan better than you will execute. You like to know why things are as they are, but are not disposed to push your investigations too closely. [114.]

(4.) AVERAGE.—Your planning and reasoning ability depends greatly upon the influence of other and larger organs, but in general it is only fair. *Cultivate.* [115.]

(3.) MODERATE.—You are rather deficient in the ability to discern and apply principles, and possess no great originality or planning capacity. *Cultivate.* [115.]

(2.) SMALL.—You are decidedly deficient in reasoning power and ability to contrive, plan, and adapt means to ends. *Cultivate.* [115.]

(1.) VERY SMALL.—You are almost utterly destitute of originality. *Cultivate.* [115.]

LII.—COMPARISON.

(7.) VERY LARGE.—You possess remarkable powers of analysis; ability to reason from analogy and to discover new truths by induction; can clearly trace out relations between the known and the unknown which escape common investigators, and with Individuality, Eventuality, and Causality well developed, will manifest great capacity for making discoveries and a passion for analytical investigations most useful to the phrenologist. [115.]

(6.) LARGE.—Your capacity for inductive reasoning is excellent; you manifest great ability in tracing the connection between known facts and phenomena and the laws or principles which govern them; a disposition to analyze, resolve combinations into elements, dissect, criticise, compare, and classify; to observe similarities and dissimilarities; to trace analogies; to explain by illustration; and in speaking, to use many comparisons, metaphors, and similes. With large Language, Continuity, Constructiveness, and Ideality, should write and speak with great fluency, correctness, and elegance, and in a style distinguished for clearness as well as for beauty; but with these organs moderate or small, there will be a liability to broken metaphors and imperfect and confusing comparisons. You would make a good chemist. [115.]

(5.) FULL.—You appreciate fine comparisons and sound inductive reasoning, and are inclined to make use of the analogical and analytical methods of arriving at the truth, but are not remarkably developed in this faculty. *Cultivate.* [117.]

(4.) AVERAGE.—Your analogical ability is fair, when called into activity by the larger organs, but otherwise is rather weak in its manifestations. *Cultivate.* [117.]

(3.) MODERATE.—You are not much inclined to institute comparisons or to observe resemblances or differences, and neither make use of nor appreciate metaphors and similes, but may enjoy a simple and direct comparison. Your ability to illustrate one case or point by another involving similar principle is poor. *Cultivate.* [117.]

(2.) SMALL.—You seldom observe likenesses or dissimilarities, have no skill in tracing analogies, and are content to take things as you find them in their combinations, instead of pulling them in pieces or resolving them into elements to find out how they are made or the proportions of their parts. *Cultivate.* [117.]

(1.) VERY SMALL.—You manifest little or none of this element of character. *Cultivate.* [117.]

LIII.—HUMAN NATURE.

(7.) VERY LARGE.—You are a natural physiognomist, or, rather, an intuitive discerner of character, forming correct estimates of the disposition and moral status of those you meet at a single glance, especially if they be of the opposite sex. You can trust your first impressions of character. With large Comparison, would make an excellent practical phrenologist and physiognomist. It is usually large in our North American Indians, and should be so in our police and in all detectives. [117.]

(6.) LARGE.—You have an excellent judgment in matters of character; read men and women intuitively; love to study the "Signs of Character" in the features, voice, walk, manners, etc., and could become a good practical delineator of character. [117.]

(5.) FULL.—Your first impressions of character are generally correct; but you are liable to make occasional mistakes. You love to study character, and with practice may become a good practical phrenologist or physiognomist. *Cultivate.* [118.]

(4.) AVERAGE.—Your talents for reading character are fair, but your first impressions are not to be fully trusted. *Cultivate.* [118.]

(3.) MODERATE.—You have no great natural capacity for character-reading, and often form incorrect estimates of people, but with study and practice may do tolerably well. *Cultivate.* [118.]

(2.) SMALL.—You are a poor judge of character and are easily imposed upon—do not know how to take people. *Cultivate.* [118.]

(1.) VERY SMALL.—You have little or no appreciation of human nature. *Cultivate.* [118.]

LIV.—AGREEABLENESS.

(7.) VERY LARGE.—You are remarkably bland, winning, and persuasive; very conciliatory; and generally please everybody. Are more like a Frenchman than an Englishman. [118.]

(6.) LARGE.—You have an agreeable and fascinating manner, and a way of saying and doing even disagreeable things at which no one can take offense, and which makes everything you say and do acceptable. You are conciliatory and persuasive, and are almost universally liked. "Are all things to all men." [118.]

(5.) FULL.—You are pleasing and bland in your manners, and, with large Ideality, polite and agreeable; but when angry, may make use of blunt and sharp expressions. *Cultivate.* [119.]

(4.) AVERAGE.—You are generally pleasant in conversation and manners, but may when excited become very brusque and repulsive. Are more like an Englishman than a Frenchman. *Cultivate.* [119.]

(3.) MODERATE.—You are rather deficient in Agreeableness, and have little ability to smooth over your words or actions. *Cultivate.* [119.]

(2.) SMALL.—You have an unpleasant way of saying even pleasant things, and often quite unnecessarily provoke the ill-will of those around you. *Cultivate.* [119.]

(1.) VERY SMALL.—You manifest no desire or ability to please. *Cultivate.* [119.]

NOTE.—The literature of Phrenology is not very voluminous. Some of the most important works are the following: Sur les Fonctions du Cerveau par Dr. Gall, 6 vols., Paris, 1825 (price, $125); Gall's Complete Works (in English), 6 vols. ($15); Spurzheim's Phrenology, 2 vols.; Cours de Phrénologie par Dr. Broussais; Traité de Phrénologie Humain et Comparée, 2 vols, 4º, avec Atlas in fº de 120 Planches, par Dr. Vimont; Combe's Lectures on Phrenology; Combe's Constitution of Man; Phrenology Proved, Illustrated, and Applied; and Boardman's Defence of Phrenology. On Physiognomy: Lavater's great work, Essays on Physiognomy (various editions), and New Physiognomy, by S. R. Wells, are the only books of much value now accessible.

PHRENOLOGY AND PHYSIOGNOMY.

American Phrenological Journal and SCIENCE OF HEALTH.—Devoted to Ethnology, Physiology, Phrenology, Physiognomy, Psychology, Sociology, Biography, Education, Literature, etc., with Measures to Reform, Elevate, and Improve Mankind Physically, Mentally, and Spiritually. Monthly, $2 a year; 20 cents a number.

Bell (Sir Charles).—Expression: its Anatomy and Philosophy. With the original Notes and Illustrations by the author, and additional Notes and Illustrations by SAMUEL R. WELLS. $1.25.

Boardman (Andrew, M.D.)—Defence OF PHRENOLOGY; Containing an Essay on the Nature and Value of Phrenological Evidence; A Vindication of Phrenology against the Attack of its opponents. $1.25.

Bray (Charles).—The Education of THE FEELINGS AND AFFECTIONS. Edited, with Notes and Illustrations, by NELSON SIZER. Cloth, $1.50.
This work gives full and definite directions for the cultivation or restraining of all the faculties relating to the feelings or affections.

Combe (George).—A System of PHRENOLOGY; With One Hundred Engravings. Cloth, $1.50.

——**Constitution of Man**; Considered in Relation to external objects. The only authorized American edition; with twenty engravings, and a portrait of the author. $1.50.
The "Constitution of Man" is a work with which every teacher and every pupil should be acquainted.

——**Lectures on Phrenology**; with Notes, an Essay on the Phrenological Mode of Investigation, and an Historical Sketch, by A. BOARDMAN, M.D. $1.50.
These are the lectures delivered by George Combe in America.

——**Moral Philosophy**; or, the Duties of Man considered in his Individual, Domestic, and Social Capacities. $1.50.
Uniform Edition, 4 vols., extra cloth, $5.00. Library Edition, 4 vols., $10.

——**On Education.**—Papers on Educational Subjects. One vol. 8vo, Edinburgh Edition. Cloth, $5.00.
This volume consists of valuable Essays written by Mr. Combe, and should be found in the library of every teacher.

——**The Life of.** By CHARLES GIBBON. 2 volumes, 8vo, with two portraits. London Edition. $5.00.
These two works are not published in this country, but we can furnish from our stock, or import to order.

Capen (Nahum, LL.D.)—Reminis-CENCES OF DR. SPURZHEIM AND GEORGE COMBE, and a Review of the Science of Phrenology from the period of its discovery by Dr. GALL to the time of the visit of GEORGE COMBE to the United States, with a new portrait of Dr. SPURZHEIM. 12mo, extra cloth, $1.50.

Drayton (H. S., A.M.), and McNeil (JAMES, A.M.)—Brain and Mind; or, Mental Science Considered in Accordance with the Principles of Phrenology and in Relation to Modern Physiology. Ill. $1.50.
This is the latest and best work published. It constitutes a complete text-book of Phrenology, is profusely illustrated, and well adapted to the use of students.

Drayton (H. S., A.M.)—The Indi-CATIONS OF CHARACTER, as manifested in the general shape of the head and the form of the face. Illustrated. 15 cents.

——**How to Study Phrenology.**—With Suggestions to Students, Lists of Best Works, Constitutions for Societies, etc. 12mo, paper, 10 cents.

Fowler (O. S.)—Education and Self-IMPROVEMENT COMPLETE; Comprising "Physiology, Animal and Mental," "Self-Culture and Perfection of Character," "Memory and Intellectual Improvement." One large vol. Illustrated. $3.50.

——**Self-Culture and Perfection of** CHARACTER; Including the Management of Children and Youth. $1.25.
One of the best of the author's works.

——**Physiology, Animal and Mental**: Applied to the Preservation and Restoration of Health of Body and Power of Mind. $1.25.

I

WORKS ON PHRENOLOGY.

Fowler (O. S.)—Memory and In-TELLECTUAL IMPROVEMENT, applied to Self-Education and Juvenile Instruction. $1.25. The best work on the subject.

——**Maternity**; or, the Bearing and Nursing of Children, including Female Education and Beauty. $1.25.

——**Matrimony**; or, Phrenology and Physiology applied to the Selection of Congenial Companions for Life, including Directions to the Married for living together Affectionately and Happily. 50c.

——**Love and Parentage.** Applied to the Improvement of Offspring; including Directions to Lovers and the Married, concerning the strongest ties and the most sacred relations of life. 50 cents.

——**Hereditary Descent**; Its Laws and Facts applied to Human Improvement. Illustrated. $1.25.

——**Amativeness**; or, Evils and Remedies of Excessive and Perverted Sexuality; including Warning and Advice to the Married and Single. 25 cents.

——**Phrenology Proved, Illustrated,** AND APPLIED. Embracing an Analysis of the Primary Mental Powers in their Various Degrees of Development, and location of the Phrenological Organs. The Mental Phenomena produced by their combined action, and the location of the faculties amply illustrated. By the Fowler Brothers. $1.50.

——**Self Instructor in Phrenology** AND PHYSIOLOGY. With over One Hundred Engravings and a Chart for Phrenologists, for the Recording of Phrenological Development. By the Fowler Brothers. Paper, 50 cts.; cloth, 75 cts.

——**Synopsis of Phrenology, and** Charts for Describing the Phrenological Developments, for the use of Lecturers and Examiners. Paper, 10 cents.

Fowler (L. N.)—Marriage, its His-TORY AND CEREMONIES, with a Phrenological and Physiological Exposition of the Functions and Qualifications for Happy Marriages. Illustrated, $1.25.

——**Lectures on Man**, as explained by Phrenology, Physiology, Physiognomy, and Ethnology. Cloth, $1.50.

Sizer (Nelson).—Choice of Pursuits; or, What to Do and Why. Describing Seventy-five Trades and Professions, and the Temperaments and Talents required for each. With Portraits and Biographies of many successful Thinkers and Workers. $1.75.

——**How to Teach According to** TEMPERAMENT AND MENTAL DEVELOPMENT; or, Phrenology in the School-room and the Family. Illustrated. $1.50.

——**Forty Years in Phrenology**; embracing Recollections of History, Anecdote and Experience. $1.50.

——**Thoughts on Domestc Life**; or, Marriage Vindicated and Free Love Exposed. 25 cents.

Spurzheim (J. G., M.D.)—Education; ITS ELEMENTARY PRINCIPLES FOUNDED ON THE NATURE OF MAN. With an Appendix by S. R. WELLS, containing a Description of the Temperaments and a Brief Analysis of the Phrenological Faculties. Illustrated. $1.50.

——**Natural Laws of Man.**—A Philosophical Catechism. Sixth Edition. Enlarged and improved. 50 cents.

Weaver (Rev. G. S.)—Lectures on MENTAL SCIENCE. According to the Philosophy of Phrenology. Delivered before the Anthropological Society. Illustrated. $1.25.

Wells (Samuel R.)—New Physiog-NOMY; or, Signs of Character, as manifested through Temperament and External Forms, and especially in the "Human Face Divine." With more than One Thousand Illustrations. In one 12mo volume, 768 pages, muslin, $5.00; in heavy calf, marbled edges, $8.00; Turkey morocco, full gilt, $10.

"The treatise of Mr. Wells, which is admirably printed and profusely illustrated, is probably the most complete hand-book upon the subject in the language."—*N. Y. Tribune.*

Phrenological Bust.—Showing the latest classification and exact location of the Organs of the Brain. It is divided so as to show each individual Organs on one side; with all the groups—Social, Executive, Intellectual, and Moral—properly classified, on the other side. There are two sizes; the largest, not mailable, price $1. The smaller, 50 cents.

Sent by Mail, post-paid. FOWLER & WELLS, *Publishers,* 753 *Broadway, New York.*

2

PHRENOLOGY AND PHYSIOGNOMY.

Wells (S. R.)—How to Read Character.—A New Illustrated Hand-book of Phrenology and Physiognomy, for Students and Examiners, with a Chart for recording the sizes of the different Organs of the Brain in the Delineation of Character; with upwards of 170 Engravings. Paper, $1.00; Cloth, $1.25.

——Wedlock; or, the Right Relations of the Sexes. Disclosing the Laws of Conjugal Selections, and showing Who May, and Who May Not Marry. A Scientific Treatise. $1.50; fancy gilt, $2.00.

——New Descriptive Chart, for the Use of Examiners in the Delineation of Character. 25 cents; cloth, 50 cents.

Harmony of Phrenology and the BIBLE, including the Definition of the Organs, their uses, excess, and deficiency, with Quotations from the Bible recognizing every faculty and passion, sanctioning their use and warning against abuse. 10c.

The Phrenological Miscellany; or, Illustrated Annuals of Phrenology and Physiognomy, from 1865 to 1873 combined in 1 volume, the nine containing over 400 illustrations, many portraits and biographies of distinguished personages, together with articles on "How to Study Phrenology," "Resemblance to Parents," "Bashfulness," "Diffidence," "Stammering," etc., an elaborate article on "The Marriage of Cousins," "Jealousy, its Cause and Cure." 450 pages, $1.50.

Phrenology and the Scriptures.—Showing the Harmony between Phrenology and the Bible. By Rev. J. PIERPONT. Paper, 15 cts.

The Annuals of Phrenology and HEALTH ALMANAC for 1874, '75, '76, '77, '78, '79, '80, '81, and '82 in one vol. $1. The current year, 10 cents.

——Symbolical Head and Phreno- LOGICAL MAP. On fine tinted paper, 10c.

Phrenology, its History and Impor- TANT PRINCIPLES. By T. TURNER. 10c.

WORKS ON MAGNETISM.

There is an increasing interest in the facts relating to Magnetism, etc., and we present below a list of Works on this subject.

Practical Instructions in Animal MAGNETISM. By J. P. F. DELEUZE. Translated by Thomas C. Hartshorn. New and Revised edition, with an appendix of notes by the Translator, and Letters from Eminent Physicians, and others. $2.00.

History of Salem Witchcraft.—A review of Charles W. Upham's great Work from the *Edinburgh Review*, with Notes; by SAMUEL R. WELLS, containing, also, The Planchette Mystery, Spiritualism, by Mrs. HARRIET BEECHER STOWE, and Dr. Doddridge's Dream. $1.

Fascination; or, the Philosophy of CHARMING. Illustrating the Principles of Life in connection with Spirit and Matter. By J. B. NEWMAN, M.D. $1.00.

Six Lectures on the Philosophy of MESMERISM, delivered in Marlboro' Chapel, Boston. By Dr. JOHN BOVEE DODS. Paper, 50 cents.

The Philosophy of Electrical Psy- CHOLOGY, in a course of Twelve Lectures. By the same author. 12mo, cloth, $1.25.

The Library of Mesmerism and PSYCHOLOGY.—Comprising the Philosophy of Mesmerism, Clairvoyance, Mental Electricity.—Fascination, or the Power of Charming. Illustrating the Principles of Life in connection with Spirit and Matter.—The Macrocosm, or the Universe Without: being an unfolding of the plan of Creation, and the Correspondence of Truths.—The Philosophy of Electrical Psychology; the Doctrine of Impressions; including the connection between Mind and Matter; also, the Treatment of Diseases.—Psychology; or, the Science of the Soul, considered Physiologically and Philosophically; with an Appendix containing Notes of Mesmeric and Psychical experience, and illustrations of the Brain and Nervous System. 1 vol. $3.50.

How to Magnetize; or, Magnetism AND CLAIRVOYANCE.—A Practical Treatise on the Choice, Management, and Capabilities of Subjects, with Instructions on the Method of Procedure. By JAMES VICTOR WILSON. 18mo, paper, 25 cts.

The Key to Ghostism. By Rev. THOMAS MITCHEL. $1.50.

Sent by Mail, post-paid. FOWLER & WELLS, *Publishers*, 753 *Broadway, New York.*

3

HEALTH BOOKS.

This List comprises the Best Works on Hygiene, Health, Etc.

——————

Combe (Andrew, M.D.)—Principles applied to the Preservation of Health and to the Improvement of Physical and Mental Education. Illustrated. Cloth, $1.50.

——Management of Infancy, Physiological and Moral Treatment. With Notes and a Supplementary Chapter, $1.25

——Physiology of Digestion.—Considered with relation to the Principles of Dietetics. Illustrated. 50 cents.

Fairchild (M. Augusta, M.D.)—How TO BE WELL; or, Common-Sense Medical Hygiene. A book for the People, giving Directions for the Treatment and Cure of Acute Diseases without the use of Drug Medicines; also, General Hints on Health. $1.00.

Graham (Sylvester).—Science of HUMAN LIFE, LECTURES ON THE. With a copious Index and Biographical Sketch of the Author. Illustrated, $3.00.

——Chastity.—Lectures to Young Men. Intended also for the Serious Consideration of Parents and Guardians. 12mo. Paper, 50 cents.

Gully (J. M., M.D.)—Water-Cure IN CHRONIC DISEASES. An Exposition of the Causes, Progress, and Termination of various Chronic Diseases of the Digestive Organs, Lungs, Nerves, Limbs, and Skin, and of their Treatment by Water and other Hygienic means. $1.50.

For Girls; A Special Physiology, or Supplement to the Study of General Physiology. By Mrs. E. R. Shepherd. $1.00.

Page (C. E., M.D.)—How to Feed the Baby to make her Healthy and Happy. 12mo. Third edition, revised and enlarged. Paper, 50 cents; extra cloth, 75 cents.
This is the most important work ever published on the subject of infant dietetics.

——The Natural Cure of Consumption, Constipation, Bright's Disease, Neuralgia, Rheumatism, "Colds" (Fevers), etc. How these Disorders Originate, and How to Prevent Them. 12mo, cloth, $1.00.

Gully (J. M., M.D.) and Wilson (JAMES, M. D.)—PRACTICE OF THE WATER-CURE, with Authenticated Evidence of its Efficacy and Safety. Containing a Detailed Account of the various Processes used in the Water Treatment, a Sketch of the History and Progress of the Water-Cure. 50 cents.

Jacques (D. H., M.D.)—The Temperaments; or, Varieties of Physical Constitution in Man, considered in their relation to Mental Character and Practical Affairs of Life. With an Introduction by H. S. DRAYTON, A.M., Editor of the *Phrenological Journal.* 150 Portraits and other Illustrations. $1.50.

The only work on the Temperaments now before the public, and treats of this important subject in a most comprehensive manner, showing its bearings on marriage, education and training of children, occupation, health and disease, heredity, etc., all illustrated with portraits from life. It tells how to cultivate or restrain temperamental tendencies, and is a work which should be in the hands of every student of human nature.

——How to Grow Handsome, or Hints toward Physical Perfection, and the Philosophy of Human Beauty, showing How to Acquire and Retain Bodily Symmetry, Health, and Vigor, secure Long Life, and Avoid the Infirmities and Deformities of Age. New Edition. $1.00.

Johnson (Edward, M.D.)—Domestic PRACTICE OF HYDROPATHY, with Fifteen Engraved Illustrations of important subjects, from Drawings by Dr. Howard Johnson. $1.50.

White (Wm., M.D.)—Medical Electricity.—A Manual for Students, showing the most Scientific and Rational Application to all forms of Diseases, of the different Combinations of Electricity, Galvanism, Electro-Magnetism, Magneto-Electricity, and Human Magnetism. 12mo, $2.00.

Transmission; or, Variations of Character Through the Mother. By GEORGIANA B. KIRBY. 25 cts.; cloth, 50 cts.

Sent by Mail, post-paid. FOWLER & WELLS, *Publishers,* 753 *Broadway, New York.*

WORKS ON HEALTH AND HYGIENE.

Peck (J. L.)—The Human Feet.— Their Shape, Dress, and Proper Care. Showing their Natural, Perfect Shape and Construction, their present Deformed Condition, and how Flat Feet, Distorted Toes, and other Defects are to be Prevented or Corrected, with directions for Dressing them Elegantly yet Comfortably, and Hints upon Various Matters relating to General Subjects. Illustrated. $1.00.

Pendleton (Hester, Mrs.) — The PARENTS' GUIDE ; or, Human Development through Pre-Natal Influences and Inherited Tendencies. Revised Ed. $1.25.

Pereira (Jonathan, M.D., F.R.S.)— FOOD AND DIET. With observations on the Dietetical Regimen, suited for Disordered States of the Digestive Organs, and an account of the Dietaries of some of the Principal Metropolitan and other Establishments for Paupers, Lunatics, Criminals, Children, the Sick, etc. Edited by CHARLES A. LEE, M.D. $1.40.

Shew (Joel, M.D.)—The Family PHYSICIAN.—A Ready Prescriber and Hygienic Adviser. With Reference to the Nature, Causes, Prevention, and Treatment of Diseases, Accidents, and Casualties of every kind. With a Glossary and copious Index. Illustrated with nearly Three Hundred Engravings. $3.00.

——Letters to Women on Midwifery AND DISEASES OF WOMEN.—A Descriptive and Practical Work, giving Treatment in Menstruation and its Disorders, Chlorosis, Leucorrhea, Fluor Albus, Prolapsus Uteri, Hysteria, Spinal Diseases, and other weaknesses of Females, Pregnancy and its Diseases, Abortion, Uterine Hemorrhage, and the General Management of Childbirth, Nursing, etc. $1.50.

——Pregnancy and Childbirth, with Cases showing the remarkable Effects of Water Treatment in Mitigating the Pains and Perils of the Parturient State. 50 cts.

Tobacco : its Physical, Intellectual, and Moral Effects on the Human System. By Dr. Wm. Alcott. 15 cents.

Shew (Joel, M.D.)—Children, their Hydropathic Management in Health and Disease. A Descriptive and Practical Work, designed as a Guide for Families and Physicians. $1.50.

Sober and Temperate Life.—The Discourses and Letters of LOUIS CORNARO on a Sober and Temperate Life. With a Biography of the Author by PIERO MARONCELLI, and Notes and Appendix by JOHN BURDELL. Paper, 50 cents.

The Story of a Stomach.—An Egotism by a Reformed Dyspeptic. 75 cents.

Philosophy of the Water-Cure : a Development of the True Principles of Health and Longevity. By John Balbirnie, M.D. Illustrated. With the Confessions and Observations of Sir Edward Lytton Bulwer. 50 cents.

Chronic Diseases.—Especially the Nervous Diseases of Women. 25 cents.

Teeth : their Structure, Disease, and Management, with Engravings. 25 cts.

Consumption, its Prevention and Cure by the Swedish-Movement Cure. With Directions for its Home Application. By David Wark, M.D. 30 cents.

Notes on Beauty, Vigor, and Devel- OPMENT ; or, How to Acquire Plumpness of Form, Strength of Limb and Beauty of Complexion, with Rules for Diet and Bathing, and a Series of Improved Physical Exercises. By William Milo, of London. Illustrated. 10 cents.

Facts About Tobacco. Compiled by Prof. E. P. THWING. 25 cents.

Tea and Coffee.—Their Physical, Intellectual, and Moral Effects on the Human System. By Dr. Alcott. 15 cts.

Heredity.—RESPONSIBILITY AND PARENTAGE. By Rev. S. H. Platt. 10 cts.

Special List.—We have in addition to the above, Private Medical Works and Treatises. This Special List will be sent on receipt of stamp.

Sent by Mail, post-paid. FOWLER & WELLS, *Publishers,* 753 *Broadway, New York.*

MISCELLANEOUS WORKS.

Hand-books for Home Improve-MENT (EDUCATIONAL); comprising, "How to Write," "How to Talk," "How to Behave," and "How to do Business." One 12mo vol., $2.00.

How to Write: a Pocket Manual of Composition and Letter-Writing. 75 cts.

How to Talk: a Pocket Manual of Conversation and Debate, with more than Five Hundred Common Mistakes in Speaking Corrected. 75 cents.

How to Behave: a Pocket Manual of Republican Etiquette and Guide to Correct Personal Habits, with Rules for Debating Societies and Deliberative Assemblies. 75 cents.

How to Do Business: a Pocket Manual of Practical Affairs, and a Guide to Success in Life, with a Collection of Legal and Commercial Forms. 75c.

How to Read.—What and Why; or, Hints in Choosing the Best Books, with Classified List of Best Works in Biography, Criticism, Fine Arts, History, Novels, Poetry, Science, Religion, Foreign Languages, etc. By A. V. Petit. Clo., $1.

How to Sing; or, the Voice and How to Use it. By W. H. Daniell. 50c; 75c.

How to Conduct a Public Meeting; or, The Chairman's Guide for Conducting Meetings, Public and Private. 15 cts.

Hopes and Helps for the Young of BOTH SEXES.—Relating to the Formation of Character, Choice of Avocation, Health, Amusement, Music, Conversation, Social Affections, Courtship and Marriage. By Weaver. $1.25.

Aims and Aids for Girls and Young WOMEN, on the various Duties of Life. Including Physical, Intellectual, and Moral Development, Dress, Beauty, Fashion, Employment, Education, the Home Relations, their Duties to Young Men, Marriage, Womanhood and Happiness. $1.25.

Ways of Life, showing the Right Way and the Wrong Way. Contrasting the High Way and the Low Way; the True Way and the False Way; the Upward Way and the Downward Way; the Way of Honor and of Dishonor. 75 cts.

The Christian Household.—Embracing the Husband, Wife, Father, Mother, Child, Brother and Sister. $1.00.

Weaver's Works for the Young, Comprising "Hopes and Helps for the Young of Both Sexes," "Aims and Aids for Girls and Young Women," "Ways of Life; or, the Right Way and the Wrong Way." One vol. 12mo. $2.50.

The Right Word in the Right Place. —A New Pocket Dictionary and Reference Book. Embracing extensive Collections of Synonyms, Technical Terms, Abbreviations, Foreign Phrases, Chapters on Writing for the Press, Punctuation, Proof-Reading, and other Information. 75 cts.

How to Learn Short-Hand; or, The Stenographic Instructor. An Improved System of Short-hand Writing arranged specially for the use of those desirous of acquiring the art without the aid of a teacher. By Arthur M. Baker. 25 cents.

Phonographic Note-Book. — For Students and Reporters. Double or Single ruled. 15 cents.

The Emphatic Diaglott, Containing the Original Greek Text of THE NEW TESTAMENT, with an Interlineary Word-for-Word English Translation; a New Emphatic Version based on the Interlineary Translation, on the Readings of the Vatican Manuscript (No. 1,209 in the Vatican Library): together with Illustrative and Explanatory Foot Notes, and a copious Selection of References; to the whole of which is added a valuable Alphabetical Index. By Benjamin Wilson. 884 pp. $4.00; extra fine binding $5.00.

History of Woman Suffrage.—Illustrated with Steel Engravings. Edited by Elizabeth Cady Stanton, Susan B. Anthony, Matilda Joslyn Gage. Complete in Three Octavo Volumes. Price per Volume, Cloth, $5.00. Sheep, $6.50.

Life at Home; or, The Family and its Members. Including Husbands and Wives, Parents, Children, Brothers, Sisters, Employers and Employed, The Altar in the House, etc. By Rev. William Aikman, D.D. 12mo, $1.50; full gilt $2.

A New Theory of the Origin of SPECIES. By Benj. G. Ferris. $1.00.

Man in Genesis and in Geology, or, the Biblical Account of Man's Creation tested by Scientific Theories of his Origin and Antiquity. By Joseph P. Thompson, D.D., LL.D. $1.00.

Sent by Mail, post-paid. FOWLER & WELLS, *Publishers,* 753 *Broadway, New York.*

MISCELLANEOUS WORKS.

The Conversion of St. Paul.—By Geo. Jarvis Geer, D.D. In three Parts. 1st. Its Relation to Unbelief. 2d. Its False Uses and True. 3d. Its Relation to the Church. $1.00.

The Temperance Reformation.—Its History from the first Temperance Society in the United States to the Adoption of the Maine Liquor Law. $1.50.

Man and Woman, Considered in their Relations to each other and to the World. By H. C. Pedder. Cloth, $1.

Æsop's Fables.—With Seventy Splendid Illustrations. One vol. 12mo, fancy cloth, gilt edges, $1. People's Edition, bound in boards, 25 cents.

Pope's Essay on Man, with Illustrations and Notes by S. R. Wells. 12mo, tinted paper, fancy cloth, full gilt, price $1. People's Edition, bound in boards, 25c.

Gems of Goldsmith: "The Traveler," "The Deserted Village," "The Hermit." With notes and Original Illustrations, and Biographical Sketch of the great author. One vol., fancy cloth, full gilt, $1. People's Ed., bound in boards, 25c.

The Rime of the Ancient Mariner. In Seven Parts. By Samuel T. Coleridge. With new Illustrations by Chapman. One vol., fancy cloth, full gilt, $1. People's Ed., bound in boards, 25 cents.

Footprints of Life; or, Faith and Nature Reconciled.—A Poem in Three Parts. The Body; The Soul; The Deity. Philip Harvey, M.D. $1.25.

How to Paint.—A Complete Compendium of the Art. Designed for the use of Tradesmen, Mechanics, Merchants and Farmers, and a Guide to the Professional Painter, Containing a plain Common-sense statement of the Methods employed by Painters to produce satisfactory results in Plain and Fancy Painting of every Description, including Gilding, Bronzing, Staining, Graining, Marbling, Varnishing, Polishing, Kalsomining, Paper Hanging, Striping, Lettering, Copying and Ornamenting, with Formulas for Mixing Paint in Oil or Water. Description of Various Pigments used: tools required, etc. By F. B. Gardner. $1.00.

The Carriage Painter's Illustrated Manual, containing a Treatise on the Art, Science, and Mystery of Coach, Carriage, and Car Painting. Including the Improvements in Fine Gilding, Bronzing, Staining, Varnishing, Polishing, Copying, Lettering, Scrolling, and Ornamenting. By F. B. Gardner. $1.00.

How to Keep a Store, embodying the Experience of Thirty Years in Merchandizing. By Samuel H. Terry. $1.50.

How to Raise Fruits.—A Hand-book. Being a Guide to the Cultivation and Management of Fruit Trees, and of Grapes and Small Fruits. With Descriptions of the Best and Most Popular Varieties. Illustrated. By Thomas Gregg. $1.

How to be Weather-Wise.—A new View of our Weather System. By I. P. Noyes. 25 cents.

How to Live.—Saving and Wasting; or, Domestic Economy Illustrated by the Life of two Families of Opposite Character, Habits, and Practices, full of Useful Lessons in Housekeeping, and Hints How to Live, How to Have, and How to be Happy, including the Story of "A Dime a Day," by Solon Robinson. $1.25.

Oratory—Sacred and Secular, or the Extemporaneous Speaker. Including a Chairman's Guide for conducting Public Meetings according to the best Parliamentary forms. By Wm. Pittenger. $1.25.

Homes for All; or, the Gravel Wall. A New, Cheap, and Superior Mode of Building, adapted to Rich and Poor. Showing the Superiority of the Gravel Concrete over Brick, Stone and Frame Houses; Manner of Making and Depositing it. By O. S. Fowler. $1.25.

The Model Potato.—Proper cultivation and mode of cooking. 50 cents.

Traits of Representative Men. With portraits. By Geo. W. Bungay. $1.50.

Capital Punishment; or, the Proper Treatment of Criminals, 10 cents. "Father Matthew, the Temperance Apostle," 10 cents. "Good Man's Legacy," 10 cents. Alphabet for Deaf and Dumb, 10 cents.

Sent by Mail, post-paid. FOWLER & WELLS, *Publishers,* 753 *Broadway, New York.*

DOWSING-PHYSICAL RADIESTHESIA · A rare 1920's massive work covering all areas of dowsing from a scientific view point. Very rare detailed review of · Instruments, Radiation of Inanimate matter, Waves, Mental Rays, Solar Rays, Radiation points, Magnetic Fields, Treasure Hunting for minerals, Treasure Hunting from a distance & by using maps, Astro-dowsing and much more. A must for the serious dowser. 210 pages. Reprint · **Hardcover · Item # RP-11-511 · $29.95**
· **Spiral Bound · Item # SP-76-016 · $19.98**

MAGNET DOWSING · Dowsing with the help of magnets. A wealth of usual practical information, drawings, charts and unique devices are of-fered here. Learn:Magnet Pointer, Chart for practice, Planet Radiation, Color Hunger, Health index, Seat of disease, Magnetic Box, Permanent Magnetic box, Electro-Magnet Box and many other charts for practical dowsing. Great text! 150 pages · **Hardcover · RP-11-736 · $29.95**
· **Spiral Bound · Item # SP-76-026 · $19.95**

PHRENOLOGY · PRACTICAL GUIDE TO YOUR HEAD · by Fowler & Fowler · This classic text from 1888 explains the whole philosophy of Phre-nology in great detail but, in an easy to understand fashion. Many illustra-tions throughout the book shows the reader how shape reflects and affects character. Giving examples of famous people to prove its point. This book is very complete and should be considered a great starting point in the study of Phrenology. 200 pages · **Hardcover · RP-11-582 · $29.95**
· **Spiral Bound · Item # SP-76-027 · $19.95**

THE PRACICAL PHRENOLOGIST AND RECORDER & DELINEATOR OF THE CHARACTOR & TALENTS · A COMPENDIUM OF PHRENO-ORGANIC SCIENCE · by OS Fowler · A classic text from 1869 is highly illustrated and very detailed. Covered: Proof of Phrenology · Size and measure of power · Large brains as affecting mind · Established by induc-tion · Organic conditions · Affecting mentality · The four forms · Analysis & Classification · Parental love · Rules for finding the organs and much more! Written by the master Phrenologist himself. A must for the researcher. 185 pages · **Hardcover · RP-11-584 · $34.95**
· **Spiral Bound · Item # SP-76-028 · $24.95**

FOWLER'S PRACTICAL PHRENOLOGY · GIVING CONCISE ELEMEN-TARY VIEW OF PHRENOLOGY · Seven different degrees of develop-ment · Location of the organs. This 1846 book is one of the first and fore-most books by Fowler. 435 pages of very detailed information. This is a definitive text that gives you insights other texts do not.
· **Hardcover · RP-11-585 · $69.95**
· **Spiral Bound · Item # SP-76-029 · $39.95**

HEADS & FACES · HOW TO STUDY THEM · by N. Sizer & HS Drayton · A Manual of Phrenology & Physiognomy For The People. First published 1885, lots of highly detailed drawings bring this fine work alive. This is one of the easiest Phrenology texts to follow. Well written by experts in the field, it was written for the average person to understand and follow. The hun-dreds of illustrations bring a clear understanding on how the formation of the Head/face causes certain personality traits. Excellent text not to be missed. 220 pages · **Hardcover · RP-11-586 · $39.95**
· **Spiral Bound · Item # SP-76-030 · $29.95**

THE MYSTERIES OF THE HEAD AND THE HEART EXPLAINED · AN IMPROVED SYSTEM OF PHRENOLOGY,MESMERISM, TRANCE AND THE SPIRIT DELUSION, GHOST SEEING AND MIND READING · IL-LUSTRATED · by J. Stanley Grimes · First published in 1875, this is a very unique book that covers a wide range of subjects not seen in only Phrenol-ogy books. He combines several techniques to bring this "how to" system to light. 40 years of research went into the writing of this book. LOTS OF RARE INFORMATION NOT AVAILABLE IN ANY OTHER TEXT! 368 pages · **Hardcover · RP-11-587 · $39.95**
· **Spiral Bound · Item # SP-76-031 · $29.95**

HOW TO READ CHARACTOR · WITH A DESCRIPTIVE CHART · A HAND-BOOK OF PHYSIOLGY PHRENOLOGY & PHYSIOGNOMY · ILLUS-TRATED · by S. Wells · First published in 1868, this text is easy to read and follow. Mr. Wells was a foremost Phrenologist of his time and taught hundreds of students. This book was written as a teaching tool. His views are slightly different then others. 195 pages · **Hardcover · RP-11-588 · $29.95**
· **Spiral Bound · Item # SP-76-032 · $19.95**

COMMON SENSE · HOW TO EXERCISE IT · A complete "how to" book on Common Sense and how you can make it work in your life. Great Book. 183 pages · **Hardcover · RP-11-573 · $29.95**
· **Spiral Bound · Item # SP-76-035 · $19.95**

THERAPEUTIC SARCOGNOMY · THE NEW SCIENCE OF SOUL, BRAIN & BODY-HEALTH & LONGGEVITY · A REVOLUTION IN BIOL-OGY · by J. Buchanan · This 1891 text is Phrenology for the WHOLE BODY, an accent on alternative treatments of that time. Including the use of Massage, Electricity, Nervaura, Medicine, Haemospasia, Animal Mag-netism, Spinal Treatments, Brain Vitality and much more. A very unique system of treatment is detailed here in a "how to" manner. A vast text cov-ering over 670 pages. YOU WILL NOT SEE THIS INFORMATION ANY-WHERE ELSE! A rare healing system that has been lost in time · **Hard-cover · RP-11-589 · $49.95**
· **Spiral Bound · Item # SP-76-033 · $34.95**

CHARACTEROLOGY; AN EXACT SCIENCE · by L. Hamilton McCor-mick · Fifteen lessons embracing Physiognomy, Phrenology & Pathog-nomy, Reconstructed, Amplified, and Amalgamated. Including views concerning memory and reason and the location of these faculties within the brain likewise facial and cranial indications of longevity-illustrated. This 1921 text was written as a course of study for students and even includes a test at the end of the book. A very rare text that is easy to follow and covers areas overlooked by other texts like, lip for-mation. 275 pages · **Hardcover · RP-11-590 · $39.95**
· **Spiral Bound · Item # SP-76-034 · $24.95**

THE METAPHORICAL BRAIN · An introduction to Cybernetics as Artificial Intelligence & Brain Theory. Using the metaphors, humans are animals and humans are machines as a dual framework, it presents the novel in-sights into the human brain resulting from experimental research on human and animals brains and analyzes the grain in view of the current advances in robot designs. 243 pages · **Hardcover · RP-11-562 · $29.95**
· **Spiral Bound · Item # SP-76-037 · $19.95**

BRAIN/MIND PARAPSYCHOLOGY · PROCEEDING 1978 CONFERENCE · Compiling of many papers from noted researchers in the field. Learn: Mind-Body PSI, Right hemisphere, Biofeedback & PK, and lots more. 252 pages · **Hardcover · Item # RP-11-056 · $29.95**
· **Spiral Bound · Item # SP-76-038 · $19.95**

WHAT'S ON YOUR MIND · Written by famous Mentalist "Dunninger". This book explains what Mental telepathy is. How it is done, can anyone do it? Gives 24 sim-ple training tests for the reader to try. Excellent how to text written in an easy to follow manner. 192 pages · **Hardcover · Item # RP-11-556 · $29.95**
· **Spiral Bound · Item # SP-76-039 · $19.95**

YOU AND HEREDITY · INCLUDING AN ORIGINAL STUDY OF THE INHERITANCE OF MUSICAL TALENT · written in 1939 by A. Scheinfeld · This text is filled with illustrations, charts and maps detailing what is "past on" or inherited by parents. A complete guide through the gene process and how it forms, skin color, eye color, health, illness, and good and bad traits in a person with detailed studies on musical traits. Points out Euro-pean, African cultures and the different traits of these people. A fascinating lo into the world of the human reproduction and mankind in general. Who we are and how we got the way we are. A classic text not o missed. 430 pages · **Hardcover · RP-11-599 · $39.95**
· **Spiral Bound · Item # SP-76-040 · $24.95**

THE UNIVERSAL ONE · VOL ONE · A very unique text from the 1920's detailing: An exact science of the One visible and invisible universe of Mind and the registration of all idea of thinking Mind in light, which is matter and also energy. Dynamics of Mind concerning light and matter, New concepts of electricity and magnetism, Universal pulse, Ionization, 4-17 Dimensions of the universe, Expressions of Gravitation and Radiation. A complete text of Alternative /New scientific thinking. EXCITING! 262 pages.
· **Hardcover · RP-11-609 · $29.95**
· **Spiral Bound · Item # SP-76-041 · $19.95**

Scientists of New Atlantis

"Atlantis Reborn"

POB 2088
Palm Springs, CA. 92263

Phone/Fax 760-325-5582
Email: NewAtlantis@webtv.net

ॐ Secret Healing Technologies · Tibetan Healing Elixirs · Mystery School Teachings · Atlantean Healing Elixirs · Advanced Yoga Systems · Inner Order Ascension Training · Light Body Activation · Egyptian Solar Activation · Egyptian Healing Rods · Psychic Protection Attack Courses and Instruments · Rare Radionic Books · Thousands of rare Healing, Metaphysical, and Scientific text reprints spanning over 500 hundred years · Hundreds of Electronic Plans and Kits for common and Advanced Technology Projects · Tesla Coils · Geopathic Stress Neutralizer · Scared Geometry Models · Psychic Protection Shields · Imported rare Healing Instruments · Aura Mending/Cleansing · Aura Goggles · Animal Healing Products · Hidden & Suppressed Technology never seen before · Soular Path Kits · College Degree Programs · Psionic Helmets · Wish Machine · Psionic Generators · Psionic/Radionic Instruments; Courses; Books · Astral Travel Kits · Space Technology · Alien Technology · Alternative Energy & Agriculture · Brain Enhancing Technology & Elixirs · Time Travel Machines · Psychic Power Development · Levitation · Teleportation · Invisibility · Ancient Wisdom · E.L.F. Devices · Psychotronics · Rife Technology · Scalar Instruments · Bio Energy Meters · Orgone Vests & Headbands · Anti-Abduction Tools · Earth Change Maps · Tesla Technology · Light Projectors · Sacred Energy Projector · Potentizers · Sacred Geometry Boards · Frequency Generators · Tachyon Technology · Antigravity · Thousands of Alternative Energy Reports & Plans · Light Speed-Tachyon Enhanced-Particle Beam-Scalar Wave-Super Amplified-Broadcast System and more... ॐ

FOR A HUGE NEW FREE CATALOG COMPLETE THE COUPON BELOW AND MAIL TO ADDRESS ABOVE.
You can also E-mail us for a free catalog. You need to state where you saw the Advertisement.
Check our online catalog at www.AtlanteanScience.com

I SAW YOUR ADVERTISEMENT IN THE FOLLOWING

PUBLICATION/BOOK ....

Please send me a free S.O.N.A. Catalog.
(Please Print Clearly so we can send the catalog the correct address. Thank you.

SHIP TO:

NAME _____

ADDRESS _____

CITY _____ STATE _____ ZIP _____

PHONE_____ DATE _____

COUNTRY _____ E-mail _____